THE SELF-BUILD EXPERIENCE

Urban Policy, Planning and the Built Environment

Series Editors:

Nick Gallent, Bartlett School of Planning, University College London, UK

Pierre Filion, University of Waterloo, Canada

Nicole Gurran, University of Sydney, Australia

This international series embraces the interdisciplinary dimensions of urbanism and the built environment – extending from urban policy and governance, to urban planning, management, housing, transport, infrastructure, landscape, heritage and design. It aims to provide critical analyses of the challenges confronting cities around the world at the intersection between markets, public policy and the built environment, as well as the responses emerging from these challenges.

The series looks in particular at the contested nature of government intervention in the urban land and housing market, and how urban governance, planning and design processes respond to increasing social complexity, social-spatial diversity and the goal of democratic renewal.

Urban Policy, Planning and the Built Environment

Editorial Board:

Karen Chapple, University of California, Berkeley, USA

Marco Cremaschi, Sciences Po, Paris, France

Robyn Dowling, University of Sydney, Australia

Jill L. Grant, Dalhousie University, Canada

Umberto Janin Rivolin, Politecnico di Torino, Italy

Markus Moos, University of Waterloo, Canada

Libby Porter, RMIT University, Australia

Mike Raco, University College London, UK

Mark Scott, University College Dublin, Ireland

Quentin Stevens, RMIT University, Australia

Igor Vojnovic, Michigan State University, USA

Laura Wolf-Powers, City University of New York, USA

Forthcoming in the series:

The New Urban Ruins: Vacancy, Urban Politics and International Experiments in the Post-Crisis City, edited by Cian O'Callaghan and Cesere Di Feliciantonio

Find out more at
www.policy.bristoluniversitypress.co.uk

THE SELF-BUILD EXPERIENCE
Institutionalisation, Place-Making and City Building

Willem Salet, Camila D'Ottaviano, Stan Majoor
and Daniël Bossuyt

With a foreword by
Oren Yiftachel

First published in Great Britain in 2021 by

Policy Press, an imprint of
Bristol University Press
University of Bristol
1-9 Old Park Hill
Bristol
BS2 8BB
UK
t: +44 (0)117 954 5940
e: bup-info@bristol.ac.uk

Details of international sales and distribution partners are available at
policy.bristoluniversitypress.co.uk

© Bristol University Press 2021

British Library Cataloguing in Publication Data
A catalogue record for this book is available from the British Library

ISBN 978-1-4473-4844-3 paperback
ISBN 978-1-4473-4842-9 hardcover
ISBN 978-1-4473-4843-6 ePdf
ISBN 978-1-4473-4847-4 ePub

The right of William Salet, Camila D'Ottaviano, Stan Majoor and Daniël Bossuyt to be identified as editors of this work has been asserted by xxxx in accordance with the Copyright, Designs and Patents Act 1988.

All rights reserved: no part of this publication may be reproduced, stored in a retrieval system, or transmitted in any form or by any means, electronic, mechanical, photocopying, recording, or otherwise without the prior permission of Bristol University Press.

Every reasonable effort has been made to obtain permission to reproduce copyrighted material. If, however, anyone knows of an oversight, please contact the publisher.

The statements and opinions contained within this publication are solely those of the editors and contributors and not of the University of Bristol or Bristol University Press. The University of Bristol and Bristol University Press disclaim responsibility for any injury to persons or property resulting from any material published in this publication.

Bristol University Press and Policy Press work to counter discrimination on grounds of gender, race, disability, age and sexuality.

Cover design: Andrew Corbett
Front cover image: 'Solidaridad Quitumbe, Quito' by
Hernan Espinoza and Janaina Marx

Dedicated to Daniela Wullers (1977–2018)

Activist for a just city

Contents

List of figures and tables — xi
Notes on contributors — xiii
Foreword — xix
Oren Yiftachel
Preface — xxi
*Willem Salet, Camila D'Ottaviano, Stan Majoor
and Daniël Bossuyt*

1   Introduction: Self-building as a right to the city — 1
     *Willem Salet, Camila D'Ottaviano, Stan Majoor
     and Daniël Bossuyt*

Part I   The changing décor of governance

2   The institutionalisation of self-build — 23
     governance: exemplifying governance relationships
     in São Paulo/Brazil/Latin America
     *Camila D'Ottaviano, Suzana Pasternak, Jorge Bassani and
     Caio Santo Amore*

3   Contested governance of housing for low- and — 43
     middle-income groups in European city-regions:
     the pivotal role of commissioning
     Willem Salet and Daniël Bossuyt

4   Self-building in contested spaces: livelihoods and — 57
     productivity challenges of the urban poor in Africa
     Nicky Pouw and Marina Humblot

Part II   Changing housing regimes

5   My House, My Life Programme – Entities: two — 79
     self-management experiences in the city of São Paulo
     *Camila D'Ottaviano, Adelcke Rossetto Netto, Cecília Andrade
     Fiúza, Flávia Massimetti and Juliana do Amaral Costa Lima*

6   The Solano Trindade housing occupation as an urban — 101
     self-management project in metropolitan Rio de Janeiro
     *Luciana Corrêa do Lago, Fernanda Petrus and Irene de
     Queiroz e Mello*

7	Self-management and the production of habitat: a case study of the Alianza Solidaria Housing Cooperative in Quito Hernán Espinoza Riera, Andrés Cevallos Serrano, Bernardo Rosero, Irina Godoy and Janaina Marx	121
8	Residents' experiences of self-build housing Daniël Bossuyt	143
9	Residential experiences in times of shifting housing regimes in Istanbul Zeynep Enlil and İclal Dinçer	167
10	The experience of an African city: urban areas in Ouagadougou, Burkina Faso Adama Belemviré	191
11	The implications of self-build for the social and spatial shape of city-regions: exemplifying the cases of São Paulo and Amsterdam Camila D'Ottaviano, Stan Majoor, Suzana Pasternak and Willem Salet	209
12	From neighbourhood self-organisation to city building: the case of Bathore, Kamëz (Albania) Ledio Allkja	229
13	Conclusion: The normalisation of moral ownership Willem Salet, Camila D'Ottaviano, Stan Majoor and Daniël Bossuyt	245
Index		269

List of figures and tables

Figures

2.1	Vistas Moravia, Medellin	24
2.2	Jardim Lapenna, São Paulo	25
2.3	Villa 31, Buenos Aires	26
4.1	Urban area sub-division, 1932–2003	67
4.2	Selected food producers groups in urban and peri-urban Ouagadougou	68
4.3	Self-built food production systems in (peri-)urban agriculture	69
4.4	Self-built water irrigation system in (peri-)urban agriculture	70
5.1	Dandara building	90
5.2	Maria Domitila Assembly	91
6.1	Solano Trindade map	107
6.2	Timber roof design course	108
6.3	Participatory project: families and the technical advisory team	111
6.4	BET construction process	115
6.5	Vegetarian cookery course	116
7.1	The 'Solidaridad Quitumbe' social housing project is located in the south of the city of Quito, enclosed by the Ortega and El Carmen *quebradas* (5 November 2018)	131
8.1	Aerial view of Homeruskwartier in the early stages of construction	150
8.2	Aerial view of Homeruskwartier in the current stage of construction	150
9.1	Former *gecekondu* densified by low-quality apartment buildings following the amnesties (in between, it is possible to detect one- to two-storey *gecekondus*)	175
9.2	In the foreground is an apartment building from the pre-1980s built through *yap-sat*, while in the background are high rises of the urban transformation era	180
9.3	Different generations of housing	182
9.4	Different generations of housing with new CBD in the background	183
10.1	Traditional habitat	199
10.2	Modern habitat	200
12.1	State-led development and voluntary housing	233

12.2	Urban expansion of Tirana	234
12.3	Process of informal development	238
12.4	Multi-actor community improvement	240

Tables

1.1	Alternative forms of self-building	5
2.1	Brazilian housing programmes and institutions, periods and abbreviations	30
4.1	Urban populations living in slums and informal settlements (%)	63
4.2	Urban productivity index and informal settlement change	65
5.1	PMCMV, July 2009 to July 2018	85
5.2	PMCMV-E, July 2009 to July 2018	89
11.1	Housing programmes SFH/BNH, 1964–85	216
11.2	Total households and *favela* households, and annual growth, per region	217

Notes on contributors

Ledio Allkja works as a lecturer of Planning Systems and European Spatial Planning at POLIS University, Tirana (Albania). He has conducted his studies on property development and planning (University of the West of England), then on European spatial and environmental planning (Radboud University Nijmegen), and is currently doing his PhD on the Europeanisation of the Planning System in Albania (TU WIEN). Since 2012, has worked at POLIS University in teaching and research, and has been a member of different groups for the preparation of spatial plans at local, regional and national levels. During 2014–16, Ledio worked as the Head of Sector of Regional and Local Planning at the Ministry of Urban Development. Currently, Ledio also works at Co-PLAN, Institute for Habitat Development, as a planning and territorial governance expert and researcher.

Cecília Andrade Fiúza is an undergraduate student of architecture and urban planning at the Faculty of Architecture and Urbanism, University of São Paulo (FAUUSP) since 2015. She holds a professional technical degree in Construction (2012).

Jorge Bassani is an architect and urbanist. He holds a master's degree in Architecture and Urbanism (1999) and a PhD in Architecture and Urbanism from the University of São Paulo (2005). He is a lecturer at the University of São Paulo at the Faculty of Architecture and Urbanism, Department of History of Architecture and Aesthetics of the Project. He has experience in architecture and urbanism, with emphasis on city history and urbanism, working mainly in the following subjects: art and city, urban art, contemporary city, art and environment, and architecture and culture. Since 1980, he has developed works in the area of art and city, author of sculptures and temporary interventions, mainly in São Paulo.

Adama Belemviré is a rural development engineer, water and forests option (1988–93) from the University of Ouagadougou (Burkina Faso), with a specialisation in remote sensing at the Agronomic University of Wageningen (WAU 1998). He spent two years (1993–94) as a researcher in the Sahelian Antenna Research Programme in partnership with WAU and the University of Ouagadougou. Since then, he has coordinated research (Universities of Wageningen and Amsterdam, African Studies Centre of Leiden) and development programmes.

Daniël Bossuyt is a PhD researcher at the Department of Geography, Planning and International Development Studies of the University of Amsterdam. He has a background in political science and urban studies. His PhD research deals with the relationship between regulation and the production of urban space in practices of self-build housing.

Andrés Cevallos Serrano is an architect and obtained his MSc in Urban Management and Development at the Erasmus University Rotterdam in 2014. He is currently a Titular Professor at the Faculty of Architecture and Urbanism of the Universidad Central del Ecuador, where he is also research fellow at the Observatorio de la Producción del Territorio Ecuatoriano. His experience and major interests are urban development studies.

İclal Dinçer is Professor of Urban Planning at the department of Urban and Regional Planning, Yildiz Technical University. Her research and teaching interests include urban and regional geography, urban conservation, urban renewal, and urban regeneration. She has had a large number of articles and papers on these subjects published in both Turkish and English.

Juliana do Amaral Costa Lima has been an undergraduate student of Architecture and Urban Planning at the Faculty of Architecture and Urbanism, University of São Paulo (FAUUSP) since 2015.

Luciana Corrêa do Lago is an architect with a PhD in Architecture and Urbanism from the University of São Paulo, Professor at the Núcleo Interdisciplinar para o Desenvolvimento Social (NIDES)/UFRJ and a researcher at the Observatório das Metrópoles/UFRJ, who develops research on social economy and urban policy, with an emphasis on urban self-management, solidarity economy, social movements and urban peripheries.

Camila D'Ottaviano is an architect and urban planner who holds a master's degree (2002) and Doctorate in Architecture and Urbanism (2008) from the Faculty of Architecture and Urbanism at University of São Paulo (FAUUSP). She is experienced in architecture and urban planning, with an emphasis on the areas of housing, urban design, city history, habitat and demographics. She is a faculty member of FAUUSP.

Zeynep Enlil is Professor of Urban Planning at the Department of Urban and Regional Planning, Yıldız Technical University. She holds a professional degree in City Planning from METU and a PhD from the University of Washington. Her teaching and research interests include neoliberal urbanism, urban regeneration, cultural and creative economy, and heritage conservation and management.

Hernán Espinoza Riera is currently Titular Professor at the Faculty of Architecture and Urbanism of the Universidad Central del Ecuador and a research fellow at the Observatorio de la Producción del Territorio Ecuatoriano. Currently, he is a PhD candidate at Universidade de Sao Paulo and obtained his master's degree in Materials Science at the Universidade Federal de Ouro Preto, Brazil. His research interests are social technologies and university extension theorisation.

Irina Godoy is Titular Professor at the Faculty of Architecture and Urbanism of the Universidad Central del Ecuador and research coordinator at the Observatorio de la Producción del Territorio Ecuatoriano. She holds a Msc in Heritage Conservation at the Universidad Politécnica de Valencia. She has experience and interest in heritage conservation and architectural rehabilitation projects in rural areas.

Marina Humblot holds a bachelor's in Business Administration from HEC Montreal, Canada, where she specialised in social entrepreneurship in 2015. In 2016, she graduated from the University of Amsterdam, the Netherlands, where she completed a Master of Science in International Development Studies. As part of her thesis, she stayed several months in Ouagadougou, Burkina Faso, to study how female farmers adapt to climate variability in peri-urban agriculture, using various participatory methods to index and illustrate all used agro-ecological practices within targeted groups. Since 2017, she has been working in the communication department of the International Labour Organization and the World Meteorological Organization, United Nations in Geneva.

Stan Majoor is Professor of Coordination of Urban Issues at the Amsterdam University of Applied Sciences in the Netherlands and is director of their interdisciplinary Urban Management research programme. He previously worked as assistant professor and programme director of the bachelor in Geography and Planning at the University of Amsterdam.

Janaina Marx is Titular Professor at the Faculty of Architecture and Urbanism at the Universidad Central del Ecuador and research fellow at the Observatorio de la Producción del Territorio Ecuatoriano. She is a PhD candidate at Universidade de São Paulo and obtained her master's degree in Architecture at the Universidade Federal de Minas Gerais, Brazil. Her area of expertise is urban and regional planning.

Flávia Massimetti is an architect and urban planner and master's candidate at the Faculty of Architecture and Urbanism at University of São Paulo (FAUUSP) (2016), and researcher of the Laboratório de Habitação e Assentamentos Humanos (Housing and Human Settlements Laboratory) (LabHab-FAUUSP). She coordinates the university outreach project 'Revisitando o território: novas percepções sobre o Grajaú' ('Revisiting the territory: new perceptions about Grajaú').

Suzana Pasternak received an undergraduate degree in Architecture and Urbanism from Mackenzie Presbyterian University (1966), an undergraduate degree in Public Health from University of São Paulo (1970), a specialisation in Urbanism from Université Paris 1 (Panthéon-Sorbonne) (1968), a specialisation in Public Health from University of São Paulo (1970), a Master's in Public Health from University of São Paulo (1975) and a Doctorate in Public Health from University of São Paulo (1983). Pasternak is currently a Full Professor at the University of São Paulo and is on the editorial staff at Cadernos Metrópole (PUCSP). She has experience in the area of urban and regional planning, with an emphasis on fundamentals of urban and regional planning. She mostly works with the topics of *favela*s, low-income housing and urban studies.

Fernanda Petrus is an architect and holds a master's degree in urbanism at the Federal University of Rio de Janeiro (2019). She is a researcher of the Observatório das Metrópoles UFRJ and develops research on urban social movements, urban self-management and urban occupation.

Nicky Pouw is Associate Professor in the Economics of Wellbeing at the University of Amsterdam, within the Governance and Inclusive Development research programme. Her areas of expertise are: poverty and inequality; inclusive development; gender; social protection; food and nutrition security; and well-being economics. She has published two books: *Local Governance and Poverty in Developing Nations* (2012, edited with Isa Baud) and *Introduction to Gender in Microeconomics* (2017), with Routledge. She has edited two special issues on inclusive development (2015, *European Journal of Development Research*; and

2017, *Current Opinion in Sustainable Development*) and managed several international research programmes in African countries.

Irene de Queiroz e Mello is a social scientist with a master's degree in Urban and Regional Planning at IPPUR/UFRJ and researcher at the Observatório das Metrópoles/UFRJ, who develops research on urban social movements, urban self-management and solidarity economy.

Bernardo Rosero is an architect at the Catholic University of Quito, Master of Architecture, with a specialisation in 'Complex Project', and a specialist in Cultural Heritage at the Catholic University of Chile. He has experience in territorial and urban planning of touristic and historical areas and has worked for the Ministry of Tourism and the Ministry of Urban Development and Housing.

Adelcke Rossetto Netto is an architect and urban planner who holds a master's degree (2017) in Architecture and Urbanism from the Faculty of Architecture and Urbanism at University of São Paulo (FAUUSP). Adelcke is the founder and architect of Integra Desenvolvimento Urbano (Integra Urban Development), and has experience in architecture design, urban design and urban planning.

Willem Salet is Emeritus Professor of Urban and Regional Planning at the University of Amsterdam. He was President of the Association of European Schools of Planning (AESOP) and was awarded a membership of honour. Salet specialised in institutions and planning and investigated the meaning of political, cultural and legal institutions in planning.

Caio Santo Amore is Associate Professor at the Department of Technology of the Faculty of Architecture and Urbanism of the University of São Paulo, where he graduated (1997) and obtained master's degrees in 'Environmental and Urban Structures' (2005) and doctorate in 'Urban and Regional Planning' (2013). He is an architect, urban planner and associate of the Peabiru Technical Assistance non-governmental organisation (Community and Environmental Work) since 1998, where he has held positions of financial and general coordination. He has experience in the area of architecture and urbanism, with emphasis on higher education and architectural projects, plans and urban studies, and team coordination, working mainly on issues related to housing of social interest, areas of precarious urbanisation and technical assistance to social and popular movements.

Foreword

Oren Yiftachel

As is widely known, the current wave of urbanisation is unprecedented. Rapidly urbanising human society is fundamentally changing our lives, mostly, though not solely, in what is known as the 'Global South-East'. Yet, most of the knowledge framing and guiding our understanding of the city emerges from the Global North-West. Planning is thus still guided by the perception that space can be tightly regulated through plans, laws and disciplined practices.

However, the 'neat' and organised representation of urban development and its 'translation' to urban theories have failed to describe, let alone prescribe, the manner in which urban development occurs in the vast majority of world cities. This is mainly because leading expertise, knowledge and concepts have continued to be generated by scholars and thinkers from the Global North-West.

As a response, in recent years, a growing body of knowledge about contemporary cities began to emerge from other regions of the world, most typically Latin America, Africa and Asia. These have told very different stories of development, social transformation and political conflict emerging from the process of rapid urbanisation.

One such insight regards the 'self-built city' on which this welcome book is focused. The act of self-construction frames a process of urban development and social transformation rarely covered in the leading literature, yet profoundly influential in the lives of billions worldwide. It represents both the incessant agency and resistance of the masses against their exclusion from urban land and planning, and a technology of control and separation used by elites against large groups of the oppressed and excluded.

The book refreshingly treats self-construction as a right to the city. As many of the chapters show, this practice, which emerges 'from below', has become an integral, often institutionalised, part of the urban self-regulation process. This should not be romanticised as simply 'the power of the poor' or 'deep democracy', as some have suggested, but understood within the geometry of powers and oppressions produced in contemporary cities. However, as the book shows, self-construction, often in defiance of formal authority, now provides an entry point to resources, institutions and circuits that only cities can offer at this historical juncture.

As scholars, activists and practitioners, our task is now to follow the welcome lead of *The Self-Build Experience*, and extend the analysis to all parts of the world in constant conversation and learning, based on grounded experience and struggle. This will hopefully assist ordinary people, so often excluded, evicted and dispossessed, in attaining the right to have a right to their cities.

Preface

Willem Salet, Camila D'Ottaviano, Stan Majoor and Daniël Bossuyt

The dense interconnectivity of the informational economy has made cities – once more – the nerves of international society. The economic prosperity of cities generates material wealth and job opportunities for their inhabitants, and it shapes the conditions, worldwide, for the continuing migration to cities, but it does not come without a price. Urban land is a current good in the hands of international capital. Nowhere else is the price of land increasing so rigorously as in the economically well-connected urban spaces. However, the 'triumph of cities' is a catastrophe for the ordinary inhabitants. Attracted by the potential of income and jobs, they are the first to be expulsed from the new urban affluence. There are enormous differences in the social and economic position of such cities as Rio de Janeiro, Addis Ababa, Istanbul or Amsterdam (cities to be analysed in this book) but they all feel the pressure and social expulsion of the selective economic processes. Yet, urban land is not just a resource of economic capital. Throughout the 20th century, low-income residents and social movements mobilised cities and states. They organised social resilience via public opinion, social organisation and political representation in order to provide opportunities for ordinary citizens to shape their access and their own qualities of 'urban place' rather than being dependent on the lone commercial exploitation of land.

This book posits the meaning of self-build initiatives within this field of tension between the selective processes of economic accretion on the one hand, and the social rights of participation in and the appropriation of the city on the other. Central attention goes to the commissioning role of the residents in shaping their own opportunities at the micro level and in their active shaping of favourable conditions at the level of urban regimes. This active social participation leads in our analyses but it cannot operate alone. The commissioning role of residents has to be manifested in the behaviour of the other involved actors in the processes of urban development: the public sector; organised social and commercial developers; and financial investors. Throughout the 20th century, cities navigated between the two poles: being dependent for their income generation on the increase of social and economic wealth at the one pole; and distributing social opportunities according to the directives of the electorate at the other. By focusing on the regime questions of contested urban governance, we hope to compare self-build initiatives from the extremely different cultures and social and economic circumstances of city-regions in three continents: Latin America, Europe and Africa.

A considerable part of this publication has been enabled via the sponsoring of the research project 'Between Self-Regulation and Formal Government' (BESEFEGO), conducted by a research consortium consisting of the University of Amsterdam and the University of São Paulo. The editors would like to thank the scientific organisations of the Netherlands, Brazil and United Kingdom (Nederlandse Organisatie voor Wetenschappelijk Onderzoek [now], Fundação de Amparo à Pesquisa do Estado de São Paulo [FAPESP] and Economic and Social Research Council [(ESRC] for this contribution. We would also like to thank Maarten Sluiter for the superb editing of the manuscript.

1

Introduction: Self-building as a right to the city

Willem Salet, Camila D'Ottaviano, Stan Majoor and Daniël Bossuyt

Introduction

Defining self-building is not an easy task. It varies from place to place, from time to time and according to the dwellers' income. Self-building may be an evident option for high-income residents but remains highly challenging for low- and moderate-income households all over the world, in particular, in densely urbanised city-regions with their characteristic scarcities of land and contested uses of space. This book investigates the self-build initiatives of low- and middle-income residents in city-regions in international comparison. We are interested in these particular experiences because of the pivotal role that urban citizens play with respect to claiming moral ownership over urban space. This necessitates an incorporation of social, cultural and instrumental use values in the production of urban spaces. In this sense, the claim of a 'right to build' is far more than an individual interest; it is an expression of public action, well framed in urban literature as the social manifestation of a 'right to the city' (Lefebvre, 1996; Purcell, 2003; Harvey, 2008). It is a claim of public participation and a claim of public appropriation by urban residents. The right to build forms an antidote to the selective exploitation of urban space for the sake of capital and commercial land and property values. It is also an antidote to the supply-led modernisation of the built environment. Many countries further social housing programmes in order to accommodate the housing needs of lower- and middle-income groups in society. However, even these socially directed programmes often tend to be based on government-led allocation, rather than enabling culturally embedded practices of accessibility (Salet, 2018). Actors may include the United Nations (UN), national and local public agencies, non-governmental organisations, and large developers, all of which more often than not face difficulties in terms of meeting needs on the ground. The needs, power and potential of citizens are at the core of this book. The book recognises the role of governmental programmes and developers' plans as long as they make room for the commissioning role of residents. In all case studies, the public responsibility of residents vis-a-vis the other relevant actors is put centre stage.

The book empirically investigates a diverse mix of self-build experiences of housing by low- and middle-income groups in urbanised regions of three different continents: Latin America (São Paulo, Rio de Janeiro, Quito), Europe (Almere/Amsterdam, Istanbul and Kamza/Tirana) and Africa (Ouagadougou). The socio-economic and cultural conditions in terms of social and economic welfare, city and society could hardly be more different in these international city-regions. The rapid urbanisation of city-regions in the urban South highlights a wide variety of self-building. Only gradually may these institutionalise over time, overcoming challenges in terms of poverty, security, safety and access to basic needs such as sanitation, energy, water and mobility (Pasternak and D'Ottaviano, 2014, 2018). The public manifestation of residents' power is widely active in these contexts; it is a matter of social survival. Circumstances are completely different in economically advanced urban regions, such as in North-Western Europe, where historic experiences of self-building have been curtailed by processes of social and urban modernisation and supply-side publicly provided programmes. However, we also see growing attention here, and paradoxically even embryonic policies, to enhance the self-building of houses in order to foster the quality and identity of place and to create more affordable, user-tailored housing options for low- and middle-income people. In all cases – North and South – initiatives of self-building by low- and middle-income residents struggle with the selective spatial tendencies of capitalist systems to absorb surplus values of property and land, which enforce the spatial displacement of commercially lower-valued uses of urban space (Harvey, 1989, 1990, 2003).

Despite the international differences of social and economic prosperity and the related housing and urban contexts, there is a recurring theme of 'contested urban governance'. This reflects the tension between the initiatives of social self-regulation, market forces and governmental regulation. Self-building for low- and middle-income residents is a public endeavour. It not only requires the active involvement of the public in terms of self-organisation at the micro level, but also demands public action with respect to the resistance of the commercial drivers of urban development, the appropriation of urban space for social use and the mobilisation of enabling conditions. In all cases covered by this book, self-building is not just self-regulation by individuals and social organisations; it also constitutes an active manifestation of the right to the city as a struggle of residents over the public control of the city (Lefebvre, 1996).

By focusing the analysis of social and institutional conditions on the transient micro-context of urban neighbourhoods in the context of contested urban governance, we unravel the potentials and the margins of self-building initiatives in order to detect the robust variables that might enhance durable strategies for more socially sustainable forms of urban development. Special elements in this approach are the following:

- emphasising the 'commissioning' role in self-building and the alternative arrangements of governance (for example, including the participation of housing movements);
- the focus on institutional conditions of contested governance, including the dilemma of regulation and self-regulation;
- the multi-scalar approach (moving the lens from neighbourhood to city building and investigating multi-scalar conditions of self-building); and
- the border-crossing perspective of comparison (North and South).

Definition of self-build housing

The concept of self-build housing means that residents bear responsibility for the production and management of housing for their own use (Turner, 1972). This book is particularly interested in specific groups of residents: low- and middle-income residents. The social relevance of self-building by these groups differs widely over different states, which also applies to the particular forms that are used in practice. Self-build housing has always accounted for a large segment of housing production across the world, both in the Global North and the Global South. While the role of self-build housing has hardly been acknowledged in the housing systems of advanced capitalist societies of the Global North, self-build housing practices have been considered a regular part of housing systems of the Global South (Pasternak and D'Ottaviano, 2018). A wide variety of production and management forms have been shared under the label of 'self-build housing'. For this reason, the meaning of self-build housing has become rather ambiguous in the international literature. The concept is not unequivocally established; as a result, it is difficult to capture in established international housing statistics. National statistics often privilege statistics regarding tenure and value over the relations of production. Moreover, self-build housing is sometimes lazily equated with informal housing. While a degree of informality characterises some incidents of self-build housing, this is not necessarily the case. This makes it necessary to be careful with respect to our definition and operationalisation of self-build housing. Rather than summing up a lot of different definitions, we pay attention to our own definition of the concept.

We take an institutional perspective to analyse the different sorts of governance of resident-led housing production. 'Self-build' is defined as the practice by which residents '*commission* the production of housing and neighbourhood facilities for their own use' (Bossuyt et al, 2018: 525). By conceptualising the practice of self-building in this way, we take account of the large variety of self-building arrangements in and within different states. This definition differs to the uses of the verb 'self-build' in daily conversation. In daily language, 'self-building' usually refers to individual residents owning and building their homes themselves. Although this basic meaning of self-building belongs to the wide spectrum of alternative self-build forms, it would not make sense to use this basic definition for an international comparison because it would exclude a wide number of self-build practices. In many cases, self-build residents do not own the land and the resources to build their home. There is a diversity of conditions and constraints (in terms of capital, regulation or land release) in different contexts (Mathéy, 1992; Benson and Hamiduddin, 2017). Thus, in defining self-build housing, we have to take into account that resident responsibility does not necessarily equate with formal ownership. A further widening of the concept of self-building is needed with regards to the 'building' of the home. Residents often do not have the professional and technical capabilities (in terms of finance, urbanism, construction and social capabilities) to build decent homes or housing complexes themselves; in most cases, they have to mobilise or contract out the required expertise. Finally, the meaning of 'self' must be abstracted because the act of self-building is not always produced by a singular resident, but often pursued by a plurality of (cooperative) residents. In particular, this applies to self-building practices in city-regions where the uses of land are expensive and dense, urging the self-builders to arrange housing in (multi-storey) complexes rather than exploiting individual parcels. Our research explicitly addresses self-building practices in city-regions.

Taking the diversity of international self-build practices into consideration, the unit of research of this comparative study has to be defined in a wide sense. The definition has to include different positions of ownership, different constituencies and different degrees of resident involvement. In order to demonstrate the range of our definition of self-building, Table 1.1 contains the margins of alternative forms of self-building. In practice, even more subdivisions are possible, for instance, when the different sub-aspects of property relationships are considered, or when different legal titles of collective organisations are exposed, or when historical changes are included. The function of Table 1.1 is to explain the margins of self-build alternatives.

A caveat to this typology is that alternative forms of self-building tend to change over time; they are sensitive to changing circumstances (social or political conditions). For instance, self-building in Brazil often starts as the illegal occupation of public land or individual plots at peripheral and irregular settlements or empty factories, to be followed by individually improvised basic constructions of shelter; however, they may end up – after years of social struggle – as legally recognised, joint constructions (developed by involved expert organisations) where residents rent from cooperative or collective associations, usually with

Table 1.1: Alternative forms of self-building

Ownership	Commissioning structure		
	Build	Procure	Promote
Ownership *Ownership by individual resident*	Individually owned, resident builds and designs project.	Individual resident in charge of development, contracts construction professionals.	Individual resident hires professional-commercial actors to develop and deliver the project.
Cooperative *Shared ownership through an organisation*	Residents build and design project.	Residents collectively in charge of development, contract construction professionals.	Group of residents hires professional-commercial actors to deliver the project.
Rent *Private or public actor (profit or non-profit) owns, residents rent from this actor*	Public or private actor owns. Residents completely build and design project.	Public or private actor is the developing actor. Construction professionals are hired to carry out works. Residents exercise control over design.	Public or private actor pays professional actors to deliver the project. Residents exercise control over design decisions.

Source: Daniël Bossuyt

public funding. Some housing associations in the Netherlands started a hundred years ago as cooperatively owned or rented associations but changed into collective organisations – being recognised as 'housing associations' and subsidised by the government for providing public home services. Whether these organisations might still be considered as a form of self-building depends on the intensity of residents' involvement as (co-)commissioners in commissioning and management. Recently, new initiatives and experiments have been taken to render the management of housing renovation processes to cooperative residents. These examples may demonstrate, first, that the definition of self-building must contain a wide range of particular forms (certainly in international comparison) and, second, that the actual form of self-building often tends to change over the course of time; in particular, cooperatives are sensitive to change over time.

By including the wide variety of alternative forms of self-building practices, we extend our focus to the social and institutional dimensions of the concept. The focus of the analysis will be on the ways in which different actors involved in the building process are related to one another. In respect of the institutional dimension, the definition of self-building is sharp as it investigates the social relations of housing production from the perspective of the constituent role of residents' responsibilities vis-a-vis other involved actors. The prioritisation of residents' control over the production and management of housing through the notion of commissioning renders it a distinctive definition in internationally diverse housing contexts.

Self-building against the changing décor of economy, city and state

The challenge of commissioning housing by low- and middle-income residents in city-regions must be analysed against the transformation of urban systems and their spatial changes instigated by the dialectic proceedings of international capitalism. Due to their inherent tendency towards destruction, capitalist systems are forced time and again to reorganise the relationships of productivity and division of labour, as well as the spatial organisation of urban activities, in order to shape new pathways of economic growth (Harvey, 1990). Under the globalising and liberalising conditions of the 1990s, the accumulation of international capitalism grew to a new stage of 'post-Fordist' relationships of capital and labour, characterised by a new specialisation of productivity and division of labour. The industrial mass economies and large-scaled office industries made space for fast-expanding financial, business and informational economies. Productivity has been increasingly rescaled and embedded in international hierarchies, but the organisation of corporations has become simultaneously more vertically disintegrated and deregulated, generating new markets for small- and medium-sized firms in sophisticated producer services in urban agglomerations (Scott, 2000; Fainstein et al, 2011). The division of labour specialised accordingly and involved new cohorts of flexible and highly skilled knowledge workers in urban economies. In the internationally connected urban concentrations of finance and business, physical proximity and face-to-face encounters created the conditions for new knowledge-based, agglomerative networks and urban concentrations of culture, information, communication, tourism, higher education and health services (Scott, 2000; Fainstein et al, 2011). New hierarchies have arisen in economic networks, involving many city-regions in the networks of new productivity but leaving other city-regions further behind. The wealth of cities was never evenly distributed. The better-connected cities profited from the economic prospects (Glaeser, 2011) but their social and spatial organisation tended to become increasingly selective. In well-connected cities, new service industries grew for increasingly affluent minorities.

Relational geographies called attention to the structural change of rescaling economic and social activities, making urban systems more dependent on external relationships. Furthermore, the territorial organisation of cities also transformed dramatically under the new economic and social conditions. Cities expanded into city-region-wide urban complexes, far exceeding the municipal borders of the central cities. The new city-regional complexes are not demarcated by sharp borderlines; rather, their boundaries – also of their administrations – have become increasingly elusive (Scott, 2001; Soja, 2015; Brenner and Schmid, 2014; Balducci et al, 2017). The spatial patterns of the city-regional complexes have lost the sharp hierarchy of core and periphery, and have grown into polycentric and discontinuous urban landscapes combining concentrations of specialised services (Hall and Pain, 2006), privileged growth nodes (dispersed over the region) (Balducci et al, 2017), wealthy suburban places (Phelps and Wu, 2011) and polarised concentrations of poverty dispersed all over the city-region. The accessibility of well-situated urban places for low- and middle-income groups has become more challenging in this highly selective proliferation of the city. Processes of social repression are often uncontrolled in these explosive circumstances.

This volume addresses the challenges of self-building at the lower side of housing markets. The international trends of urbanisation, such as those mentioned earlier, raise the fundamental question as to what self-building might mean in the context of the increasing global dependencies of urban economies, cities and states, where – in particular in the case of economic success – social repression and urban exclusion tend to increase because of rising commercial rates of land use and rising prices of urban land itself. Is it realistic to isolate 'self-provision' in a world where the self has become interconnected and interdependent more than ever?

In recent decades, urban growth has been characterised by the liberalisation and deregulation of cities and states. However, liberalisation has not delivered its promise of empowering self-regulation by citizens at the bottom end of urban societies. In recent urban literature, the potential of self-regulation (housing, energy, food and so on) has been discussed as a way to enable alternative enclaves with romantic lifestyles in a hostile urban world of modernisation; however, it is not the idealised isolation of the 'Walden enclave' that will be addressed in this volume (Thoreau, 2006 [1854]). For many, self-build housing is the only way to make a living. The position of the self (specifically defined here as low- and middle-income residents) will be studied not in isolation, but as an active social constituent in urban society vis-a-vis other actors involved in the production and management of housing. The process and outcomes of self-building will not be studied in a disaggregated manner as an isolated cosmos at the micro level of urban society, but positioned in social organisation and as an active part of urban and national policies (Savini, 2017).

Related to this question is the issue of civic capability. When self-building is perceived as a social constituency – a civic act – would it be realistic to expect to find the capabilities to equip this commissioning and entrepreneurial spirit exactly at the lower-income side of urban society? This is a burning issue in civic and social participation theory – an issue where theory and empirical reality might easily diverge (Putnam et al, 1993 2000; Uitermark, 2015). Low-income residents often lack not only the material and technical resources, but also the social competences and experience, to employ this civic and entrepreneurial attitude in operational practice. The act of self-building as a form of social participation is persistent in complex urban societies. This is certainly the case in cities of the Global South, where rural-to-urban migrants may lack social and economic resources. However, this challenge also extends to affluent urban spaces of the Global North, where residents face increasing difficulties in terms of arranging their own housing solutions. These considerations present an argument as to why self-build housing should not be considered as an isolated process. Rather, self-building requires social and political organisation and mobilisation at several levels to organise the empowerment that enables practices of self-building. This social and institutional configuration of self-building is at the heart of the matter in this investigation.

The framework of analysis: contested urban governance

Property presents a crucial variable in the analysis of the contested urban governance of self-build processes. It is the most critical determinant of urban development. There are two interrelated but highly distinctive dimensions of this variable: the *material* and the *cultural* dimensions of property. The material dimension of property is mostly investigated in critical political-economic studies that expose the optimisation of the commercial value of property as the permanent drive of economically optimising capitalist systems to search for new material surpluses in processes of economic growth. When existing trajectories of economic growth are hampered (because of saturation, unemployment, social conflicts and so on), new trajectories have to be carved out and facilitated in order to enable new processes of economic growth. Spatial displacement is one of the most effective strategies to cope with this challenge (Harvey, 1989). The economic innovation of liberal economies, countries or cities depends on the competitive race to gain material surpluses while destructing the lower-valued land and other properties. This is exactly what happens when lower-valued self-build areas in cities are rejected repressed by new office or selective housing development, or when processes of gentrification create new selective spaces in economically advanced cities. The economic selections divide the winners and the losers, a process termed by David Harvey (2008: 12) as the tendency of 'accumulation by dispossession'.

Social movements for self-building for people on low and moderate incomes – in North and South – always suffer of this selective economic pressure in liberal economies. If this is the reality of economic growth and economic innovation (not only in the behaviour of economic actors, but also in cities and states, as well as for individual owners), then why should the same mechanisms not apply to self-building? If one cannot beat capitalism, why not join it? The promotion of capitalist standards in response to the needs of the poor appears to be the key strategy of a number of international organisations, including most UN programmes. The arguments are provided by economists such as, for instance, Hernando de Soto (2000). De Soto rebated investigated the dominance of informal economies – including many illegal, semi-legal and non-representative self-building activities – in economically developing countries. He recognised modes of entrepreneurship and a hidden, non-productive capital in informal economies. However, he claims that it is dead capital because it is not documented and not formally legalised, and because of this lack of representation and institutionalisation, it cannot be made productive in processes of economic growth and innovation. While most entrepreneurs mortgage their homes in order to finance their enterprises in the US, in informal local economies, it is hidden and thus constrains explicit growth. Normalising market relationships in order to capitalise properties is a widely applied strategy in economically developing countries. De Soto advises making individual residents and citizens independent by providing titles of land, protecting their properties, stimulating projects of economic growth and so forth. This line of reasoning finds a lot of applications but is also highly controversial. The economic explanation of giving the poor title to property as the key to enabling economic growth is too simple and monistic an explanation, concludes Skidelsky (2000) in an assessment of this strategy. Moreover, it does not unconditionally respond to the social needs of low-income groups. It obviously ignores the fact that the poor do *not* possess the properties. However, when properties would be provided in the low segments of the housing market, it might also lead to a repulsion of those who are not in this privileged position. Normalising market relationships makes sense but the sole focus on unconditionally providing titles is not effective because of its propensity to create new separations with those who are not privileged.

Yet, the fascinating point of this reasoning – in the light of our framework – is that both Harvey and De Soto emphasise the active potential of the growth of capital. Capital is a potential to realise economic surplus value rather than a static stock of money. Harvey assesses this economic process as leading to 'social dispossession' and De Soto as a process of 'social elevation' but both are very convincing in explaining the workings of the same material phenomenon (even Karl Marx and Adam Smith, who differed in almost all respects, shared an analytical focus on materialist growth). The dynamic nature of material property is a permanent condition in processes of self-building, and generates many operational dilemmas on the ground, for example: in subsidising small properties and providing titles enabling self-build processes and creating commercial trades, markets and small capitalism in these areas, will the poor be excluded first? Should titles be provided under conditions of selling back to the community in order to continue the accessibility of the poor? Should hybrid mixes of economic entrepreneurship and public goals be arranged? The local case studies will provide a lot of insights into how local initiatives of self-build deal with this very tense material condition.

Thus far, we have discussed the first dimension of property: the material dimension. The second dimension with regard to the social and cultural meaning of property focuses the lense on the *use values* of property. It addresses how properties are used, whether you own them or not. Two sorts of use value are very relevant for self-building processes: the social aspects related to the accessibility of property for people on low and moderate incomes; and the cultural aspects related to the cultural embedding and appropriation of the property. Lefebvre (1996) champions the use values of property and urban development. His book, *Writings on Cities*, is completely devoted to the cultural and social uses of urban development, in this way counteracting the material explanations of commercial value. Lefebvre recapitulates his argument as following:

> The city is itself *'oeuvre'*, a feature which contrasts with the irreversible tendency towards money and commerce, towards exchange and *products*. Indeed the *oeuvre* is use vale and the *product* is exchange value. The eminent use of the city, that is, of its streets and squares, edifices and monuments, is *La Fête* (pleasure and prestige). (Lefebvre, 1966: 66)

The urban is a cultural way of life that includes a kind of 'imaginary transcendence' (Lefebvre, 1996: 103): 'Social needs have an anthropological foundation. The need for creative activity, for the oeuvre (not only products and consumable material goods), of the need of information, symbolism, the imagery and play' (Lefebvre, 1996: 147). The use values of property and urban evolution are not based on wishful thinking; they are part of changing reality, not less real than the material drives mentioned earlier. Lefebvre recognised the impact of material production and its inherent laws of economic growth on the growth of cities but refused to take the material perspective as the only or even as the hegemonic explanation of human and urban change. By upgrading use values to the explanatory conditions of urban research, he helps us to widen our framework of investigating processes of self-building. Therefore, in this book, we try to investigate the dialectic between the exchange values and the use values of property and urban development.

Excavating the contributions of Lefebvre concerning the rights to the city, Purcell (2003: 99) qualified this approach as the 'urban politics of the resident'. Through this notion, Lefebvre proposes that the production of urban space should reach beyond the state and include citizens. Lefebvre emphasises the lived space (as a combination of the perceived and conceived space) of residents, which encompasses both the material and immaterial production and reproduction of urban life. Purcell (2003: 102) distinguishes between two basic rights of residents in Lefebvre's concept of 'the right to the city': (1) the right to participation; and (2) the right to appropriation. The right to participation belongs to all residents of a city and concerns decisions made not only by the state, but also by (international) firms and organisations that are active in a city. The resident should have a pivotal say in all decisions that contribute to the production of space. The right to appropriation includes the right of residents to physically access, occupy and use urban space, which should meet the needs of residents (Purcell, 2003: 103).

The formulation of these rights constitutes a wide framework to study the potential of residents to produce a city as lived space. One might object that this is only a matter of 'claiming rights'; it does not recognise the real powers that reign over urban space. However, the claiming of rights also bears the historic power of reality. The power and social mechanisms of material exchange values are often addressed as the only powers as they concern the (globalised) exploitation of capital, investment and surplus value. They are manifest in daily practices and are also well embedded in institutional settings. However, the immaterial use rights of residents also provide power, both in daily practices and in institutional settings: the power of self-manifestation and social organisation (social movements); the power of public opinion and public media; the power of the law; and the power of mobilising political representation and public policymaking. The practical meaning of all these sources is 'potential' in the sense that empirical reality explains how these sources are actually used. However, this also applies to the potential validation of material capital: their manifestation may advantage the commercial values of property and land or the use values, or – more probably – some sort of combination. The dialectic between the two dimensions of urban properties is often asymmetric (such as Stephen Elkin [1987] convincingly demonstrated in a 200-year historic analysis of local evolution in the US). However, it is never fixed; its manifestations depend on time- and place-bounded encounters of participation and appropriation versus commercial capitalisation. Municipalities depend for income generation on the exploitation of material capital but political existence depends on public opinion and the vote of the electorate. Control over the use of urban spaces is a permanent social struggle. The empirical investigation of urban self-build experiences in this book will be situated in the struggle between these competing powers.

This book will analyse both sides of these processes and their mutual interrelationships in the concrete context of international cases. Navigating through this intricate field of tension under conditions of globalising economies and modernisation requires a rethinking of urban governance related to the moral and managerial ownership of the city. Crucial in this tension is the capacity for residents, in particular, low- and moderate-income groups, to arrange their own place in a city, requiring rights of access, basic facilities and protection against misuse or crime via public manifestation, law and politics on the one hand, and the material production of the city on the other. The main question that all the chapters will comprehend is: 'How is the capacity for self-regulation in practices of self-build housing and facilities related to the formal domains of governance and regulation, and how can this relationship be optimised to create more socially sustainable forms of urbanisation?'

Methodology

International research into the subject matter of this book – 'the contestation of urban governance with regards to the experiences of self-building of low- and moderate-income residents in city-regions' – is still embryonic and urges the adoption of an explorative methodology of research. The definition of the scope of exploration warrants a choice between a general theme or a particular object of research. There is a category of worldwide studies (often UN related) with a general focus. Some researchers, for instance, focus on the conditions of national policy systems (Gurran and Bramley, 2017). Others include general and interdisciplinary trends (financial, demographic, social and so on) (Tiwari et al, 2016). Our demarcation of the research subject is far more specific and includes the particularities of institutional and operational missions in local experiences of self-organisation processes, ranging from neighbourhood to trans-scalar relationships. This makes it necessary to conduct individual case studies in depth in order to pay tribute to the significant particular conditions of local contexts.

Yet, we aim to undertake a systematic investigation enabling us to compare and to learn from the different experiences. Generalisation of findings is impossible in this premature stage of international institutional research. This is not due to the relatively limited number of ten local case studies; even doubling or tripling the amount of cases would not enable generalisation in this explorative stage. We aim to involve very different cases in order to see how the underlying institutional tensions are contextualised in different circumstances. One of the most delicate choices in the comparative research of international case studies is the question of how to select the different cases. Do you select cases based on similarities or on differences? Most existing comparative studies on self-building have addressed empirical case studies of a similar background; these often focus on similar input conditions (economic, cultural, administrative) of regions in the Global South (see, for instance: Aldrich and Sandu [2015], *Housing for the Urban Poor in Developing Countries*; Bredenoord, Van Lindert and Smets [eds] [2014], *Affordable Housing in the Urban Global South*; and Ward, Huerta and Di Virgilio [2015], *Housing Policy in Latin American Cities: A New Generation of Strategies and Approaches for 2016 UN-Habitat III*). Alternatively, they have focused on self-building practices in the limited context of North-Western Europe (Benson and Hamiduddin, 2017). These researchers have good reasons to select cases of relative similarity because different circumstantial conditions already make for large differences in cases on the ground. However, both similarity and difference are necessary aspects of comparative studies. We emphasise the possibility of creating connections across empirical differences.

The comparative methodology in this book aligns with ongoing aspirations in urban studies to conceive of the urban through the diverse histories of the urban (Robinson and Roy, 2016). An increasing number of voices have berated the low quality of comparative research, in which Northern researchers lazily focus on their cases at home and apply theoretical insights to cases abroad. The hegemony of global models of urban theory has been challenged by a series of papers that call for recognising the complexity and difference of divergent contexts (Nijman, 2015). In response, some urban scholars have voiced fear with respect to the displacement of earlier dominant approaches, and to departing from a certain degree of universalism in urban theory (Scott and Storper, 2015). These voices suggest that a focus on specificity and particularity forecloses any chance for theory development.

In our adopted methodology, we propose to follow Ward's (2010) suggestion of adopting a relational-comparative perspective: places are dynamic and contradictory trans-scalar entities that must be understood through dialectics and motion. Robinson (2011, 2015) suggests that instead of considering and controlling each case 'for difference', we should pay attention to repeated instances that occur among numerous urban contexts. The approach adopted here turns the methodological advice of controlling for difference around. Understanding self-building practices in the context of difference forms the basis for the generation of conceptual insights. Thus, we underline the relevance of a case selection in different urban contexts and adopt a dynamic-relational view of the selected case studies. The comparability of the cases is sought not in selecting cases with similar conditions, but in using the same conceptual methodology (that is, the framework of contested urban governance detailed earlier) as a conceptual format in empirically different cases. In this way, we take difference as a productive opportunity for developing ingredients and hypotheses of a more global urban theory and innovative comparative insights. While local contexts are undeniably different, we take the governance tension between the arrangements of social self-building, inter-scalar pressures of the market and state regulation to be manifest in all cases. The manifestation and shape of the aforementioned field of tension is spatio-temporally variable.

The empirical conditions of the cases differ over time and place but the aforementioned field of tension is permanently active and urges dialectical practices. We hope to compare these tense experiences (crossing the North and the South) and to learn from the different practices.

The organisation of the book

The aim of the book is to explore – by comparing international cases of contrast– the social and institutional physiognomy of self-building practices by low- and middle-income residents in urban city-regions. The definition of self-building centres around the commissioning role of residents in arranging their housing situation vis-a-vis other players on city-regional housing markets (including social movements, market actors and the state). Residents navigate between the inter-scalar pressures of governmental and market conditions at the interface of regulation and self-regulatory initiatives. We are particularly interested in how social and institutional practices of self-build evolve over time and how social institutions of self-build capacity grow in relation to changing governmental and market conditions. In the context of commercial and dense city-regions, self-build practices are very rarely stand-alone practices. Rather, they require committed processes of social organisation and public and political involvement to sustain bottom-up initiatives in durable ways. We want to explore the different types of social and political commitment, and the margins of these processes of social organisation.

In order to explore the full potential of social organisation and to learn from contextual differences, a set of contrasting international cases is selected. To this end, international experts from several continents have conducted case studies of self-building in different national contexts. The book is organised in two parts. Part I contains an introduction to the three continents involved. This part of the book addresses the different constellations of contested urban governance in the tension between social self-regulation, state and market, and the included interrelationships of regulation and self-regulation. This introduction is needed to provide a general understanding of self-build practices in extremely different parts of the world. In three oversight chapters, concerning Latin America, Europe and Northern Africa, indicative overviews are given of the recent histories of urban and housing practices characteristic of the continents. They include the typical range of self-build initiatives and general ways of social organisation, as well as the relevant governmental programmes. Some of these overview chapters indicate a brief case study in order to underline the general argument.

Part II features in-depth empirical case studies. These case studies start at the level of individual projects and neighbourhoods (such as in Sao Paulo, Rio de Janeiro, Quito and Almere-Amsterdam) but in the latter part also include examples of the self-build of complete urban districts (for example, Ouagadougou and Istanbul), and even a completely new town (Bathore in Albania). The latter examples also pay attention to the spatial implications of self-build initiatives for large-scaled urban processes. The case studies characteristically assume the following pattern of mapping:

- the historical development of self-building practices in relation to governmental and market relations;
- the description of the case: the type of self-building, the motivations of the residents, how they fulfil the commissioning role and in what way residents give shape to place;
- the social organisation empowering the self-build initiative: social movement, mobilisation and the building up of social expertise (technical, financial and social expertise);
- the social struggle to involve the public and politics;
- the governmental conditions and policy programmes in relation to market circumstances; and
- the institutionalisation of social organisation (and its margins).

The concluding chapter recapitulates and generates the findings of the empirical case studies. In that chapter, we also deliberate on the implications of contested urban governance by assessing the findings from different contexts against the conceptual framework outlined in this introduction. We draw lessons on the struggling institutionalisation of self-build initiatives in the context of contested governance. The very different ways in which low- and middle-income residents in different contexts appropriate the production of urban space in difficult circumstances generates useful lessons for the experience and social organisation of self-building practices.

References

Aldrich, B.C. and Sandu, R.S. (2015) *Housing for the Urban Poor in Developing Countries*, New Delhi: Rawat Publications.

Balducci, A., Fedeli, V. and Curci, F. (eds) (2017) *Post-Metropolitan Territories: Looking for a New Urbanity*, London: Routledge.

Benson, M. and Hamiduddin, I. (eds) (2017) *Self-Build Homes: Social Discourse, Experiences and Directions*, London: UCL Press.

Bossuyt, D., Salet, W. and Majoor, S. (2018) 'Commissioning as the cornerstone of self-build. Assessing the constraints and opportunities of self-build housing in the Netherlands', *Land Use Policy*, 77: 524–33.

Bredenoord, J., Van Lindert, P. and Smets, P. (eds) (2014) *Affordable Housing in the Urban Global South*, New York, NY: Routledge.

Brenner, N. and Schmid, C. (2014) 'The "urban age" in question', *International Journal of Urban and Regional Research*, 38(3): 731–55.

De Soto, H. (2000) *The Mystery of Capital: Why Capitalism Triumphs in the West and Fails Everywhere Else*, New York, NY: Basic Books.

Elkin, S.L. (1987) *City and Regime in the American Republic*, Chicago, IL: Chicago University Press.

Fainstein, S.S., Gordon, I. and Harloe, M. (2011) 'Ups and downs in the global city: London and New York in the twenty-first century', in G. Bridge and S. Watson (eds) *The New Blackwell Companion to the City*, Hoboken, NJ: Blackwell, pp 38–47.

Glaeser, E. (2011) *Triumph of the City*, Basingstoke: Pan MacMillan.

Gurran, N. and Bramley, G. (2017) *Urban Planning and the Housing Market: International Perspectives for Policy and Practice*, London: Palgrave.

Hall, P. and Pain, K. (2006) *The Polycentric Metropolis. Learning from Mega-City Regions in Europe*, London: Earthscan.

Harvey, D. (1989) *The Urban Experience*, Oxford: Blackwell.

Harvey, D. (1990) *The Condition of Postmodernity*, Oxford: Blackwell.

Harvey, D. (2003) *The New Imperialism*, Oxford: Oxford University Press.

Harvey, D. (2008) 'The right to the city', *New Left Review*, 53 (September–October), https://newleftreview.org/II/53/david-harvey-the-right-to-the-city

Lefebvre, H. (1996) *Writings on Cities*, Oxford: Blackwell.

Mathéy, K. (1992) *Beyond Self-Help Housing*, London: Mansell.

Nijman, J. (2015) 'The theoretical imperative of comparative urbanism: a commentary on "Cities beyond compare?" by Jamie Peck', *Regional Studies*, 49(1): 183–6.

Pasternak, S. and D'Ottaviano, C. (2014) 'Half a century of self help housing in Brazil', in J. Bredenoord, P. Van Lindert and P. Smets (eds) *Housing the Poor in a Urbanizing World*, Amsterdam: Earthscan.

Pasternak, S. and D'Ottaviano, C. (2018) 'Paradoxes of the intervention policy in *favelas* in São Paulo: how the practice turned out the policy', in W. Salet (ed) *The Routledge Handbook of Institutions and Planing in Action*, London and New York, NY: Routledge, pp 315–30.

Phelps, N.A. and Wu, F. (eds) (2011) *International Perspectives on Suburbanization: A Post-Suburban World?*, Basingstoke: Palgrave MacMillan.

Purcell, M. (2003) 'Excavating Lefebvre: the right to city and its urban politics of the resident', *Geojournal*, 58: 99–108.

Putnam, R.D. (2000) *Bowling Alone: The Collapse and Revival of American Community*, New York, NY: Simon & Schuster.

Putnam, R.D., Leonardi, R. and Nanetti, R. (1993) *Making Democracy Work: Civic Traditions in Modern Italy*, Princeton, NJ: Princeton University Press.

Robinson, J. (2011) 'Cities in a world of cities: the comparative gesture', *International Journal of Urban and Regional Research*, 35(1): 1–23.

Robinson, J. (2015) 'Thinking cities through elsewhere: comparative tactics for a more global urban studies', *Progress in Human Geography*, https://journals.sagepub.com/doi/abs/10.1177/0309132515598025?journalCode=phgb. Published as article in 2016: 40(1):3-29.

Robinson, J. and Roy, A. (2016) 'Debate on global urbanisms and the nature of urban theory', *International Journal of Urban and Regional Research*, 40(1): 181–6.

Salet, W. (2018) *Public Norms and Aspirations: The Turn to Institutions in Action*, London and New York, NY: Routledge.

Savini, F. (2017) 'Self-organization and urban development: disaggregating the city-region, deconstructing urbanity in Amsterdam: self-organization and urban development', *IJURR*, DOI: 10.1111/1468–2427.12469

Scott, A.J. (2000) *The Cultural Economy of Cities: Essays on the Geography of Image-Producing Industries*, Thousand Oaks, CA: Sage.

Scott, A.J. (2001) 'Globalisation and the rise of city-regions', *European Planning Studies*, 9: 813–26.

Scott, A.J. and Storper, M. (2015) 'The nature of cities: the scope and limits of urban theory', *International Journal of Urban and Regional Research*, 39(1): 1–15.

Skidelsky, R. (2000) 'The wealth of (some) nations', *New York Times Books*, 30 May, https://www.nytimes.com/2000/12/24/books/the-wealth-of-some-nations.html

Soja, E.W. (2015) Accentuate the regional, *International Journal of Urban and Regional Research*, 39(2): 372–81.

Thoreau, H.D. (2006 [1854]) *Walden; or Life in the Woods*, New Haven, CT: Yale University Press.

Tiwari, P., Rao, J. and Day, J. (2016) *Development Paradigms for Urban Housing in BRICS Countries*, London: Palgrave.

Turner, J. (1972) *Freedom to Build*, Basingstoke: MacMillan.

Uitermark, J. (2015) 'Longing for Wikitopia: the study and politics of self-organisation', *Urban Studies*, 52(13): 2301–12.

Ward, K. (2010) 'Towards a relational comparative approach to the study of cities', *Progress in Human Geography*, 34(4): 471–87.

Ward, P.M., Huerta, E.R.J. and Di Virgilio, M.M. (2015) *Housing Policy in Latin American Cities: A New Generation of Strategies and Approaches for 2016 UN-HABITAT III* (1st edn), New York, NY: Routledge.

PART I

The changing décor of governance

2

The institutionalisation of self-build governance: exemplifying governance relationships in São Paulo/Brazil/Latin America

Camila D'Ottaviano, Suzana Pasternak, Jorge Bassani and Caio Santo Amore

Introduction

In 2012, a report drafted by the United Nations Human Settlements Programme (UN-Habitat) pointed out that Latin America was the most urbanised region of the world, with 23–75 per cent of its population living in cities.[1] In 2010, the total population of the region totalled 588 million, with 468 million inhabitants living in cities. In Brazil alone, the largest country of the region, a third of the region's population is concentrated. The intense regional process of urbanisation occurred mostly in the second half of the 20th century, when in addition to intense rural–urban migration, most of the countries of the region went through a demographic transition process. With this, the cities of the region received 305 million new inhabitants in only a period of 40 years between 1970 and 2010 (UN-Habitat, 2012).

Beyond intense demographic growth, another characteristic common to Latin American countries is profound social inequality, with great income concentration and a significant portion of the population living below the poverty line.[2] Within this scenario of demographic growth and deep social inequality, the formal real estate market is inaccessible to the low-income population, who have historically used informal[3] practices to access housing. The intense urban growth of the last decades was based overall in the consolidation and densification of irregular and precarious settlements, whether irregular and clandestine peripheral allotments or *favelas* and invasions in central areas as well. What defines an irregular, clandestine or *favela*-like area[4] varies in each

Figure 2.1: Vistas Moravia, Medellin

Source: Bassani (2015)

one of the Latin American countries; however, all of those areas are characterised by housing precariousness, where buildings do not have licences, are not inspected by the authorities, have hazardous access to urban infrastructure (water supply, sanitary exhaustion, power, garbage removal) and are self-constructed. Pictures like those of the *favelas* in Rio de Janeiro, the irregular allotments in permanent protection areas on the borders of water supplies to São Paulo's dams, the *comunas* in Medellin's slopes or the *villas* alongside the railway tracks in Buenos Aires are paradigmatic examples of the day-to-day housing of the low-income population in Latin American cities (see Figures 2.1, 2.2 and 2.3).

In 2005 (the last date with available data for all countries), the concentration of the urban population living in precarious areas[5] varied from 9 per cent in Chile to 50.4 per cent in Bolivia, reaching 36.1 per cent in Peru, 32 per cent in Venezuela, 29 per cent in Brazil, 17.9 per cent in Colombia and 14.4 per cent in Mexico (UN-Habitat, 2012). In the Brazilian case, research published by the Ministry of the Cities about precarious housing pointed out that at the beginning of the 2000s, there was a total of 1,618,836 dwellings (6.65 per cent) located in subnormal sectors[6] (*favelas*) and 1,546,250 (6.35 per cent) in precarious sectors,[7] indicating that 13 per cent of the total of 24,364,375 Brazilian dwellings had some kind of precariousness (Marques,

Figure 2.2: Jardim Lapenna, São Paulo

Source: D'Ottaviano (2015)

2007). The study considered as precarious houses located in *favelas*, clandestine and/or irregular allotments, and tenements. In addition to the physical conditions of the houses, the research considered such variables as access to the infrastructure network, neighbourhood facilities and public services, the effective urbanisation of the plot, and the entitlement of the property. Data from the 2010 Brazilian Census pointed out that 11.4 million inhabitants (5.61 per cent of the total) lived in 3.2 million dwellings located in the 6,329 *favelas* scattered throughout the national territory (Pasternak and D'Ottaviano, 2016). This is an enormous volume of families living in houses with diverse degrees of precariousness, mainly in the big cities and metropolitan regions of the country.

As proposed in Chapter 1, the purpose here is to advance an analysis of contested urban governance, especially considering the role of inhabitants facing the tension between capitalism and market pressures, the role of the state, and social forces. Although the struggle for decent housing by the urban poor in all of Latin America is important for this discussion, its diversity from country to country or even in some local experiences hampers a general analysis. Due to that, this chapter focuses analysis on the Brazilian reality and more specifically the city

Figure 2.3: Villa 31, Buenos Aires

Source: D'Ottaviano (2016)

of São Paulo,[8] where the first self-help municipal programme took place in Brazil. Even though the reality of social inequality and urban housing precariousness is present in all Latin American countries, the detailed analysis of the São Paulo experience is important in illustrating the characteristics and strategies adopted, and also because it has been the model adopted by many municipalities and the federal government, as well as by other cities and countries in the region over the following decades.

Self-building and self-management in Brazil

Historically, the access to housing of the low-income population was always very precarious, with practically no intervention by the authorities until the last decades of the 20th century. During the period of slavery (until 1888), the solution to housing was the *senzala* (slave quarters). In the first stage of industrialisation (1889–1929), tenements appear as a spontaneous solution, as well as workers' villas as a private initiative solution supported by the authorities. Access to housing was mostly by rent, with policy stimulated by the federal government. After 1930, major south-east cities – São Paulo, Rio de Janeiro and Belo Horizonte – experienced an intense growth process due to high demographic growth and rural–urban migration. In 1942, a federal law (the Tenement Law) froze all rental prices, discouraging the building of new rental housing. It is precisely at this moment of intense urban population growth that the form of access to housing changed with the self-building of privately owned houses in peripheral popular allotments, usually irregular or clandestine. This model was known as the 'tripod peripheral allotment–privately owned house–self-building'. This new model was responsible for the peripheral horizontal expansion of urbanised areas, expanding and consolidating the 'poor periphery'. The self-building of houses in alleged spontaneous occupation areas – the *favelas* – was also consolidated as an important form of access to housing, mainly in the city of Rio de Janeiro and later in the urban areas of practically every big Brazilian city.

Housing provision via the real estate market, usually associated with legal production, is only accessible to the middle- and high-income populations. To the low-income population, it is only accessible through public provision, offered directly by the state, even though the building is still the responsibility of private construction companies and subsidised public funding. Since the middle of the 20th century, 'informal' provision by self-building in irregular or clandestine allotments, in *favelas* and areas rejected by the market, or through the occupation of empty buildings has been the main form of access to housing of the low-income population in Brazil, as in other Latin American countries.

The concept of self-building employed throughout this chapter concerns all those processes by which a certain resident manages the building of their own housing, where they may use a paid workforce (hiring construction workers or small building contractors), free workforce (friends and relatives working in a collective effort regime) or mixed workforce for its execution, but without the presence of technicians like architects or engineers. Usually, these processes present no distinction between the stages of project execution and present low levels of budget and planning as they are executed with few resources and in stages that keep the house in a state of construction for many years (Cabral, 2017: 17).

Self-construction and official public policies

In the post-war period since the 1950s, many countries officially integrated self-construction practices into their public policies, combining a critique of massive and standardised state housing production initiatives, as advocated by modernism in architecture. In this context, English architect John Turner's tour of Latin America was an important landmark for the internationalisation of the concept of houses 'built by the people' and the power of users in the individualisation of their needs, in the identity they establish with their houses and in their participation in decision-making and construction processes. His participation as a consultant for the World Bank influenced other international development and funding agencies, as well as the course that banks and local agencies followed in housing policies. Offering the incomplete house – by means of the so-called 'embryos' with a single room, bathroom and kitchen, or, worse, only urbanised plots – and reckoning on the participation of users with their own financial resources and workforce to construct proper houses became the recipe for success because, in theory, with smaller (public) investments, it would be possible to produce a greater number of houses. The decrease of public financial inputs would be compensated by the intensive use of the popular workforce.

Self-building began to be integrated into Brazilian housing policies in the 1970s, when the National Housing Bank (BNH) began to finance 'alternative' programmes that offered incomplete houses as a solution for low-income families. The first federal programme – the Urbanised Allotments Financing Programme (Profilurb) – was created in 1975. Profilurb was intended to prevent the growth of *favelas*, with new financing lines at a lower cost. The financing was intended for the production of urbanised plots and the acquisition of building supplies and technical assistance, and to answer the pressures for greater popular participation in public housing programmes. Other programmes followed this one, like the Programme of Sub-Housing Eradication (Promorar) in 1979, which promoted the opening of new popular allotments with the implementation of basic infrastructure and housing embryos, and also allowed *favela* urbanisation projects, financing the acquisition of building supplies for housing unit restorations and improvements. In 1985, the last year of operation of the BNH, the national Self-Building Programme/Ovenbird Project was instituted. While the volume of resources employed in the alternative programmes has not reached 6 per cent of the BNH's history of investments, it seems important to understand that this was a moment at which the integration of popular practices of self-building began to transform the logic of operation of the authorities in housing policies, not only in Brazil (see Table 2.1 for Brazilian housing programs and policies).

The dissolution of the BNH in 1986 and the municipalisation of the housing policies defined by the 1988 Constitution, ratified after the end of the military dictatorship (1964–85), allied with the lack of federal funds for housing, popularised the so-called 'alternative programmes' even more. A pioneer experience was made in the municipality of São Paulo by the Social Welfare Office (SEBES), which supported the construction of around 41 housing units by collective effort in 1974. In this experience, the future residents alone chose the housing project and supplied the workforce. City government experts supervised the work and, at each stage, authorised funds for the acquisition of building supplies for the next stage. Gomide and Tanaka (1997: 11) affirm that:

> the pilot experience of Family Collective Effort of building houses through the process of mutual help of the families themselves, found strong obstacles to its development given the irregularity of the allotments and the delay of the Regional Administrations Coordinator in the approval of the projects, and to the delay of the COHAB-SP [São Paulo's municipal housing agency] in liberating resources to the acquisition of the building supplies.

Self-management in São Paulo: popular conquest or illusion?

During the late 1970s and early 1980s, popular movements organised around the struggle for housing were already very strong in São Paulo. According to Gohn (1991), there were at least four agendas that mobilised the poorest population in different ways. In the *favelas* and precarious allotments, the mobilisation happened around the demand for urban improvements, water and power infrastructure, roads, alleys and stairways, and urban interventions without removals. In the tenements and consolidated neighbourhood yards, the mobilisation happened around the relations with owners and intermediaries over negotiations about rent and improvements in living conditions.

Table 2.1: Brazilian housing programmes and institutions, periods and abbreviations

Period or year of creation	Institution or programme	Abbreviation
BRAZIL		
1937–45	Institutes of Pensions and Retirements	IAPs
1946–64	Popular House Foundation	FCP
1966–	Financial Housing System	SFH
1964–85	National Housing Bank	BNH
1975–85	Urbanised Allotments Financing Programme	Profilurb
1979–85	Programme of Sub-Housing Eradication	Promorar
1985–85	Self-Building Programme	–
1987–90	Special Office of Communal Action	SEAC
1991–	National Popular Housing Movement	MNMR
1993–	Social Development Fund	FDS
1994–	National Popular Housing Union	UNMP
2001–	Residential Leasing Fund	FAR
2003–	Ministry of Cities	MCidades
2004–09	Solidary Loan Programme	PCS
2009–	My House, My Life Programme	PMCMV
2009–	My House, My Life Programme – Entities	PMCMV-E
SÃO PAULO STATE		
1984–	Housing and Urban Development Company	CDHU
1995–	São Paulo State Collective Effort Programme	–
SÃO PAULO CITY		
–	Municipal Housing Office	SEHAB
1989	Superintendence of Popular Housing	HABI
1965–	São Paulo Housing Agency	COHAB
1974	Social Welfare Office	SEBES
1979–94	Fund for Service to the Population in Sub-Normal Housing	FUNAPS
1989–92	FUNAPS Communal	FUNACOM
1989–92	Interventions in Risk Areas and Urbanisation of *Favelas*	URBANCOM

There were also squatter-organised movements in the periphery that fought for urban improvements and land tenure, as well as groups of tenants that lived in individual units in the back of allotments in the periphery that began to claim special housing funds. Part of those groups received support from young architects, engineers and other professionals who were close to the popular demands and organised themselves around unions, strike commands, architecture and urbanism schools, with the decisive support of some Catholic Church sectors. This was the context in which the Workers Party (PT) and the central unions were born. It was a broad civil society movement that had already pressured the military and authoritarian regime, demanding direct elections and greater participation in the guidance of public policies.

The popular self-management and production of housing in São Paulo derives from this broad movement, with at least three embryonic experiences that guided public policies until today: the Vila Nova Cachoeirinha neighbourhood in São Paulo's Northern Zone, an experience with a notorious influence of Uruguayan housing cooperatives, and with collective housing production enabled by collective acquisitions with public resources from the municipal government of São Paulo; the Communitarian Village in the city of São Bernardo do Campo, the birthplace of Brazilian unionism, which was a project with the participation of professionals from the so-called Housing Team, organically linked to the housing organisation (the housing construction began with resources from the workers' strike fund and proceeded with the negotiation of funding by the state housing company); and Recanto da Alegria (Joy Place) and Vila Arco Íris (Rainbow Vila) in São Paulo's Southern Zone, a project led by a group of professors and students from the Housing Lab of the College of Architecture and Fine Arts (the experience trained many professionals who would later participate in São Paulo's municipal government). It is important to notice that these actions were strongly connected with popular organisations. Two meetings between technical advisory teams and housing movements in the first half of the 1980s were important milestones of this growing articulation. It was a much broader movement that was responsible for the birth of organised civil society in Brazil, defining a series of guidelines for social rights that were integrated within the debates and in the text of the new Federal Constitution, including the chapter about urban policy. The movement was responsible for the inclusion of collective effort, mutual help, self-management and policy participation, among other concepts, into the re-democratisation process, and for overcoming the housing policy of the military period. The title of a booklet developed in the Communitarian Village in São Bernardo do Campo is very representative of this effort: 'How to get out of BNH and build houses through collective effort?'

The victory of the social assistant Luiza Erundina (PT) in the municipal elections of São Paulo in 1988 led to the government of many of the technicians that were already working with alternative housing production by mutual help (collective effort) and self-management. Without any federal budget, the resources came from the city budget, which funded the first municipal housing programme designed for the population living in subnormal housing (the Fund for Service to the Population in Sub-Normal Housing [FUNAPS]). This first municipal self-help programme – FUNACOM (or FUNAPS-Communal) – was structured as a tripod. First, the state, represented by the city government, offered public land and local technical support to organise housing construction; second, residents associations were created specifically for each enterprise, formed by the precise number of associated families that were going to live in the housing complexes; and, third, technical advisory entities, constituted as non-profit associations and registered with the city government to operate the programme, designed the projects and monitored the construction according to contracts established directly with the residents associations. They allowed the associations to receive the resources in advance, hire the technical advisory entities (up to 4 per cent of the total resource) and specialised workforce (10 per cent limit), buy equipment, build the worksites (4 per cent limit), and, finally, negotiate and buy the supplies for the housing construction.

During four years, the Erundina administration contracted more than 90 projects with more than 12,000 housing units (Ronconi, 1995). The FUNACOM experience and projects were responsible for three important legacies. The first was a strengthened popular movement. Since that time, the movement has kept its mobilisation capacity and formed generations of participants that see in collective effort a more direct access to quality housing, and fight for self-management in public policies. The second was the formation of 25 technical advisory entities, although most of them went extinct in the following years. However, the third and most important legacy was a new programme paradigm that to this day influences all Brazilian self-management public policy experiences and programmes.

At the beginning of the 1990s, the government of São Paulo state implemented the São Paulo Collective Efforts Programme through the Housing and Urban Development Company (CDHU), which kept the municipal movement–state–technical advisory tripod as its structure, increasing the percentages for hiring specialised workforce and technical advisory entities. Reference sets were introduced, which altered the typological pattern, with high-rise buildings. Gradually, this type of production became interesting to some construction companies. To the 'collective effort' or to the autonomous management of the residents associations remained only some less specialised services. The CDHU started to adopt more and more standardised projects. Programmes that advocate the principles of self-management as a form of participation of future residents in the whole housing production process are usually considered a less important alternative to mass production. Mass production programmes, on the other hand, have no social control or transparency, and focus on demands that can be solved, with debt capacity according to the existing financing rules. Of course, the fights of social movements for alternative housing had many achievements. However, the housing policies encouraged by multilateral agencies in Latin America since the 1970s were guided by 'participation' as a means for the 'unaccountability' of the state concerning the assurance of a fundamental right. In some ways, collective effort and self-management are part of the same history.

However, two questions still need reflection: would collective effort be an antiquated remnant of the super-exploitation of the workforce, or a popular conquest of housing production and management, and therefore an important asset to the worker? Moreover, does self-management enable the full exercise of citizenship or is this be an illusion?

Public policies and housing programmes: FUNACOM, São Paulo Collective Effort Programme, Solidary Loan Programme and My House, My Life Programme – Entities

FUNACOM (1989–2002)

At the beginning of the 1990s, the new housing policy implemented by the municipal administration in the city of São Paulo represented a radical change in what was occurring in Brazil. Mayor Luiza Erundina (1989–92) reorganised the Municipal Housing Office (SEHAB) and constituted a new technical framework with agents historically involved with the fight for urban reform and with self-managed popular movements. For the first time, the municipal authorities adopted the principle of recognising the real city, elaborating a programme of action that faced urban and housing problems in accordance with their specificities: *favela* urbanisation and land tenure; housing improvements and interventions in tenements; the production of new housing; access to urbanised land; and land property safety. The municipal government used the FUNAPS fund created in 1979. The fund was created as an answer to the pressure from the Catholic Church and popular movements for housing, and was intended to respond to the demands of very poor precarious housing dwellers. The resources could be applied as grant assistance, turning the municipal administration into an alternative for those who did not have access to the federal Financial Housing System (SFH), created in the 1960s by the government during the military dictatorship.

After its creation, during two municipal administrations in the period between 1982 and 1988, the resources of the fund were used for the actions of land acquisition, *favelas* removals, collective effort and intervention in risk areas. By then, the sole alternative to federal financing for very poor families was the National Collective Efforts Programme of the Special Office of Communal Action (SEAC). Created in 1987 with the goal of financing 550,000 housing units, the programme was interrupted in 1990, with many of the approved projects not built due to high inflation, the low amounts of finance and bad management.

During the Luiza Erundina administration, the FUNAPS became the main funding source for housing, financing the FUNACOM, interventions in risk areas and *favela* urbanisation (URBANCOM). FUNACOM was an answer to the housing movement's demands for a programme that included self-management production. Developed in an experimental way by the technical team of SEHAB, the FUNACOM ended up becoming the main programme of the Superintendence of Popular Housing (HABI) due to its agility and range.[9] Through the programme, neighbourhood associations in precarious areas could themselves hire technical advisory teams to design projects, always in a participatory process with the beneficiary families. The technicians were also responsible for monitoring the collective construction of the housing and, sometimes, the neighbourhoods' facilities. The collective effort included the management of the whole building process – construction, administration and finance (Pasternak and D'Ottaviano, 2014). In a little more than three years, 93 projects were signed off and 12,351 housing units were built, all of them through self-managed collective effort (Ronconi, 1995).

Beyond quantitative results, the experience in the city of São Paulo was responsible for the consolidation of a new form of housing provision made viable by cooperation between the authorities and housing movements. The FUNACOM was extrapolated from the local sphere and became a model for the proposition of new national policies. Due to the actions of housing movements, the government of the state of São Paulo negotiated the creation of the Collective Effort Programme, later transformed in the São Paulo State Collective Effort Programme. The new state programme was responsible for the continuity of municipal programmes of self-management after 1992.

São Paulo State Collective Effort Programme (since 1995)

In the Brazilian context, both the city and the state of São Paulo have special characteristics concerning housing policies. The municipal government of São Paulo has its own housing agency (COHAB-SP), with an exclusive budget and basic structure. The state, in turn, has the CDHU, with a budget derived from the transfer of part of the state Tax on Commerce of Goods and Services. With a fixed budget greater than that of many cities, the CDHU has been responsible for a considerable amount of housing provision in cities all over the state since its creation in 1984. After some experiences that anticipated popular participation, in 1995, during the Mário Covas administration (1995–2001), the São Paulo State Collective Effort Programme was created. According to statements from the governor at the time, the programme was created as collective effort was 'based in the incentive to the population organization, as well as to the reduction of costs and production deadlines' (Royer, 2002: 103). By the end of the first year, in its preliminary evaluation, the CDHU indicated the following characteristics of the programme as important:

> (1) indication of the participant associations by the UMM [Union of Housing Movements]; (2) selection of families with proper criteria; (3) hiring of technical advisory without any interference of the CDHU and free choice of the architectural project by the movements; (4) building of housing units with areas and/or patterns of workmanship superior to those adopted in the traditional CDHU production, with scale gains being obtained through the process of self-construction management. (Royer, 2002: 109)

However, the programme encountered difficulties inside the CDHU as it required operational adaptation and new technical routines. Routines were solely structured around a mass production model and, although innovative, production through the Collective Effort Programme was not very significant, representing only 6 per cent of the total. Although not very significant in numerical terms, the CDHU's Collective Effort Programme existed for more than three decades as an important alternative for housing access, mainly in the largest cities where housing movements are present in a more organised way.

Solidary Loan Programme (2004–09)

During the 1990s, housing movements organised a national manifestation. In 1991, the National Popular Housing Movement was created, and in 1994, the National Popular Housing Union (UNMP). This institutionalisation process of housing movements at the national level amplified the self-management agenda and empowered the debates and fights for housing. The UNMP had an important role in the national expansion of the self-management option, having the experience of the Uruguayan housing cooperatives as a paradigmatic model. In 2001, for example, the UNMP organised a tour of Uruguay so that the movements could see the cooperative experiences of mutual help housing production.

As the result of the national mobilisation of housing movements, in 2004, during the first Lula government (2003–06) the Solidary Loan Programme (PCS) was created. The PCS represented the concrete possibility of expansion to a national level of self-management. The PCS was intended for very poor families who were organised in associations, though not necessarily linked to the housing movements. According to the Ministry of Cities, the PCS had as main goals:

> to provide access to regular housing to the low-income population who does not have the capacity for savings, by means of special conditions and subsidized loans; to contribute effectively to the reduction of the housing deficit, reaching, as a priority, families with monthly income inferior to three minimum wages and, exceptionally, admitting the service of families with income between three and five minimum wages; to stimulate the cooperate housing model and the principle of mutual help, guaranteeing the participation of the population as protagonist in the solution for its common housing, observing local needs, characteristics, uses and traditions. (Moreira, 2009: 85)

The programme had four different modalities: (1) *land*, which included the acquisition of land; (2) *construction*, on proprietary or third-party land; (3) *restoration*, with funding for the conclusion, expansion or restoration of an existing housing unit; and (4) *building acquisition*, funding for the acquisition of an existing unit or of buildings for urban rehabilitation.[10] The PCS was structured according to the housing movements' demands, made possible using resources from the Fund for Social Development (FDS) and operated by Caixa, being the federal bank and the programme's financial agent. Between 2004 and 2007, the PCS constructed 203 projects in 21 Brazilian states, comprising 12,199 housing units (Moreira, 2009: 85).[11] In the second stage of the programme between 2007 and 2010, 21,223 new units were contracted with associations and cooperatives.

From the point of view of housing programmes, the PCS represented a paradigm change. According to Evaniza Rodrigues, leader of the UNMP:

> And in this story we enhance the proposal ... but what was still missing? It missed to those states (to the movements of state representation) that were arriving the opportunity to live, to have such an experience.... Because ok, one goes to another one's house and thinks it is all pretty, very pretty, but comes back home and nothing.... So, for us, it was fundamental to build solidary loan. That is, to build a program at national level that could make self-management in other places. (Moreira, 2009: 82)

With the PCS, self-management ceased being an experience made viable only through exceptional pilot programmes, and instead became a model of housing provision to the low-income population with national coverage.

My House, My Life Programme – Entities (since 2009)

In 2009, the federal government launched the My House, My Life Programme (PMCMV) (Law no. 11.977 of July 2007) with the goal of building 1 million new houses. Amid the economic crisis, the government of the then President Luis Inácio Lula da Silva (2003–10) used on public investment to reverse the impacts generated by the North-American subprime crisis of 2008. The programme was intended to tackle two different problems: to resolve the housing deficit (around 5.5 million houses) and to boost the construction industry, generating new jobs and increasing capital investments. PMCMV[12] is the biggest and most comprehensive housing programme created in Brazil since the extinction of the BNH in 1986. Up to 31 July 2018, PMCMV contracted 5.3 million units for different income ranges, supplanting other housing programmes, which disappeared or were incorporated into it. PMCMV offered unprecedented public subsidy for families without enough income to access regular housing loans. This segment, benefiting from a very high subsidy (up to 95 per cent of the unit's value), was named PMCMV Segment 1,[13] and although it served families that represent the largest part of the country's housing deficit (approximately 90 per cent), it only accounted for 25 per cent of the total investment of the programme, or 38.8 per cent of the contracted units.

PMCMV Segment 1 originally anticipated two models of operation: the first one based on local government actions associated with construction companies, fed by the Residential Leasing Fund (FAR); the second one based on self-management by housing associations and cooperatives, fed by the FDS. The programme was conceived mainly for big construction companies, enabling gains through the production of large housing complexes (scale gains) in the outskirts of big cities (a way to capture the increase in value by transforming rural areas into urban space). Standard typologies were systematically replicated, minimising project costs and increasing scale and land gains.

As a response to organised social housing movements' demands, the federal government created a sub-programme, My House, My Life Programme – Entities (PMCMV-E).[14] PMCMV-E incorporated the characteristics and intentions of the PCS and was structured in a similar way, including the target public (very poor families) and the form of access to the programme (through organised entities) with FDS funding (Moreira, 2009; Pasternak and D'Ottaviano, 2014; D'Ottaviano and Rossetto Netto, forthcoming). PMCMV-E will be analysed in a more detailed way in Chapter 5.

Conclusion

Self-building, on proprietary or occupied land, is still the main form of access to housing for low-income families in Brazil and Latin America. Low salaries, high land prices and high construction prices hamper access to decent housing for low-income families and workers. With no alternative, the acquisition of a peripheral plot (irregular or illegal) or land invasion is the sole option for the Latin American poor. Even in the city of São Paulo, Brazil's financial hub, the percentage of *favela* houses has continuously increased (in 1973, it was 1.2 per cent; in 1991, it climbed to 5.58 per cent; in 2000, it was 7.41 per cent; and in 2010, it was 9.95 per cent).

Historically, the path of Brazilian housing policy was always that of the continuous transference of production costs from the owners of capital (farmers, entrepreneurs) to society as a whole, with *senzalas* or slave quarters (in the late 19th century) to worker villages (in the early 20th century). In 1988, after the military dictatorship, the new Constitution ratified the municipalisation of housing policy as a response to the struggles of popular urban movements. As already stated, the existence of municipal resources in São Paulo guaranteed its use for grant assistance. *Favelas* were urbanised and new units were built, mainly by self-management. *Favela* urbanisation and land tenure programmes represented important innovations in tackling the housing question, where pre-existence was respected and invasions were tolerated (with exemptions in risk areas). For the first time in Brazilian history, funding was used to guarantee housing for the very low-income population. Housing began to be understood as a right. In 2009, the federal government resumed large popular housing programmes, with national resources. However, this time, there was an important paradigm change: units were almost wholly subsidised for very low-income families. The use of such a subsidy is a novelty in times of extreme liberalism.

Currently, in countries such as Chile, Mexico, Venezuela and Brazil, housing policy generally continues to be structured mainly through mass production in large peripheral projects with high subsidy for the lower-income population, with the primary goal of stimulating the economy and generating jobs. In this context, PMCMV-E self-managed production in Brazil, as well as Uruguayan mutual aid cooperatives and previous projects, continue to be exemplary cases from the point of view of the participation of residents in design and construction processes, of architectural and urban quality, and of social mobilisation. However, this housing production logic has severe limits regarding disputes over land and location within the city. Besides this, experiences are hardly representative in quantitative terms. Nevertheless, self-construction in irregular settlements and *favelas* is still the major form of access to housing for the urban poor in all of Latin America.

Notes

1. Research developed with the support of the São Paulo Research Foundation (FAPESP).
2. According to the report of UN-Habitat (2012), in 2009, 27.8 per cent of the population of Latin America lived in conditions of urban poverty.
3. Here, we use the terms 'informality' and 'irregularity' with reference to common sense while not ignoring the argument made by Roy (2005: 148) that informality 'is not a separate sector, but a series of transactions that connect different economies and spaces'.
4. '*Favela*' is the name given in Brazil to housing clusters built in invaded areas, with precarious urbanisation and without basic infrastructures. The first Brazilian *favelas* date back to the end of the 19th century in the city of Rio de Janeiro (Pasternak and D'Ottaviano, 2016). In other countries, some of the terms used to designate these precarious housing areas are: '*Villa Miséria*' (Argentina); '*Ciudadela*' (Bolivia); '*Campamento*' (Chile); '*Barrios Bajos*' or '*Comuna*' (Colombia); '*Tugurio*' (Costa Rica); '*Llega y Pon*' (Cuba); '*Guasmo*' or '*Invasión*' (Ecuador); '*Champerío*' (El Salvador); '*Arrabales*' or '*Champas*' (Guatemala); '*Barrio*' (Honduras); '*Barriada*' (México); '*Barracón*' (Peru); '*Cantegril*' (Uruguay); and '*Rancho*' (Venezuela).
5. In accordance with the methodology of the UN-Habitat (2012), which considers data about households on four variables used to identify precarious areas: the supply of drinking water; basic sanitation; permanent housing; and enough space to live.
6. 'Subnormal sector' is the definition used by the Demographic Census. For academic studies and demographic analyses, we use this census category as a proxy for '*favela*'.
7. In accordance with the methodology developed by CEM-CEBRAP for the Ministry of the Cities (Marques, 2007).
8. For an analysis of self-management experiences in the city of Rio de Janeiro, see Chapters 6 and 7.
9. On the collective effort actions developed in this period, see Ronconi (1995).
10. See: www.caixa.gov.br/poder-publico/programas-uniao/habitacao/credito-solidario/Paginas/default.aspx
11. See: www.cidades.gov.br
12. The PMCMV had three distinct phases: PMCMV 1 (2009), with the goal of building 1 million new housing units; PMCMV 2 (2011), with the goal of 2 million new units; and PMCMV 3 (2016), with the goal of 2 million new units. Each phase defines partial goals without indicating if the previous goal had already been reached. In 2017, PMCMV 3 was reviewed, with the expansion of the income segments served by the programme and of the values of units, and with a goal of contracting 610,000 units. In practice, Segment 1 of the programme, which depends on public subsidy to access financing, practically ceased to exist with the decrease of resources, the increase of financing values and the restriction of financing to situations tied to urban programmes and risk.
13. Segment 1 – families with income below R$1,395.00/US$697.50; Segment 2 – families with income from R$1,396.00 to R$ 2,790.00/US$698.00 to US$1,395.00; Segment 3 – families with income from R$2,791.00 to R$4,900.00/US$1,395.50 to US$2,450.00 (the conversion to US dollars used the exchange rate on 9 July 2009, release date of PMCMV 1 [Source: UOL Economy]).
14. Specific analyses of PMCMV-E are presented in Chapters 5 and 6.

References

Cabral, G. (2017) *Autoconstrução da Habitação Urbana: um estudo de caso em Paraisópolis* [*Self-Construction of Urban Housing: A Case Study in Paraisópolis*], São Paulo: FAUUSP.

D'Ottaviano, C. and Rossetto Netto, A. (forthcoming) 'Programa Minha Casa Minha Vida – Entidades. Edifício Dandara – moradia de interesse social de qualidade na área central São Paulo', in F. Córdova Canela, V.L. Díaz Núñez and T.A. Moreira (eds) *Miradas Cruzadas de Vivienda Social Brasil-México*, Guadalajara: Universidad de Guadalajara.

Gohn, M. da G. (1991) *Movimentos sociais e a luta pela moradia*, São Paulo: Loyola.

Gomide, R. and Tanaka, M. (1997) *A política heterodoxa de habitação popular. Operacionalização em São Paulo através do FUNAPS (Fundo de Atendimento à População Moradora em Habitação Subnormal)* [*The Heterodox Policy of Popular Housing. Operationalization in São Paulo Through FUNAPS*], Caderno de Pesquisa do LAP, no. 22, São Paulo: FAUUSP.

Marques, E. (ed) (2007) *Assentamentos Precários no Brasil Urbano* [*Precarious Settlements in Urban Brazil*], Brasília: Centro de Estudos da Metrópole/CEBRAP e Secretaria Nacional de Habitação/Ministério das Cidades.

Moreira, F. (2009) 'O lugar da autogestão no governo Lula' ['The place of self-management in the Lula's government'], master's thesis, FAUUSP, São Paulo.

Pasternak, S. and D'Ottaviano, C. (2014) 'Half a century of selfhelp in Brazil', in J. Bredenoord, P. Van Lindert and P. Smets (eds) *Affordable Housing in the Urban Global South* (vol 1), London: Routledge, pp 241–55.

Pasternak, S. and D'Ottaviano, C. (2016) 'Favelas no Brasil e em São Paulo: avanços nas análises a partir da Leitura Territorial do Censo de 2010' ['Squatter settlements in Brazil and in São Paulo: improvements in the analyses from the 2010 Census Territorial Reading'], *Cadernos Metrópole*, 18(35): 75–99.

Ronconi, R. (1995) *Mutirões autogestionados: levantamento de obras 1989–1995* [*Self-Managed Mutirões: Survey of Works 1989–1995*], São Paulo: FASE-SP.

Roy, A. (2005) 'Urban informality: towards an epistemology of planning', *Journal of the American Planning Association*, 71(2): 147–58.

Royer, L. (2002) 'A Política Habitacional no Estdo de São Paulo: estudo sobre a Companhia de Desenvolvimento Habitacional e Urbano do Estado de São Paulo, CDHU' ['The housing policy in the state of São Paulo: study on the Housing and Urban Development Company of the state of São Paulo, CDHU'], PhD dissertation, FAUUSP, São Paulo.

UN-Habitat (United Nations Human Settlements Programme) (2012) *Estado de las Ciudades de América Latina y el Caribe 2012. Rumbo a una nueva transición urbana* [*State of the Cities of Latin America and the Caribbean 2012. Towards a New Urban Transition*], Brazil: ONU-Habitat.

3

Contested governance of housing for low- and middle-income groups in European city-regions: the pivotal role of commissioning

Willem Salet and Daniël Bossuyt

Introduction

This chapter explores whether and how low- and middle-income residents in European city-regions employ an active commissioning role in the contested governance of the dominant players of the market, the public sector and the established providers of housing. The position of residents in European city-regions varies vastly in terms of tenure, access and affordability.

From a global perspective, housing in North-Western Europe occupies a unique position because of the historic trajectories of housing regimes through the welfare state. While capitalism is established as a general economic order, it is mitigated and differentiated under the influence of social movements and professionalising policy regimes of welfare capitalism (Esping-Andersen, 1990; Kemeny, 1995). Throughout the 20th century, low- and middle-income residents have been able to exert power through social organisation and political representation. As a result, most North-Western European states – with strong regional variation – are characterised by social housing sectors, which peaked particularly in the immediate post-war period, offering affordable and secure housing to large numbers of residents on below average incomes. Since the end of the 1980s, the size of the organised social sector has been reduced and its working areas have become more selective after almost half a century of universal growth. In this process of social residualisation (Harloe, 1995), the social housing sector also mirrors the differentiation of social and political regimes throughout Europe. Lower- and middle-income groups have conventionally depended on collectively arranged varieties of social or private rent.

The first part of this chapter will give an overview of the most significant characteristics of housing for low- and middle-income groups with regards to tenures, differences of accessibility and recent tendencies. The different parts of Europe go through their own processes of transformation. As a result of recent liberalisation, homeownership is increasingly an alternative tenure throughout Europe. However, this remains only limitedly accessible for lower-income segments on the housing market. There are vast differences across European regions. In some North-Western European states, such as the Netherlands, Sweden or France, social housing constitutes an important component of a universalist housing approach. In other countries, such as the UK and Western Germany, social housing has increasingly exclusively catered to low-income groups. Eastern European housing figures diverge from North-Western European patterns because of their socialist legacies. Here, the privatisation or restitution of state-owned or social housing has resulted in the extension of homeownership to large echelons of society (Hegedűs, 2008; Lux, 2011).

The second part of the chapter will pay attention to the position and active involvement of low- and middle-income residents in the creation of housing in city-regions. We wonder how residents organise their commitment in an epoch of political and economic liberalisation. As outlined in the general introduction to this book, our focus on self-building is oriented to the active commissioning role (Bossuyt et al, 2018) and moral ownership of urban residents (Lefebvre, 1996). This commissioning role entails a variety of tenures, ranging from rented dwellings, to owner-occupied, cooperatives or other forms of hybrid ownership that actively include residents. The right to the city refers to the rights that residents have to control their everyday lives, which is enmeshed within the wider production of urban spaces, as Purcell summarises following Lefebvre (2003). From this point of view, the relevant setting of governance is always dynamic and socially and politically contested because the interrelationships between residents, organised providers, the state and the market are frequently changing. The position of residents is not given; it is a continuous challenge, and it is highly contextually bounded, varying over time and space (Kemeny, 1995). Facing the vast variation of local experiences, we will select a number of significant cases.

Mapping arrangements of housing for low- and middle-income groups in Europe

Research on housing in Europe is very well documented, both at the level of individual states and the European comparative level (Housing Europe , annually) ; Whitehead and Scanlon, 2007; Scanlon and Whitehead, 2008; Houard, 2011; Poggio and Whitehead, 2017). Housing statistics keep track of tenure percentages in European states, indicating the dominance of homeownership and wide differences in social sector, ranging from 35 per cent in the Netherlands to 4 per cent in Hungary (Scanlon and Whitehead 2007: 1; for recent oversight of tenures detailed by country, see Housing Europe, 2017). However, careful consideration of individual countries is necessary to make sense of the realities behind these general categories. The meaning and organisation of different tenures differs strongly for both owner occupation and the social sector. Social housing may be owned by local authorities (England), arm's-length municipal housing companies (Sweden, Germany), housing associations (Denmark, the Netherlands) or private landlords (Germany) (Stephens, 2008: 28). The different arrangements of social housing have in common that rents are set or subsidised by 'non-market criteria' and 'allocations are made by administrative criteria' (Stephens, 2008: 31).

Since the 1990s, the tenure composition of the housing stock has been increasingly subject to liberalisation. The trend has been to transfer ownership from social or municipal organisations to individual or privatised ownership. Private rent often operates as a quasi-social sector (under market conditions and sometimes sponsored by municipalities for specific purposes, for instance, hostels). For instance, private rent in France and Denmark is more accessible for the very poor than social rent or arm's-length municipal organisations. The access to social rented housing is bound to a maximum income limit of tenants in most countries but these limits are so high in some countries (France, Austria, the UK and Sweden) that high echelons of middle-income groups may easily qualify (Scanlon and Whitehead, 2007: 17): 'These countries had to "Europe-proof" their social housing sectors by creating a clear division between services that are eligible for governmental subsidies and those that are not' (Scanlon and Whitehead, 2007: 19).

In most European countries, the social sector decreased from the end of the 1980s. Universalist systems of social housing, serving a wide array of low- and middle-income groups, often not primarily the very poor, were not uncommon until 1990. They still exist in Scandinavian countries, the Netherlands, France and Austria but conditions have continuously tightened under the political liberalisation of recent decades (financial liberalisation, decreasing subsidies, shifts from object subsidies to subject subsidies, income limits for new constructions, buy-out programmes and so on). The general trend has been directed towards the residualisation of mass systems that used to serve the broader public, but there are still remarkable differences between countries. The most radical residualisation took place in England and Germany. In 1980, England had a huge proportion of good-quality council homes (31 per cent, which is quite comparable to the 34 per cent of social rented homes of European frontrunner the Netherlands) serving both middle-class and low-income residents, while urging most of the very poor to private rent (Mullins and Murie, 2006; Murie, 2008). The Thatcher government introduced the Right to Buy and promoted the sale of council homes to tenants (under market prices). Next, a large number of council housing stocks were transferred (sold) from municipalities to social landlords (stock transfer). As a result, the more affluent tenants and the better housing left, and the status of council housing shifted 'from affluent working class to housing the poor' (Murie, 2008: 243). At present, after selling about one third of housing stock, councils still exploit a considerable number of homes (some 20 per cent) but this sector now functions as a 'safety net' for the (in England substantive) group of very poor. It is also more difficult to manage collectively because of the individual buy-outs and spread ownership (Murie, 2008).

The other case of radical residualisation in North-Western Europe is Germany. Germany traditionally had a diverse system of providing homes for low- and middle-income groups. The government funded different organisations, in particular, municipal companies, private landlords and cooperatives (Stephens et al, 2008: Fitzpatrick and Stephens, 2008); some of these organisations also made use of client saving systems but the government drastically reduced funding in the 1990s. The social sector contained a fifth of the German housing stock in 1980 but has been reduced to less than 5 per cent nowadays. Remarkably, social estates were often sold to private equity funds, making them dependent on the forces of speculation. The housing of the poor is mainly dependent on the highly different policies of local organisations.

Besides the radical transformation of the social rented sector in England and Germany, more gradual trajectories of change took place in Scandinavia, France, Austria and the Netherlands. Here, programmes of privatisation (via buy-outs) are indicative, and pressed via rather indirect ways. The universal ambitions of the past have become more hybrid, tightening the norms of income at the entrance of social dwellings (also in response to European legislation) but not taxing residents' growth of income after their entrance. As a result, these social housing stocks are still mixed but the structural quality of the stock is becoming marginalised because of the low level of new constructions (where one might expect the better qualities and higher incomes of mixed sectors). New constructions are also hampered by the tightening of financial conditions. The proportion of the social housing stock has stayed relatively stable under modest buy-outs and modest new investments in new construction but the veil of stability hides a long-term weakening of housing quality and gradual residualisation. Increasingly, residualisation is becoming the underlying trend, as well as recently in Denmark and Sweden (Poggio and Whitehead, 2017). With regard to the state of governance, the most general trend is that housing associations are loosening the previously closed ties with governments and operate more directly on markets (making them vulnerable for new commercial dependencies). With regard to intergovernmental relationships, there is a general tendency of decentralisation, making local government – in all its variation – more directly involved than the retreating central administrations.

The cultural and institutional backgrounds in Eastern and Southern states of Europe differ from the tendencies outlined earlier. In Eastern Europe, social housing is almost non-existent after the structural devolution and privatisation of the socialised housing estates of the communist epoch. Owner occupation has become the new general standard, including for the lower-income segments of the market. There are some embryonic indications of new arrangements of social organisation and grass-roots collaborative housing initiatives (needed because of accessibility problems, in particular, for young residents). In Southern European states (Greece, Italy, Spain and Portugal), housing is culturally and institutionally bound up with family systems. These countries only have a small tradition of social housing and tend to organise housing in owner-occupied family housing. In these contexts, the global financial crisis has made young people even more dependent on family networks (Arundel and Ronald, 2015; Lennartz et al, 2015). A recent report by Housing Europe (2018) observed the 'generational phenomenon that the majority of people aged 18–34 still live with their parents: 66 per cent of them in Italy, 58 per cent in Portugal, 55 per cent in Spain, 74 per cent in Slovakia, etc'.

The commissioning of residents

What is the role of the residents in the changing décor of governance? In the epoch of the welfare state regimes, the role of residents had become rather passive, wedged between the forces of the market and the solid supply-side coalitions of the government and organised providers of housing. The tenant had become a recipient of public provision. However, the arrangements of the welfare regimes have become very dynamic and changeable since the early 1990s. Following decades of stagnating urban economies, markets rediscovered the cities and city-regions as attractive economic spaces; the political powers of the states decentralised housing and urban policies to local echelons, and the post-war supply-side alliances between national states and professional developers have dissolved (Poggio and Whitehead, 2017). It remains to be seen to what extent low- and middle-income residents of city-regions will manage to re-conquer these vacant spaces. Have they been able to foster new alliances within the context of decentralising politics and claim new conditions from the market? Practically speaking, there are two ways to materialise these opportunities within the domain of urban housing policies: the first is to enlarge the commissioning and control opportunities of residents within existing supply-side arrangements of the social sector; and the second is to enlarge the social power of residents' autonomy in order to develop grass-roots or collaborative initiatives. The first strategy is increasingly found in advanced European welfare economies, in particular, when existing housing stocks have to be refurbished. Examples of the second strategy are only gradually unfolding here. In Eastern and Southern parts of Europe, residents might more often feel urged to a strategy of (cooperative) self-management. New hybrids of these strategies are also emerging.

Enlarging resident control

England is the exemplary political case of empowering and commissioning the users of public facilities. Labour's citizens' initiative set the stage for the attack on welfare paternalism by creating new options for users in policy fields as health and education, but also housing (Clarke, 2005; Pawson, 2008). New citizenship initiatives aimed at transferring 'managerial accountability to tenants in a collective sense ... such as tenant charters, stock transfer ballots, and tenant management co-operatives' (Pawson, 2008: 85). New Labour promoted tenant choice rather than voice; the basic incentive was to make tenants more accountable for their living circumstances, motivated by the expectation of 'better allocating sources, upgrading management standards, and the intrinsic meaning of choice' (Pawson, 2008: 85). A range of instruments were introduced, among them 'the right to manage', enabling tenant groups to take over the management of council estates (applied in 2006 to 84,000 homes) (Pawson, 2008: 89). An important target (mirroring the practice in Dutch housing associations) was also the enlargement of the individual choice of tenants to elect dwellings according to their own preferences (in particular, considering the situation of the neighbourhood in a city). Many initiatives have been taken to enable a more choice-driven management in England's citizen-empowering programmes, some with success. However, the largest problem is that it proved difficult to enlarge tenant choices in a residualising market where residents tend to have structurally less choice. Councils manage to house large groups of England's poor but creating choice at this level appears to be highly challenging.

The Netherlands employs the largest proportion of social housing in Europe, a public task provided by publicly adopted but privately based housing associations. It originated more than a century ago in grass-roots initiatives, but in the post-war epoch, it culminated in professional and very close cooperation between the government and housing associations, with tenants in a passive role of receiving welfare (Bossuyt et al, 2018). The associations lost sight of the preferences of their own clients. Controlled liberalisation was accomplished in the housing policy reform of 1990 but the government lost control in the booming economy over the course of the 1990s. The new prosperity enlarged the classic risk profile of affluent non-governmental organisations (NGOs), not being controlled by politics nor by the market, resulting in fat offices, high managerial incomes, speculative behaviour on capital markets (beyond the legal margins) and even corruption. Scandals made the housing associations easy prey for an ideological politics of residualisation. The tenants and their social movements kept quiet (surprisingly, in the epoch of scandals and marginalisation) but new initiatives are welling up, attempting to re-establish the choice of residents as a cornerstone in the supply of social housing. A wide number of local initiatives have arisen, sometimes instigated by housing associations and by groups of tenants, to enable participation in the commissioning of housing. A change of law in 2015 enabled housing cooperatives, but in practice, this is still waiting for normalisation at a more general scale under the current policy conditions of residualisation. Most experiments relate to the refurbishment of existing housing stocks. An interesting case of a housing association in Rotterdam (Woonbron) created the option for different rent regimes (traditional, fixed rent for a certain period, fixed rent increase) but also socially bound ownership and ownership with a buy-back option (Gruis et al, 2005). Recent examples include many options to provide groups of tenants with the opportunity to commission the structural renovation of a block of dismantled homes, or to buy and renovate them themselves ('*klussenflats*'). Also, new hybrid constructions of buy and rent are being tried out, for instance, selling the homes to tenants but keeping the services and facility care with housing associations.

Grass-roots initiatives of home-building

Most literature in Europe on grass-roots or collaborative housing builds on individual (promising) cases. Several attempts to upgrade this analysis to more general and comparative levels wrestle with the fact that these practices in European states are still small in scale and highly diversified (Dol et al, 2012; Tummers, 2015; Czischke, 2018). This literature underlines the necessity of mainstreaming and normalising promising practices of resident-led housing production. There has been a re-emergence of such housing practices in the aftermath of recent trends of liberalisation, privatisation and growing pressures on housing affordability. Self-build construction initiatives are recognised as responding to growing social needs. Both individual and collective varieties resonate with social tendencies of both pluralisation and individualisation, calling for the innovative and differentiated organisation of different groups of residents. This extends to all parts of Europe, including less economically affluent parts of Eastern Europe, where this may not always be consistently acknowledged in statistics of owner occupation (Hegedűs et al, 2018). Hence, this book gives special attention to European cases from urban regions in Albania and Turkey, where self-provisioning through owner building and collaboration, sometimes through informal means, has been highly significant (see Chapters 9 and 12). In this chapter, we keep attention on some remarkable cases in Western Europe: Germany and Belgium.

Germany is the country of private rent. Social housing in Germany has historically been provided by a range of public and private organisations, but by the 1980s, all public sector agencies had already been privatised. A crucial downturn of performance by private rent organisations was the withdrawal of public subsidies. In 2006, the option of governmental contributions was made completely dependent on the (highly different) policy attitudes and capabilities of local governments and the overall figures of private rent decreased (from 18 per cent to some 4 per cent). In the major cities, many new experiments in inhabitant-led housing have emerged, usually on a small scale, both in the domain of private rent and in the domain of owner-occupied self-build initiatives. Knorr-Siedow (2008) and Droste (2015) provided a broad oversight of experiments in major cities, in particular, Berlin, with similar projects in Leipzig, Hamburg and Munich. Sometimes, these collective self-build initiatives started with wealthier end users in collaboration with architects, but over the course of time, other groups with a vulnerable condition or specific requirements (dependent elder residents, Aids patients and so on) were included (Knorr-Siedow, 2008: 135). Often, they qualify for particular subsidies, such as in cases of refurbishment or specific disabilities. Knorr-Siedow (2008: 138) also makes mention of homesteading initiatives and particular collaborations of residents with municipalities, such as in the case of the appeasement of radical squatters, where initial conflict situations were solved in joint objectives and gradually normalised. Special lifestyles require a differentiated response in diversifying cities.

Belgium is a nation of homeowners. However, unlike other countries in North-Western Europe that have only more recently transitioned to homeownership, the dominance of homeownership can be traced well back to the early 20th century. Historically, the liberal Belgian constitution coupled with a Christian political hegemony has guaranteed the strong protection of individual property rights and a housing politics oriented around the promotion of homeownership. Since the late 19th century, political elites have nurtured social aspirations to homeownership through a consistent reinforcement of a system consisting of tax exemptions, cheap loans and financial subsidies (De Decker, 2008). Coupled with a weak, or absent, planning tradition and abundant land, this has had tremendous effects on the housing landscape. Notable in this regard is the role of residents, who have been responsible for commissioning their own privately built single-family homes. Belgium is the country in Europe in which self-building is most predominant: more than half of all dwellings are constructed through self-building (Halleux et al, 2002; Halleux, 2005). Private rent (23.8 per cent) is hardly considered an alternative because of a lack of rent control and minimal quality rules, leading to a poor price–quality ratio (De Decker, 2008). Social rent is similarly peripheral to the housing system, accounting for 8.5 per cent of total stock. The withdrawal of public institutions from housing production is a defining feature of Belgian residential housing production (Dessouroux and Romainville, 2011).

Public bodies have financially supported homeownership through individual owner building. This has resulted in differences between peri-urbanised areas and more densely built areas such as inner-cites and the coast (De Meulder et al, 1999). While self-build owner-occupied homes are a notable feature of peri-urban and suburban residential housing production, real estate developers are more important in urban cores such as Brussels (Romainville, 2017). It is in the context of these urban cores that we also witness the emergence of various forms of community-based housing schemes as a response to problems of affordability for low- and middle-income households and minority groups. In urban cores such as the Brussels Capital Region, affordable and good-quality rental housing is scarce and neither the state nor the market is able or willing to provide this. Activists and community organisations confronted with housing affordability problems have established various novel housing initiatives in relation to claiming the right to housing (Aernouts and Ryckewaert, 2019 These often build on rental cooperatives, which can be traced back to the early 20th century and 'garden-city' principles, but have been overshadowed by the dominance of individual owner building. Although quantitatively still lacking, there is an emergence of novel initiatives in which residents are actively involved in the development and management of their dwelling throughout Belgium.

Conclusion: a new stage of transition

The housing of low- and middle-income groups is well established in many European city-regions thanks to the intermediating welfare state regimes. Yet, the social sector is not a quiet asset on the European housing markets. After half a century of expanding social sectors, the last two decades manifested a general tendency of residualisation, including even radical shifts, such as in England and Germany. Rent is the most common structure for low- and moderate-income groups in North-Western Europe. It provides generally more relief than countries without these facilities (where starters and low-income groups depend on family structures and/or the lower segments of private markets). Rent is provided via different tenures: municipal (largely disappeared), delegated municipal, social and private. The social accessibility of the rented facilities differs over countries. Paradoxically, the most residualised system (in England) excludes middle-income residents but provides the strongest legal guarantees of accessibility for the large group of very poor. However, this housing system has been dramatically marginalised after the selling off of the better parts. The position of social housing in other economically advanced countries has become more hybrid, reducing the social housing stock (by sales and lower investment) and narrowing the eligibility of social housing while neglecting the growth of incomes after entrance. It is a sort of 'slow motion marginalisation' of previously affluent social housing positions.

The commissioning role of residents vis-a-vis the powerful public and private stakeholders of housing markets is in stage of transition. The passive receivers of the welfare state arrangements (municipalities, local housing agencies and residents) have been alerted by the retreat of central government. Concerns are particularly growing in the core areas of economically advanced city-regions, where the tendencies of spatial disposition have become increasingly selective to low- and middle-income groups . New arrangements are not yet solidly established, but emerging, highly diverse and bounded to different local contexts. New opportunities for active residential commissioning are being created in collective initiatives of housing management, in the joint refurbishment of social estates and in new hybrid forms of rent/ownership. Furthermore, the self-management of new home construction and cooperative initiatives of self-build are increasing, albeit not yet in large amounts. The empowering of residential commissioning faces both the residualisation of social sectors and the increasing exclusivity of urban spaces.

References

Aernouts, N. and Ryckewaert, M. (2019) 'Reproducing housing commons. Government involvement and differential commoning in a housing cooperative', *Housing Studies*, 34(1):92-110

Arundel, R. and Ronald, R. (2015) 'Parental co-residence, shared living and emerging adulthood in Europe: semi-dependent housing across welfare regime and housing system contexts', *Journal of Youth Studies*, 19(7): 885–905.

Bossuyt, D., Salet, W. and Majoor, S. (2018) 'Commissioning as the cornerstone of self-build. Assessing the constraints and opportunities of self-build housing in the Netherlands', *Land Use Policy*, 77: 524–33.

Clarke, J. (2005) 'New Labour's citizens: activated, empowered, responsibilised, abandoned?', *Critical Social Policy*, 25(4): 447–63.

Czischke, D. (2018) 'Collaborative housing and housing providers: toward an analytical framework of multi-stakeholder collaboration in housing co-production', *International Journal of Housing Policy*, 18(1): 55–81.

De Decker, P. (2008) 'Facets of housing and housing policies in Belgium', *Journal of Housing and the Built Environment*, 23(3): 155–71.

De Meulder, B., Schreurs, J., Cock, A. and Notteboom, B. (1999) 'Sleutelen aan het Belgische stadslandschap' ['Patching up the Belgian urban landscape'], *Oase*, 52: 78–113.

Dessouroux, C. and Romainville, A. (2011) 'La production de logements en Belgique et à Bruxelles – Acteurs, dynamiques, géographie', *EchoGéo*, 15: 1–19.

Dol, K., Lennartz, C. and De Decker, P. (2012) 'Self-provided housing in developed societies', in S. Smith, M. Elsinga, L. Fox Mahoney, O. Seow Eng, S. Wachter and R. Ronald (eds) *International Encyclopedia of Housing & Home. Volume 6.* Oxford: Elsevier, pp 310–15.

Droste, C. (2015) 'German co-housing: an opportunity for municipalities to foster socially inclusive urban development?', *Urban Research & Practice*, 8(1): 79–92.

Esping-Andersen, G. (1990) *The Three Worlds of Welfare Capitalism*, Cambridge: Polity Press.

Fitzpatrick, S. and Stephens, M. (2008) *The Future of Social Housing*, London: Shelter.

Gruis, V.H., Elsinga, M., Wolters, A.G. and Priemus, H. (2005) 'Tenant empowerment through innovative tenures', *Housing Studies*, 20(1): 127–47.

Halleux, J.-M. (2005) 'Le rôle des promotions foncières et immobilières dans la production des périphéries: application à la Belgique et à ses nouveaux espaces résidentiels', *Revue Géographique de l'Est*, 45(3/4): 161–73.

Halleux, J.-M., Brück, L. and Mairy, N. (2002) 'La périurbanisation résidentielle en Belgique à la lumière des contextes suisse et danois: enracinement, dynamiques centrifuges et régulations collectives', *Belgeo. Revue Belge de Géographie*, 4: 333–54, https://doi.org/10.4000/belgeo.16086

Harloe, M. (1995) *The People's Home?*, Oxford: Blackwell.

Hegedüs, J. (2008) 'Social housing in transition countries: the case of Hungary', in K. Scanlon and C. Whitehead (eds) *Social Housing in Europe II: A Review of Policies and Outcomes*, London: London School of Economics and Political Science, pp 145–61.

Houard, N. (2011) *Social Housing across Europe*, Paris: Ministère de l'Écologie, du Développement durable, des Transports et du Logement.

Housing Europe (2017) 'Housing markets in the European Union 2017' in Housing Europe (ed) *The State of Housing in the European Union*, Brussel: Housing Europe, www.housingeurope.eu/resource-1000/the-state-of-housing-in-the-eu-2017

Housing Europe (2018) The state of housing in the EU 2015, www.housingeurope.eu/event-447/the-state-of-housing-in-the-eu-2015

Kemeny, J. (1995) *From Public Housing to Social Market*, London: Routledge.

Knorr-Siedow, T. (2008) 'Innovations from below? A new concept for social housing in Germany', in K. Scanlon and C. Whitehead (eds) *Social Housing in Europe II: A Review of Policies and Outcomes*, London: London School of Economics and Political Science, pp 131–44.

Lefebvre, H. (1996) *Writings on Cities*, Oxford: Blackwell.

Lennartz, C., Arundel, R.J. and Ronald, R. (2015) 'Younger adults and homeownership in Europe through the global financial crisis', *Population, Space and Place*, 22(8): 823–35.

Lux, M. (2011) 'Social housing in the Czech Republic', in N. Houard (ed) *Social Housing across Europe*, Paris: Ministère de l'Écologie, du Développement durable, des Transports et du Logement, pp 85–97.

Mullins, J. and Murie, A. (2006) *Housing Policy in the UK*, Basingstoke: Palgrave.

Murie, M. (2008) 'Social housing privatisation in England', in K. Scanlon and C. Whitehead (eds) *Social Housing in Europe II: A Review of Policies and Outcomes*, London: London School of Economics and Political Science, pp 241–59.

Pawson, H. (2008) 'Social housing and choice', in S. Fitzpatrick and M. Stephens (eds) *The Future of Social Housing*, London: Shelter, pp 85–100.

Poggio, T. and Whitehead, C. (eds) (2017) 'Social housing in Europe: legacies, new trends and the crisis', Special Issue, *Critical Housing Analysis*, 4(1): 1–10.

Purcell, M. (2003) 'Excavating Lefebvre: the right to city and its urban politics of the inhabitant', *Geojournal*, 58: 99–108.

Romainville, A. (2017) 'The financialization of housing production in Brussels', *International Journal of Urban and Regional Research*, 41(4): 623–41, https://onlinelibrary.wiley.com/doi/abs/10.1111/1468-2427.12517

Scanlon, K. and Whitehead, C. (2007) 'Social housing in Europe', in C. Whitehead and K. Scanlon (eds) *Social Housing in Europe*, London: London School of Economics and Political Science, pp 8–33.

Scanlon, K. and Whitehead, C. (eds) (2008) *Social Housing in Europe II: A Review of Policies and Outcomes*, London: London School of Economics and Political Science.

Stephens, M. (2008) 'The role of the social rented sector', in S. Fitzpatrick and M. Stephens (eds) *The Future of Social Housing*, London: Shelter, pp 27–38.

Stephens, M., Elsinga, M. and Knorr-Siedow, T. (2008) 'The privatisation of social housing: three different pathways', in K. Scanlon and C. Whitehead (eds) *Social Housing in Europe II: A Review of Policies and Outcomes*, London: London School of Economics and Political Science, pp 105–30.

Tummers, L. (2015) 'The re-emergence of self-help co-housing in Europe: a critical review of co-housing research', *Urban Studies*, 53(10): 2023–40.

Whitehead, C. and Scanlon, K. (eds) (2007) *Social Housing in Europe*, London: London School of Economics and Political Science, pp 8–33.

4

Self-building in contested spaces: livelihoods and productivity challenges of the urban poor in Africa

Nicky Pouw and Marina Humblot

Introduction

In Africa, it is estimated that one in two people will reside in cities by 2030.[1] Africa's rapid urbanisation and continuing poverty challenges result in rising urban slum populations to unprecedented heights. For example, the urban slum population as a percentage of the total urban population is higher than 80 per cent in the following ten African countries: Chad (98.9 per cent), Sierra Leone (97 per cent), Rwanda (96 per cent), Ethiopia (95.5 per cent), Mali (94.2 per cent), Madagascar (93 per cent), Central African Republic (87.5 per cent), Angola (86.5 per cent), Niger (83.6 per cent) and Guinea-Bissau (83.1 per cent) (UN-Habitat, 2018b). Yet, at the same time, there is sustained gross domestic product (GDP) growth in some African economies, for example, in Ghana (8.5 per cent), Ivory Coast (7.8 per cent) and Senegal (6.8 per cent) in 2017. In these countries, especially in the capital cities, the emergence of a prosperous middle class and a certain opulence is now changing the face of the urban economy. Stark inequalities in close proximity of one another lead to contested urban spaces in cities (Bayat, 2000; Bayat and Biekart, 2009; O'Connor, 2013). People are pulled into cities by economic opportunities, different lifestyles and improved well-being prospects for themselves and their relatives, whom they might leave (temporarily) behind in rural areas. The larger parts of what most African cities could be have not yet been built (World Bank, 2017), leading to the overpopulation of existing urban housing, high costs and self-building on marginal land plots. Simultaneously, urban development pushes existing groups of poor and marginalised people and their practised livelihoods out of city centres and towards its fringes, or towards the new fringes of an ever-expanding city. The lack of formal jobs, housing, building spaces, facilities and services implies newly lived experiences of urban deprivation for a growing urban population (Sassen, 2018). Many fall back on family and kinship support, social networks, informality, or illegality while creating their own living spaces and livelihoods. 'The working age population of 15–64 years is the group that typically migrates', the majority of whom are young adults (UNCTAD, 2018: 17). They are transiting out of a family home towards independent living, often finding their way into the city through social and kinship ties. Their arrival puts pressure on urban household resources and living spaces at the micro level, but also on the availability of urban food, transportation and labour markets, as well as on urban planning and services, and their respective governing institutions. For this reason, African cities are often characterised as 'crowded, disconnected and costly' (World Bank, 2017: 8).

Self-build housing is a common strategy among the existing urban poor and newcomers alike because of the insurmountable high cost and/or lack of regular housing in the city. Shelters are created within slum settlements by expanding on existing buildings or new urban fringes. Mobility and resource constraints direct their preferences to finding accommodation in proximity of labour opportunities, production sites and food corridors for subsistence. In particular, those who are engaged in small-scale food production choose to live nearby land and water resources. Among the most vulnerable are many women, who play a key role as food providers in the household. Their urban gardens and communal land plots constitute well-known principal locations of food enterprises and informal home-based economic activities, thus offering potential to contribute to local economic development (Majale, 2008: 271). Their food production is vitally important for the food and nutrition security of vulnerable urban populations. On the one hand, the rising number of urban poor and marginalised people stresses the demand for increased urban food productivity, which may not suffice to 'feed the city'. On the other hand, small-scale food producers encounter new and fierce competition from imported and prepared food commodities and changing urban diets to reduce cooking time and accommodate new tastes (Noack and Pouw, 2015).

According to the United Nations (UN) *State of the World Cities 2016* report (UN Habitat, 2016) a lot of African cities are characterised by high economic vulnerability.[2] This creates challenges for the productivity gains of growing African cities as urban poverty can dampen or undermine urban economic growth. With the continent's ambition to renew African cities to the model of Singapore (UN-Africa

Renewal, 2016), this chapter hypothesises that development spaces for the livelihoods of the urban poor are shrinking, including spaces for self-building. In this chapter, self-building is comprehensively defined as any self-construction of living and working spaces to sustain a livelihood, which is broader than just housing. After a brief discussion of the contested debates on African urbanisation and poverty in the second section, we will explore recent data on informal settlements and urban productivity in the third section. In the fourth section, we will zoom in on self-building in (peri-)urban agriculture as a dominant strategy of poor urban food producers, based on a case study in Ouagadougou, Burkina Faso. The practical and conceptual policy implications of these findings are discussed in the fifth section in terms of 'shrinking spaces' for the livelihoods of the urban poor, and the sixth section concludes.

African urbanisation and productivity growth

In this section, we will discuss the shift in paradigms on urban development in Africa over the past five decades in relation to empirical data on informal settlement development and productivity. Early scholarly work on urban development in Africa portrayed the new African cities at the time as administrative and commercial centres, being 'the nexus between Africa and Europe' (McCall, 1955: 151). Congestion and overcrowding have been perceived as problems characterising African urban development from the 1960s onwards (Gutkind, 1960), and became connected to issues of a growing urban labour force (Elkan, 1960), rural–urban migration (Elkan, 1967; Caldwell, 1969) and social networks (Mitchell, 1969). These studies were soon followed by a body of literature addressing the multiple urban planning challenges of African cities (for example, Hutton, 1972; Kanyeihamba, 1973; Soja and Weaver, 1976; King, 1977; Stretton, 1978; Obudho and El-Shaks, 1979). Urban planners from the Global North teamed up with local urban planning and development institutions to mimic European city development plans in Africa. However, it proved difficult to encompass the social and political dimensions of urban development in planning practices and cultures since these were not home-grown. This led to some arguing pessimistically that urban transformation was failing in African cities, not least due to their structural dependency on high-income countries (for example, Bardinett, 1977), while the optimists, such as Collier and Lai (1980), emphasised how (small-scale) economic development in African countries was realised thanks to enhanced productivity in urban centres (see also Mabogunje, 1990).

This contestation in the international literature between more pessimistic and optimistic views on African urban slum and productivity development can still be traced in the recent debate. For example, as Majale (2008: 271) states: 'In many [African] cities, slums and squatter settlements are also the principal location of informal-sector enterprises, including micro- and small-enterprises and home-based enterprises. They consequently make a significant contribution to employment creation, local economic development, the urban economy and national growth.' Others continue to stress the land access problem in Africa's rapidly growing cities, which leads to a 'mushrooming' of informal settlements (UN-Habitat, 2010, 2011: 31) and increases the risks of African cities being prone to a 'low development trap' (World Bank, 2017: 8). More recently, there has been a shift in this debate. Scholars and policymakers have begun to argue for a new kind of 'African urbanism'[3] or, in a similar vein, an informality lens (Porter et al, 2011), whereby the urban economy is rethought from the bottom up (the slum), which might lead to a more realistic and useful framing, according to Edgar Pieterse (2011). Simply replicating the urban development examples of the world's advanced economies of the 1950s and 1960s is no longer considered a credible sustainable development path. There is no 'one-size-fits-all' solution (UN-Habitat, 2014). An alternative view is needed that recognises the 'stubborn realities' of self-building by the 'subaltern' (Roy, 2011; Watson, 2013), the 'quiet encroachment' of urban spaces (Bayat and Biekart, 2009: 545), self-organisation and management on the ground, and considers the hidden potential of 'anti-planning' strategies and approaches (Gandy, 2006). Such a view partially links up to the latest policy of the United Nations Human Settlements Programme (UN-Habitat) to develop more differentiated urban policies, including industrial zoning and assistance for transforming self-help housing into more sustainable residential areas (Parnell and Hart, 1999), instead of slum relocation or gentrification (Bredenoord and Van Lindert, 2010; Lemanski, 2014; UN-Habitat, 2018a). However, overall, the modernisation and neoliberal paradigm remains dominant in the policies of multilateral institutions and national and urban governments as far as urban development is concerned (Brenner and Theodore, 2002).

Accordingly, African cities are encouraged to 'seize a more prominent position in the world economy by enhancing their accessibility, connectivity, markets and urban attractiveness' (UN-Habitat, 2018a: 13), and to 'open their doors' to globalisation (World Bank, 2017). According to Pierre Guislain, Vice-President of Private Sector, Infrastructure & Industrialization of the African Development

Bank (AFDB), attracting more foreign direct investment is key to urban transformation:

> With a population of over 1.2 billion and a combined GDP of USD 3.4 trillion, Africa is an attractive destination for foreign direct investment (FDI), which amounted to USD 56.5 billion in 2016 […]. Benefiting from economies of scale and agglomeration, African cities can become the drivers of economic growth and productivity. (UN-Habitat, 2018a: 10)

Despite calls for more basic urban infrastructure development, poverty reduction and inclusive growth and cities in all of the aforementioned reports, an elaborated vision of how this could exactly empower and upscale the productive capacities of the urban poor remains unclear. A strategic perspective on spatial urban governance regarding the different functions of the urban economy, including the basic function of providing food to the city, with a multitude of stakeholders at multiple levels, is also lacking. According to Pouw and De Bruijne (2015: 284):

> strategic governance is then about the effective realignment of predefined strategies with performances and outcomes within a context of interactive governance. In this way, urban governance can respond and adapt effectively to the complex challenges it faces. For example, binding urban governance is needed in situations where inequality has led to conflict and violence between different population sub-groups in the city.

Existing urban governance is linked to specific interest groups that the urban poor are typically not part of. Their interests are under-represented, and their economic activities are not considered as part of the urban productivity equation. In this chapter, we will seek to learn from taking a bottom-up approach to these issues, based on an urban food producer's case study situated in Ouagadougou, Burkina Faso.

Africa's growing cities: informal settlements and productivity

Africa's rapidly growing population is increasingly living in cities, with the continent's urban population expected to reach 50 per cent by 2030, up from 36 per cent in 2016 (UN-Habitat, 2018b). In this section, we explore the nexus between informal settlements and productivity in Africa's growing cities. Urbanisation is often assumed to translate into productivity growth since urban centres are hubs for economic activity, research and innovation, as well as the advancement of human capital. However, African cities are characterised by deep poverty and growing inequality. Contested access to urban land has long been identified as one of the multiple aspects of deep poverty and socio-economic inequality in Africa (UN-Habitat, 2010). Given that many urban poor people are engaged in the basic functions of the economy, including food production, for which they require access to fertile land and water resources, the renewal of African cities threatens their livelihoods. From the perspective of the urban poor, this implies insecurity of settlement, contestations over land access and use, a polluted environment and water, and mobility, transportation and market access challenges. In the following tables, we explore the scant data[4] that are available on African city development by focusing on the following indicators: the share of urban populations in informal settlements and productivity. Urban productivity is defined as 'the average achievements of the cities in terms of creating wealth and how it's shared, or cities' contribution to economic growth and development, generation of income, provision of decent jobs and equal opportunities for all' (UN-Habitat, 2018c). In Table 4.1, the percentage shares of urban populations residing in slums and informal settlements are presented for 38 out of the 52 African countries over the period 1990–2009. Out of these, in 20 countries we observe a decreasing trend of informal settlements, compared to seven increasing, and 11 where the rate is staying more or less the same (within a 0.1 per cent margin) or is inconclusive due to a lack of data or spurious data over time. However, of great concern is the fact that the *absolute* number of people residing in slums and informal settlements is increasing in most countries, with the seeming exception of Accra in Ghana and Conakry in Niger, but this needs to be confirmed when more recent data become available. This illustrates the vast challenge for African urban management: how to accommodate the growing number of urban dwellers and their livelihoods, and to (re)connect urbanisation to urban productivity growth in order to benefit urban transformation?

For that reason, we turn to a review of urban productivity data next. Unfortunately, these data are even more scant than data on living conditions. The productivity levels of urban populations in cities in Northern and Southern Africa are relatively highest (see Table 4.2). There is a top-performing category including Cairo, Casablanca,

Table 4.1: Urban populations living in slums and informal settlements (%)

Country	1990	1995	2000	2005	2007	2009
Angola				86.5	76.2	65.8
Benin	79.3	76.8	74.3	71.8	70.8	69.8
Burkina Faso	78.8	72.4	65.9	59.5	59.9	
Burundi				64.3	64.3	
Cameroon	50.8	49.6	48.4	47.4	46.6	46.1
Central African Republic	87.5	89.7	91.9	94.1	95	95.9
Chad	98.9	96.4	93.9	91.3	90.3	89.3
Comoros	65.4	65.4	65.4	68.9	68.9	
Democratic Rep. Congo				76.4	69.1	61.7
Egypt	50.2	39.2	28.1	17.1	17.1	17.1
Equatorial Guinea				66.3		
Ethiopia	95.5	95.5	88.6	81.8	79.1	76.4
Gabon				38.7		
Gambia				45.4	34.8	
Ghana	65.5	58.8	52.1	45.4	42.8	40.1
Guinea	80.4	68.8	57.3	38.7	45.7	
Guinea-Bissau				83.1		
Kenya	54.9	54.8	54.8	54.8	54.8	54.7
Lesotho				35.1	44.4	
Liberia						68.3
Madagascar	93	88.6	84.1	80.6	78	76.2
Malawi	66.4	66.4	66.4	66.4	67.7	68.9
Mali	94.2	84.8	75.4	65.9	65.9	65.9
Morocco	37.4	35.2	24.2	13.1	13.1	13.1
Mozambique	75.6	76.9	78.2	79.5	80	80.5
Namibia	34.4	34.1	33.9	33.9	33.6	33.5
Niger	83.6	83.1	82.6	82.1	81.9	81.7
Nigeria	77.3	73.5	69.6	65.8	64.2	62.7
Rwanda	96	87.9	79.7	71.6	68.3	65.1
Senegal	70.6	59.8	48.9	43.3	41.1	38.8
Sierra Leone					97	
Somalia				73.5	73.6	73.6
South Africa			33.2	28.7	23	23
Tanzania	77.4	73.7	70.1	66.4	65	63.5
Togo				62.1		
Uganda	75	75	75	66.7	63.4	60.1
Zambia	57	57.1	57.2	57.2	57.3	57.3
Zimbabwe	4	3.7	3.3	17.9	21	24.1

Source: Elaborated by author using the UN-Habitat (2018b) database

Cape Town and Johannesburg, with productivity higher than 0.62. There is a 'middle' category with rates between 0.30 and around 0.50, including Cameroon, Accra, Addis Ababa, Abidjan, Nairobi, Niamey, Lagos, Dar es Salaam, Kampala and Lusaka. Finally, there is a distinct lower category with rates below 0.20, including Conakry, Monrovia, Antananarivo and Harare. Combining the productivity data with the changes in informal settlement populations (absolute numbers and relative change) does not show a clear pattern between the indicators. High productivity does not correlate clearly with either increases or decreases in urban informal settlement dwellers. There is a location-specific indication of high productivity combined with both the number and percentage share of urban informal settlement dwellers decreasing only in Casablanca, Morocco. In Accra, Ghana, the absolute change in informal settlement population seems to be stabilising, and coupled with medium productivity growth and a decreasing relative share of slums, this might lead to more positive figures in the nearby future. The absolute number of urban population in informal settlements is more than doubling in Addis Ababa, Ethiopia, and in Lagos, Nigeria, which is coupled with medium productivity growth in both cities. In the cities with lower productivity, the absolute rise in informal settlement populations seems to challenge urban productivity levels.

There is thus far limited evidence of cities where urban governance is successful in improving living conditions for the urban poor within rapidly growing African cities. However, given that there is significant scope for productivity improvement, it is not strategic for urban governance to overlook the productivity potential of the urban poor. Given their big numbers (and young age), neglecting their productive capacities, as well as their current livelihoods, is unwise from a purely economic perspective – let alone from a social and political perspective and the continent's ambition to build inclusive cities. The interests of the poor are currently not serviced by urban governance policies and actions, which focus one-sidedly on city renewal and attracting FDI.

Self-building by the urban poor

Self-building initiatives by the urban poor and by new urban dwellers migrating into the city is a common phenomenon across African cities (Harris, 1998; Gilbert, 1999; Landman and Napier, 2010). In large-scale cities in particular, self-building, squatting and encroachment are commonly shared strategies among the urban poor (Bayat, 2000; Baumann et al, 2004; Landman and Napier, 2010). However, in research and policy reports on self-building, the focus is commonly and exclusively on housing. Yet, if we look at the livelihoods of the urban poor, self-building strategies are not confined to housing constructions, but also encompass (temporary) constructions that facilitate their home-based economic activities, urban agriculture and other small production activities. Zooming in on the case of small-scale urban

Table 4.2: Urban productivity index and informal settlement change

Country, city	Productivity*	Informal settlement population change (absolute)	Informal settlement population change (%)
Cameroon, Yaoundé (2012)	0.492	+	–
Egypt, Cairo (2013)	0.679	+	–
Ethiopia, Addis Ababa (2013)	0.503	++	–
Ghana, Accra (2013)	0.347	+/–	–
Guinea, Conakry (2012)	0.133	+/–	–
Ivory Coast, Abidjan (2012)	0.452	No data	No data
Kenya, Nairobi (2013)	0.481	+	+/–
Liberia, Monrovia (2012)	0.048	No data	No data
Madagascar, Antananarivo (2012)	0.171	+	–
Morocco, Casablanca (2013)	0.634	–	–
Niger, Niamey (2012)	0.402	+	–
Nigeria, Lagos (2013)	0.475	++	–
South Africa, Cape Town (2013)	0.628	+	–
South Africa, Johannesburg (2013)	0.654	+	–
Tanzania, Dar as Salaam (2012)	0.427	+	–
Uganda, Kampala (2012)	0.512	+	–
Zambia, Lusaka (2012)	0.316	+	–
Zimbabwe, Harare (2012)	0.246	+	+

* The urban productivity index ranges from low (0) to high (1 and above)

** Absolute change is computed by the percentage change in the urban slum population multiplied by the absolute number of the urban population in two subsequent years, taking the most recent data points (+ indicates an increase; ++ indicates a doubling or more; – indicates a decrease; +/– indicates approximately even).

Source: Elaborated by the author from the UN-Habitat (2018b) 'Urban database'

food producers in Ouagadougou (Burkina Faso), we will argue that urban development threatens their basis for subsistence and income, and that they encounter shrinking spaces for productivity due to the entanglement of their livelihood with the spatiality of natural resource access within an expanding city.

Ouagadougou food producer groups: in search of land and water

Ouagadougou is the capital city of Burkina Faso and home to a rapidly growing urban population of 2.7 million in 2015, compared to 0.82 million in 2004 (Commune de Ouagadougou, 2018). The city has expanded its boundaries in more or less concentric circles, as indicated in Figure 4.1, and the expansion is continuing to date (although a more recent map is not available). Small-scale informal food producer groups have practised urban agriculture in the proximity of water resources over decades: in the North near Loumbila; in the (now) central area nearby the water dam in Tanghin and Tampouy; and in the South near Pissy and in Bobo-Dioulasso. However, land is increasingly becoming scarce, costly and inaccessible due to urban population growth and development (Bellwood-Howard et al, 2015). Industrial zoning in the areas of Kossodo (gas) and Bobo-Dioulasso (sugar, cotton, soap, batteries and chargers, chemicals, and plastics) has been small in scale for long time but is now expanding and claiming more land, infrastructure and access to water.

Informal food producer groups range in size and composition, from 30 to 250 members, consisting of men and women, or women only. In our study[5] on the food production livelihoods of the urban poor organised in informal groups, we located seven groups (see Figure 4.2). The groups were selected through a purposeful stratified sample covering informal settlements on all sides of Ouagadougou's greater central area, and included mixed and women-only informal food producer groups. Focus group discussions (FGDs) on each site were organised with groups of women and men (separately) of five to six members each to discuss access and control over resources (including land and water), food production, processing and marketing strategies and practices, and group governance. In addition, participatory observation and key informant interviews were held to triangulate and complement the findings from the FGDs. Although the selected groups used to practise agriculture in the peri-urban areas, many of them have now become part of the Ouagadougou central area. Their land plots and surrounding areas are increasingly encroached upon by new housing and industries. On the one hand, this brings the advantage of infrastructure being built (roads, transport, commercial centres) and nearby customers for the sale of their produce, but on the other hand, and given their insecure land titles, access to land and water is becoming more difficult. Farmers in Tanghin reported that they would soon have to leave because a road to access the new airport in Loumbila will go through their plots. The construction of infrastructures capable of welcoming the growing population overturn current city planning, and the informal settings even more so. Moreover, access to water resources is becoming increasingly difficult because of an increasing

Figure 4.1: Urban area sub-division, 1932–2003

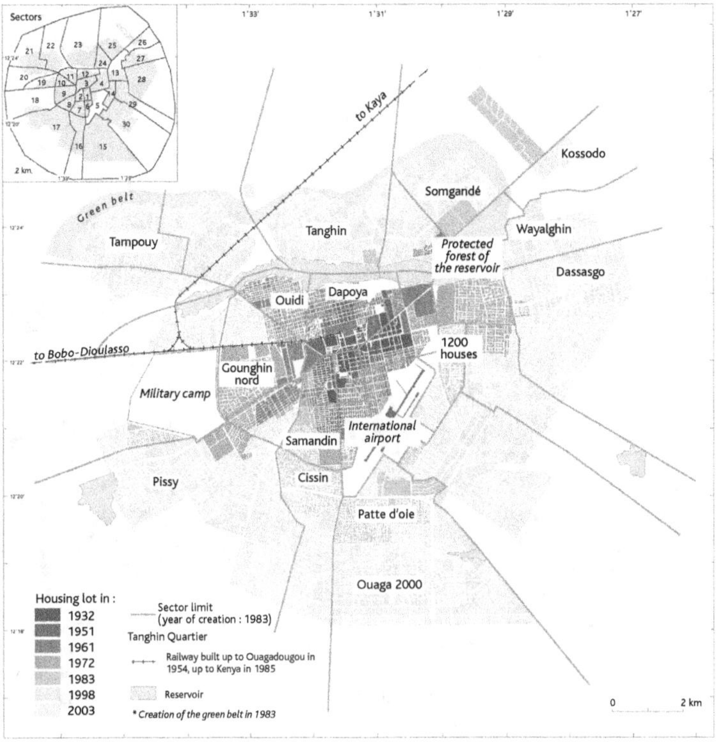

Source: Fournet et al (2008)

demand from ever more urban dwellers and because of the industrial zoning preventing the farmers from accessing and using the water resource easily and freely.

The food producer groups grow a mix of leafy vegetables (lettuce, celery, cabbage, amaranth, sorrel, spinach and parsley), fruit vegetables (strawberries, a local variant of eggplant, cucumber, beans, pepper, okra, green peas, tomatoes and zucchini) and bulb and root vegetables (onions, garlic, radish, turnip, carrot, beetroot and potatoes). Some groups combine this with growing and selling tree seedlings. Three groups out of these seven engage in food processing as well. They produce maize flour, rice flour, moringa powder, couscous, biscuits and food mixtures (for example, couscous with dried vegetables). One group, la Saisonnière, is famous for adhering to agro-ecology, not using chemicals, being a women-only group and providing food education to children in their gardens. The groups process foods nearby the land plots or in residential areas close to their homesteads. Access

Figure 4.2: Selected food producers groups in urban and peri-urban Ouagadougou

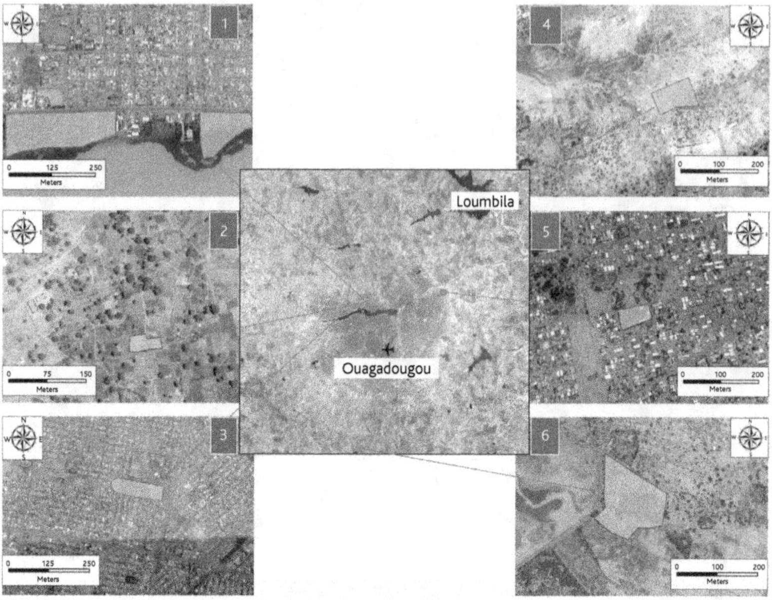

Notes: (1) Association de Léon and Namab Sanga, Tanghin, Ouagadougou, mixed, around 80 people; (2) Béo Néeré, Tanghin, Ouagadougou, mixed, 24 people; (3) Nabons-Wende, Tampouy, Ouagadougou, women, 25 people; (4) Yelemani, Loumbila (22 km north from Ouagadougou), women, eight people; (5) La Saisonnière, Sector 42, Ouagadougou, women, 50 people; (6) Riimpogb-Noonma, Kiervaoghin, Boulbi (16km south from Ouagadougou), mixed, unknown number of people.

Source: Field research by Marina Humblot (2016–17) as part of the formerly mentioned NWO-WOTRO/ Food & Business Knowledge Platform research project on 'Building Inclusive Business Models for Women Food Entrepreneurs in Burkina Faso and Kenya, 2015–2019'.

to electricity, water and technology is very limited, so their food-processing techniques remain basic. Lack of space and infrastructure for processing and storage also limits their productivity. However, perhaps the biggest challenge is secure access to clean water to irrigate their crops. Although, the groups nearby the water dam have sustainable access to water as long as they are entitled to use this stretch of land through the permission of the urban municipality (they do not hold private land titles), the other groups struggle to systematically access water for irrigation. Since the producers do not live next to their land plots, it is risky to leave water irrigation equipment unattended on their lands as it sometimes gets stolen. Instead, the food producer groups build their own, low-tech and low-cost constructions and facilities to store water and irrigate their crops. These range from planting tables and plots delimited by bricks in which the water is kept longer, water-dripping jars dug into the soil, vertical gardening in sacks, sandwich mounds and water tanks with dripping hoses (see Figures 4.3 and 4.4).

Figure 4.3: Self-built food production systems in (peri-)urban agriculture

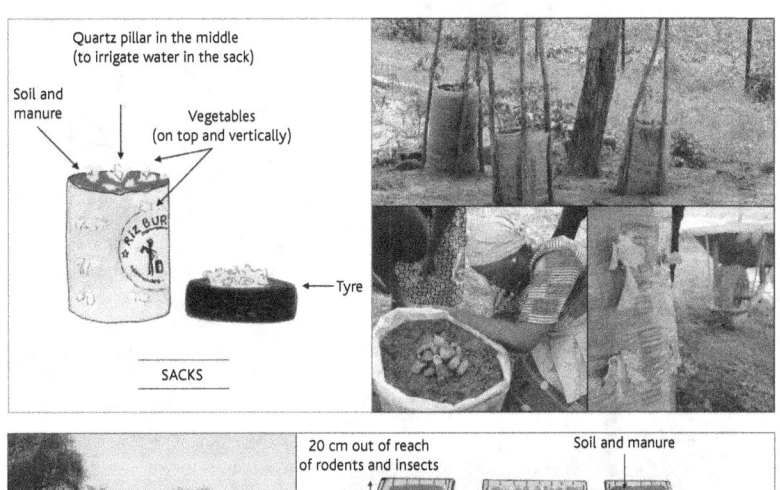

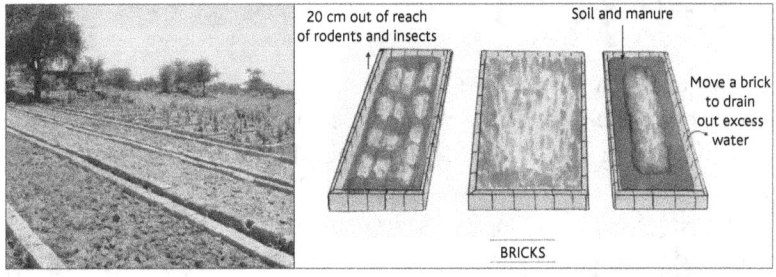

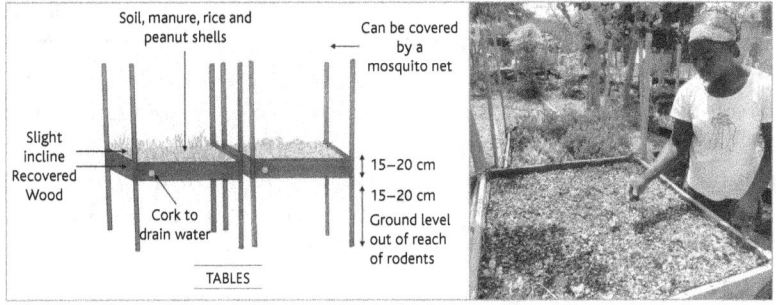

Source: Marina Humblot (2017)

The different techniques and adaptation strategies on production sites were identified through in-situ observations and within people's discourses and testimonies during key informant interviews with group leaders and FGDs with food producers.

These self-built constructions facilitate food production and processing by the urban poor, and contribute to their own food and nutrition security and that of urban communities. Yet, in the urban food chain, these production groups and their production and processing sites are rarely recognised and never supported by private and public sector

Figure 4.4: Self-built water irrigation system in (peri-)urban agriculture

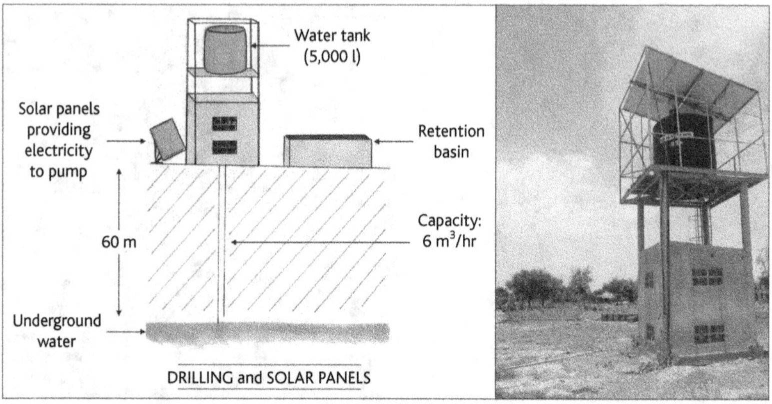

Source: Marina Humblot (2017)

investments or infrastructure. The self-built constructions and facilities are in themselves prone to destruction, replacement and damage done by bad weather conditions (for example, flooding and heavy rains). The poor bear the costs of maintenance and reconstruction themselves. By uniting as a group and seeking formalisation, some groups have managed to obtain formal credit and invest in infrastructure together. However, the risk of damage to or loss of the equipment and facilities is entirely on them. Altogether, with urban population growth and development, there is a shrinking space for the sustenance and development of the livelihoods and productive economic activities of the urban poor, such as is the case for the informal food producers in this case study. More research is needed to map out the livelihoods and productivity base of other (groups of) urban poor in order to see the full breadth and depth of their multiple essential but rather invisible basic inputs into urban productivity growth.

Discussion

From a bottom-up approach with a focus on the urban poor, the Burkinabe case study of food producer groups has demonstrated that the self-building activities of poor urban food producers typically encompass more than housing alone. Given their roles as food producers and processors, their self-building includes food production systems, water irrigation systems and food and compost production and storage sites. Opportunities and spaces for maintaining or expanding their food production activities are shrinking in a growing city environment, where urban renewal, industrial zoning and population growth take precedence over the basic functions of providing food and nutrition security to vulnerable populations. Yet, feeding the city is essential for urban productivity maintenance and growth. Focusing urban governance on professional business and attracting FDI alone is not strategic for including the poor. Addressing the insecurity of housing tenure of the urban poor as a residual problem will also not be enough to sustain their livelihoods and enhance their productivity. Self-building assistance can only be effective and responsive to social justice if urban poor people's livelihoods, and interconnections to their natural resource base, are acknowledged. Urban zoning and spatial development policies should recognise the tight entanglement of the subsistence and income earning needs of the urban poor with the spatiality of access to natural resource in and around the city. Customary law takes precedence over property law in Ouagadougou (Le Gall and Brondeau, 2012). Market gardening activities usually take place until construction or housing projects are planned, or any other new urban activity is set up by the government. The constant relocation of the poor due to urban development, as well as the prevailing land insecurity and limited access to water, as is the case in Ouagadougou, impinges the basis of existence and pushes them further into poverty and marginality. The inclusive growth and inclusive cities strategies and self-building assistance policies advocated by UN-Habitat and others (for example, Huchzermeyer and Misselwitz, 2016) should therefore be reconsidered in this light and take a more socially oriented approach (see also Cochrane, 2010). This can be achieved by critically investigating how urban development and growth ambitions can go hand in hand with inclusive strategies for urban poverty reduction and the consideration of livelihoods. First and foremost, this requires a more encompassing approach to self-building strategies that safeguards the livelihoods of the urban poor, and could be a stepping stone for enhancing their productivity levels. If the development spaces of the urban poor shrink further, their potential contribution to urban productivity can easily turn around and erode urban productivity. However, 'steering the [urban] economy towards achieving economic growth while governing a plurality of social and political actors with different interests and powers for poverty/inequality reduction and sustainability, is a daunting task' (Pouw and De Bruijne, 2015: 482). Urban policy and strategic governance initiatives are needed to counter the further marginalisation of vulnerable groups and their livelihoods within African cities.

Conclusion

Self-building by the urban poor in African cities encompasses more constructions and spaces than housing alone. On the basis of a case study of urban food producer groups in informal settlements of Ouagadougou, Burkina Faso, this chapter has demonstrated that food and nutrition security for vulnerable populations is strived for on contested land. Fresh vegetable production, processing and marketing, predominantly undertaken by women in informal associations, are economic activities by the urban poor that are currently overlooked by urban development policy. Strategic urban governance would include these food producer groups into their development policies and plans, not least because of their essential inputs into urban productivity and liveability.

Notes

[1] Acknowledgement: the authors would like to thank the NWO-WOTRO (Dutch Research Council – Science for Global Development) and the Netherlands Food & Business Knowledge Platform for subsidising the underlying research on 'Building Inclusive Business Models for Women Food Entrepreneurs in Burkina Faso and Kenya, 2015–2019', with grant number: W08.250.200.

[2] Whereby economic vulnerability is defined by the United Nations Development Programme (UNDP) by a composite index of eight indicators: population size; remoteness; merchandise export concentration; share of agriculture, forestry and fisheries in GDP; homelessness due to natural disasters; instability of agricultural production; instability of exports of goods and services; and the share of the population living in a low-elevated coastal zone.

[3] In the words of Maimunah Mohd Sharif, Executive Director of UN-Habitat in the *State of the African Cities Report* (UN-Habitat, 2018a: 8).

[4] Statistical data on urban development indicators in Africa are knowingly limited. There are only data for a limited number of cities and a limited number of years. It is not unlikely that the data presented here are biased in a sense that those countries and urban governments with a stronger data capacity base produce more and better data; these may represent better-organised countries and/or countries where large-scale external support and donor funding are provided through historical ties.

[5] The food production groups formed part of the field research in the research on 'Building Inclusive Business Models for Women Food Entrepreneurs in Burkina Faso and Kenya, 2015–2019', led by N. Pouw at the University of Amsterdam in partnership with research institutes, among others, in Burkina Faso (see Chapter 10).

References

Bardinet, C. (1977) 'City responsibilities in the structural dependence of sub-industrialized economies in Africa', *Antipode*, 9(3): 43–8.

Baumann, T., Bolnick, J. and Mitlin, D. (2004) 'The age of cities and organizations of the urban poor: the work of the South African Homeless People's Federation', in D. Mitlin and D. Satterthwaite (eds) *Empowering Squatter Citizen*, London: Earthscan, pp 193–215.

Bayat, A. (2000) 'From dangerous classes to "quiet rebels": politics of the urban subaltern in the Global South', *International Sociology*, 15(3): 533–57.

Bayat, A. and Biekart, K. (2009) 'Cities of extremes', *Development and Change*, 40(5): 815–25.

Bellwood-Howard, I., Häring, V., Karg, H., Roessler, R., Schlesinger, J. and Shakya, M. (2015) *Characteristics of Urban and Peri-Urban Agriculture in West Africa: Results of an Exploratory Survey Conducted in Tamale (Ghana) and Ouagadougou (Burkina Faso)* (vol 163), Colombo, Sri Lanka: International Water Management Institute (IWMI).

Bredenoord, J. and Van Lindert, P. (2010) 'Pro-poor housing policies: rethinking the potential of assisted self-help housing', *Habitat International*, 34(3): 278–87.

Brenner, N. and Theodore, N. (2002) 'Cities and the geographies of "actually existing neoliberalism"', *Antipode*, 34(3): 349–79.

Caldwell, J.C. (1969) *African Rural–Urban Migration: The Movement to Ghana's Towns*, Canberra: Australian National University Press.

Cochrane, A. (2010) 'Alternative approaches to local and regional development', in A. Pike, A. Rodríguez-Pose and J. Tomaney (eds) *Handbook of Local and Regional Development*, London and New York, NY: Routledge, pp 97–106.

Collier, P. and Lal, D. (1980) *Coercion, Compassion and Competition: Wage and Employment Trends and Structures in Kenya 1800–1980*, Washington, DC: The World Bank.

Commune de Ouagadougou (2018) 'Homepage', https://web.archive.org/web/20110629001118/http://www.mairie-ouaga.bf/

Elkan, W. (1960) *Migrants and Proletarians: Urban Labour in the Economic Development of Uganda*, London: Oxford University Press.

Elkan, W. (1967) 'Circular migration and the growth of towns in East Africa', *International Labour Review*, 96(6): 581–9.

Fournet, F., Meunier-Nikilema, A. and Salem, G. (2008) *Ouagadougou une urbanisation différenciée (1850–2004)*, Marseille: IRD éditions (Institut de Recherche pour le Développement).

Gandy, M. (2006) 'Planning, anti-planning, and the infrastructure crisis facing metropolitan Lagos', in M. Murray and G. Myers (eds) *Cities in Contemporary Africa*, New York, NY: Palgrave Macmillan, pp 247–64.

Gilbert, A. (1999) 'A home is for ever? Residential mobility and homeownership in self-help settlements', *Environment and Planning A*, 31(6): 1073–91.

Gutkind, P.C. (1960) 'Congestion and overcrowding: an African urban problem', *Human Organization*, 19(3): 129–34.

Harris, R. (1998) 'The silence of the experts: "aided self-help housing", 1939–1954', *Habitat International*, 22(2): 165–89.

Huchzermeyer, M. and Misselwitz, P. (2016) 'Coproducing inclusive cities? Addressing knowledge gaps and conflicting rationalities between self-provisioned housing and state-led housing programmes', *Current Opinion in Environmental Sustainability*, 20: 73–9.

Humblot, M. (2017) 'From risk to resilience', master's thesis, University of Amsterdam, the Netherlands.

Hutton, J. (ed) (1972) *Urban Challenge in East Africa*, Nairobi: East African Publishing House.

Kanyeihamba, G.W. (1973) *Urban Planning Law in East Africa: With Special Reference to Uganda*, Oxford: Pergamon Press.

King, A.D. (1977) 'Exporting "planning": the colonial and neo-colonial experience', *Urbanism Past & Present*, 5: 12–22.

Landman, K. and Napier, M. (2010) 'Waiting for a house or building your own? Reconsidering state provision, aided and unaided self-help in South Africa', *Habitat International*, 34(3): 299–305.

LeGall, L. and Brondeau, F. (2012) 'Les sites maraichers planifiés en milieu urbain: quelle sécurisation foncière pour quelle sécurisation économique? Analyse à l'échelle locale. Le cas du périmètre maraicher de Kossodo. Ouagadougou, Burkina Faso', XLIXème colloque SRDLF Industrie, ville et région dans une économie mondialisée, session speciale 'Nature et Metropole, regards croises', July, France.

Lemanski, C. (2014) 'Hybrid gentrification in South Africa: theorising across southern and northern cities', *Urban Studies*, 51(14): 2943–60.

Mabogunje, A.L. (1990) 'Urban planning and the post-colonial state in Africa: a research overview', *African Studies Review*, 33(2): 121–203.

Majale, M. (2008) 'Employment creation through participatory urban planning and slum upgrading: the case of Kitale, Kenya', *Habitat International*, 32: 270–82.

McCall, D.F. (1955) 'Dynamics of urbanization in Africa', *The Annals of the American Academy of Political and Social Science*, 298(1): 151–60.

Mitchell, J.C. (ed) (1969) *Social Networks in Urban Situations: Analyses of Personal Relationships in Central African Towns*, Manchester: Manchester University Press.

Noack, A.L. and Pouw, N.R.M. (2015) 'A blind spot in food and nutrition security: where culture and social change shape the local food plate', *Agriculture and Human Values*, 32: 169–82.

Obudho, R.A. and El-Shakhs, S. (1979) *Development of Urban Systems in Africa*, New York, NY: Praeger Publishers.

O'Connor, A. (2013) *The African City*, London and New York, NY: Routledge.

Parnell, S. and Hart, D. (1999) 'Self-help housing as a flexible instrument of state control in 20th-century South Africa', *Housing Studies*, 14(3): 367–86.

Pieterse, E. (2011) 'Grasping the unknowable: coming to grips with African urbanisms', *Social Dynamics*, 37(1): 5–23.

Porter, L., Lombard, M., Huxley, M., Ingin, A.K., Islam, T., Briggs, J. and Watson, V. (2011) 'Informality, the commons and the paradoxes for planning: concepts and debates for informality and planning self-made cities: ordinary informality? The reordering of a Romany neighbourhood. The land formalisation process and the peri-urban zone of Dar es Salaam, Tanzania. Street vendors and planning in Indonesian cities. Informal urbanism in the USA: new challenges for theory and practice engaging with citizenship and urban struggle through an informality lens', *Planning Theory & Practice*, 12(1): 115–53.

Pouw, N.R.M. and De Bruijne, G.A. (2015) 'Strategic governance for inclusive development', *European Journal of Development Research*, 27(4): 481–7.

Roy, A. (2011) 'Slum dog cities: rethinking subaltern urbanism', *International Journal of Urban and Regional Research*, 35(2): 223–38.

Sassen, S. (2018) *Cities in a World Economy*, Thousand Oaks, CA: Sage Publications.

Soja, E.W. and Weaver, C.E. (1976) *Urbanization and Underdevelopment in East Africa*, Beverly Hills, CA: Sage.

Stretton, H. (1978) *Urban Planning in Rich and Poor Countries*, London: Mansell.

UN-Africa Renewal (United Nations Africa Renewal) (2016) 'Africa's cities of the future', *Africa Renewal*, 30(1): 4–5, www.un.org/africarenewal/magazine/april-2016/africa's-cities-future

UNCTAD (United Nations Conference on Trade and Development) (2018) *Economic Development in Africa Report 2018. Migration for Structural Transformation*, New York, NY, and Geneva: UNCTAD.

UN-Habitat (United Nations Human Settlements Programme) (2010) *State of the World's Cities 2010/2011: Bridging the Urban Divide*, London: Earthscan.

UN-Habitat (2011) *Cities and Climate Change: Global Report on Human Settlements 2011*, London: Earthscan.

UN-Habitat (2014) *A New Strategy of Sustainable Neighbourhood Planning: Five Principles*, Nairobi, Kenya: United Nations Human Settlements Programme.

UN-Habitat (2018a) *The State of African Cities*, Nairobi, Kenya: UN-Habitat.

UN-Habitat (2018b) 'Urban database', http://urbandata.unhabitat.org/download-raw-data

UN-Habitat (2018c) 'City Prosperity Index', http://urbandata.unhabitat.org/estimate-cpi-your-city

Watson, V. (2013) 'Planning and the "stubborn realities" of global south-east cities: some emerging ideas', *Planning Theory*, 12(1): 81–100.

World Bank (2017) *Africa's Cities. Opening Doors to the World*, Washington, DC: The World Bank Group and UKAID.

PART II

Changing housing regimes

5

My House, My Life Programme – Entities: two self-management experiences in the city of São Paulo

Camila D'Ottaviano, Adelcke Rossetto Netto, Cecília Andrade Fiúza, Flávia Massimetti and Juliana do Amaral Costa Lima

Introduction

After understanding the general characteristics of the city of São Paulo and the logic of housing production in Brazil, this chapter presents two emblematic and marginal cases of recent self-managed housing production in the city.[1] According to the latest National Census of 2010, 84.36 per cent of the Brazilian population live in the urban areas of our cities. This has happened because Brazilian cities have experienced a process of intense population growth over the last five decades. In the case of the city of São Paulo, the population, which was 3.7 million in 1960, jumped to 8.5 million in 1980 and reached 11.3 million in 2010. For Brazil as a whole, population growth over the same period was 120 million inhabitants, reaching 190.7 million inhabitants, almost all of them living in urban areas. In general, it can be stated that the growth of Brazilian cities throughout the second half of the 20th century was characterised by the configuration of two distinct cities: a legal city, consolidated by the implementation of official (legalised) sections usually located in more central and structured areas, with available housing for the middle and upper classes; and an illegal city, destined to house the lower classes.

In large cities and metropolises, access to housing by the lower-income population usually occurs through precarious solutions, such as housing in slums, in tenements or through self-build residences in illegal (or irregular) peripheral settlements. Due to the lack of an effective housing policy for the low-income population, self-construction and the informal housing market have been decisive in shaping our cities (D'Ottaviano and Quaglia-Silva, 2010). Alongside this, the public promotion of dwellings is supplied by the construction of large housing estates intended for the low-income population. This state policy, implemented in the late 1960s, was one of the main factors responsible for consolidating the socio-spatial segregation model known as the rich city centre versus the poor periphery.

Beginnings: housing policy in Brazil

The first experience at the national level of the provision of housing for the low-income population was the Affordable House Foundation (FCP), created in 1946 through a federal decree. The foundation was created based on the activities of the Institute of Retirement and Pension for the Industry Labour Force (IAPI) of the state of Minas Gerais. It was the responsibility of the FCP to 'finance urban construction work relating to water supply, sewage, electric power supplies, social assistance and other needs aimed at improving the living conditions and well-being of the working classes' (Azevedo and Andrade, 1981: 21). At that time, after the populist government of Getúlio Vargas (1930–45), the state provision of housing was thought to be a political instrument, especially as a way of legitimising the current government to urban workers, who were the government's main political opponents.

In April 1964, with the military coup, the FCP was dissolved. Shortly afterwards, on 21 August, the National Housing Plan was established, creating the National Housing Bank (BNH) and the Federal Housing and Urbanism Service (SERFAU). The new government took over a country with strong urban population dynamics, contributing from the beginning to its intensification by encouraging the process of the industrialisation of cities and the modernisation of rural areas. Thus, the situation of the housing inventory in the country required a large-scale solution, the authoritarian state sought popular legitimisation and domestic companies sought some form of capitalisation. The financing of social housing provided by the BNH aimed to meet all these demands. For more than two decades (1964–86), the BNH, through the Financial Housing System (SFH) created in 1966, was responsible for national housing policy as a whole, producing 5 million new housing units and making housing available mainly to the middle class, who could afford the cost of housing finance.

The first policy that was not strictly for the production of new residential units took place in 1975, with the creation of the Financing for Urbanised Lots (PROFILURB). The programme was intended to be a preventive action against the growth of *favelas* (slums) and was part of a new policy of lower-cost financing lines. The funding was intended for the production of urbanised lots, the purchase of construction materials and the hiring of technical advisors, and responded to pressures for greater participation from the population in public housing programmes. Within BNH's total production, the residential units produced by this programme accounted for 10 per cent of the total units produced by the other conventional programmes. (Azevedo and Andrade, 1981). The 1980s, known as the 'lost decade', was marked by the worsening economic crisis, by the accelerated rise in the cost of urban land, by land invasions organised by housing movements and by the decrease in BNH/SFH investments, culminating in the closing of the BNH in 1986, leaving the housing issue adrift and under the responsibility of states and municipalities.

With the exhaustion of the military regime, the country initiated a long process of re-democratisation, where social organisation became an essential element. In São Paulo, this social organisation for housing would consolidate the organised movements as active and important agents within housing policy. Based on this collective effort of technicians working to effectively organise, the 1st Meeting of Housing Movements was held in São Paulo and São Bernardo do Campo in 1984. The main theme was 'In favour of a cooperative action of mutual aid and self-management', with the participation of associations active in experiences of collective efforts in the metropolitan region and representatives of the Uruguayan Federation of Cooperative Housing for Mutual Aid (FUCVAM). This meeting was the first attempt to articulate proposals for alternatives to the existing centralised housing policy. In 1985, during the second meeting, the Cooperation of Movements of Housing Associations, Mutual Aid and Self-Management was created, with the following main principles based on the Uruguayan experience: self-management, mutual aid, solidarity and common property. In this political action for housing production, the years 1987 and 1988 were marked by large land occupations (especially in the eastern part of the city of São Paulo), by the unification of the São Paulo Housing Movements (UMM/SP) and by the strong performance of the National Movement for Urban Reform, which influenced the debate around the new Constitution of 1988. The period of re-democratisation after the military dictatorship (1964–85) was accompanied by a series of legal advances and administrative restructuring regarding access to housing and public policies, both regarding local governments and the federal government. From a legal standpoint, the 1988 Constitution advanced the definition of the need for an urban policy, as indicated in Articles 182 and 183 of Chapter II on urban policy.

The end of the BNH, the process of re-democratisation and the new Federal Constitution marked a period of greater political prominence of the municipalities, including with regard to housing policies. Within an institutional framework that was still fragile and in the midst of economic difficulties, there were occasional initiatives, especially in cities with some investment capacity. The state government and São Paulo City Hall began to support alternative housing programmes, such as collective efforts for housing construction, as a way to find a possible cheap solution to the growing housing deficit, and in response to the demands made by housing movements. From a public policy perspective, the experience of the Aid Fund for the Resident Population Living in Subnormal Housing Areas (FUNAPS) from São Paulo City Hall (1989–92) is paradigmatic of the new forms of housing provision provided by cities in that period (Moreira, 2009; Pasternak and D'Ottaviano, 2014).

Besides the collective efforts that took place in the peripheral areas of São Paulo, the organised housing movements politically questioned the housing provision model that endorsed large housing complexes in the fringes of the city, demanding the inclusion of actions within central tenements, as well as the use of the large number of vacant buildings in the centre of the city resulting from the process of the displacement of higher-income families to other areas of the city. The 1980s and 1990s were characterised by various occupations and violent repossessions of these vacant buildings. This scenario was a clear demonstration of the need for well-placed housing and quality urban infrastructure, as well as a further need to point out the speculative nature of the vacant private real estate inventory in the city in addition to the actual power of private property. The housing efforts continued to focus on the municipal sphere through the financing obtained by the municipality or through the allocation of resources from the state government, with its annual budget allowing a certain continuity in the housing supply. At the beginning of this century, the lines of financing were once again put in place for families with incomes ranging from three to six minimum monthly salaries through the Residential Lease Programme (PAR) and the Federal Savings Bank (CAIXA), which is the state-owned bank that manages the Government Severance Indemnity Fund for Workers (FGTS).

In 2003, with President Lula (2003–10) taking office and the creation of the Ministry of the Cities, various housing programmes were implemented (the National Programme to Support Sustainable Land Regularisation in 2003 and the Solidarity Loan Programme [PCS] in 2004). During Lula's second mandate in 2007, the government provided massive investment for infrastructure programmes: the Growth Acceleration Programme (PAC) and PAC-Urbanisation of the Slums. The PCS,[2] created as a response to the demands of housing movements, was the first nationwide programme of self-managed housing provision. With the PCS, the construction of housing for the low-income population through self-management[3] and a partnership among the housing movements and technical advisors, combined with public financing, became a national policy rather than a one-off experience. Over the seven years of the programme, 33,422 new units were built in 21 Brazilian states. In 2009, with the launch of the My House, My Life Programme (PMCMV), the PCS ceased to exist and was encompassed into the My House, My Life Programme – Entities (PMCMV-E).

The City Statute and the social function of property

In 2001, after more than a decade of the approval of the new Constitution, the City Statute (Law No. 10,257) was approved as a direct result of two decades of political mobilisation and public participation on issues such as urban policy and the right to the city. The approval of the Statute regulating Articles 182 and 183 of the Federal Constitution represented a new regulatory framework for Brazilian urban policy and management, defining the instruments aimed at guaranteeing the right to the city, the right to decent housing, the social function of property and the democratisation of urban management.

Since then, the precise definition of the concept of the social function of property has been considered to be one of the major advances of the Statute. The social function of property was an idea already considered in several of the Brazilian Constitutions and reinforced in the Constitution of 1988; however, it only became a more explicit and easily applicable concept after the establishment of the Statute. Its aim was to provide new possibilities for technical action, especially regarding issues related to access to decent housing as one of the prerequisites of the right to the city (D'Ottaviano and Quaglia-Silva, 2010). The idea of the social function of property involves the prevalence of social interest, collective good and collective well-being, as well as the pursuit and achievement of land regularisation and the urbanisation of areas occupied by low-income populations (Statute, single paragraph of Article 1 and item XIV of Article 2) (Dallari and Ferraz, 2006: 145).

There was a great deal of expectation with regard to urban issues and, in particular, housing issues between 2000 and 2010. The approval of the City Statute generated a positive expectation that legal advances, such as the social function of ownership, the new city land-use master plan and, in particular, the utilisation of the newly regulated urban planning instruments, would change the production and growth of cities and access to housing by the low-income population in the country. In 2005, the National Housing System of Social Interest (SNHIS) and the National Housing Fund of Social Interest (FNHIS) were created, thus requiring municipal and state housing plans, as well as independent funds from the Housing of Social Interest (HIS), audited through the housing councils in the different government spheres. In 2009, the National Housing Plan (PLANHAB) was finalised, becoming rapidly unimportant with the launching in the same year of the PMCMV, which incorporated all other existing housing programmes and promised the construction of 1 million new housing units, with non-refundable subsidies for the population with incomes between zero and three minimum monthly wages.

The PMCMV

The PMCMV (Law No. 11,977 of 7 July) was introduced by the federal government in 2009 and had as its initial goal the construction of 1 million new homes. It was launched in the midst of the global economic crisis generated by the subprime mortgage crisis of 2008. The PMCMV was in fact a counter-cyclical programme: with the goal of reducing the domestic housing deficit (about 5.5 million houses), the programme invested heavily in the construction industry, generating low qualification jobs and increasing capital circulation. The programme, currently in its third phase, is the largest housing programme ever created in the country since the BNH's demise in 1986. For the first time, a housing programme had a low-income and extremely low-income population as its target, offering subsidies that exceed 95 per cent of the value of the unit. Between July 2009 and July 2018, the programme built 5,357,940 million units[4] for different income[5] brackets, superseding other housing programmes, such as the PCS, which disappeared or were incorporated into it. In the PMCMV Segment 1, to which the public subsidy was directed, 1.85 million units were undertaken (34.6 per cent). Despite the fact that it targeted families that represent the largest portion of the country's housing deficit (approximately 90 per cent of the total), as shown in Table 5.1, the amounts obtained for this income range have so far reached only 20.44 per cent of the total investment of the programme. In view of the fact that it is a counter-cyclical programme, it is intended for the large-scale production of housing by large construction companies, especially

Table 5.1: PMCMV, July 2009 to July 2018

Segment	No. of housing units obtained	%	Amount obtained (R$)	%
Segment 1	1,855,324	34.63%	89,322,835,337	20.44%
Segment 1.5	118,930	2.22%	14,702,803,395	3.37%
Segment 2	2,745,817	51.25%	272,805,424,516	62.44%
Subtotal Segment 3	637,869	11.91%	60,095,409,647	13.75%
TOTAL	5,357,940	100.00%	436,926,472,895	100.00%
PMCMV-E	78,151	1.46%	2,214,647,949	0.51%

Note: The data from Segment 1.5 relate to years 2016, 2017 and 2018. Regarding the other segments, the data relate to the entire period.

Source: Ministry of the Cities (2018), 2 October

in Segment 1, where the gain occurs through the production of large housing estates on the outskirts of large cities, where the value of land is cheaper. Due to this model, the housing types were systematically replicated, minimising project costs and increasing scale and land gains, replicating the model of the production of large peripheral housing complexes of the 1970s and 1980s.

After incorporating all the other federal housing programmes, in order to respond to the demand of organised social movements for housing, a federal self-management programme under the PCS was created: My House, My Life Entities Programme – Entities (PMCMV-E). The PMCMV-E was structured in a similar way to the PCS, including the target public (families with incomes of up to three minimum monthly salaries) and the form of access taking place only through organised entities, using funds from the Social Development Fund (Pasternak and D'Ottaviano, 2014; D'Ottaviano and Rossetto Netto, forthcoming).

According to the conception of the programme, only 2 per cent of the total resources allocated to the PMCMV were allocated to the Entities sub-programme. However, according to data supplied by the Ministry of the Cities (see Table 5.2), of the total resources undertaken by the PMCMV in its ten years of existence, only 0.51 per cent was allocated to the Entities sub-programme, totalling 78,151 units obtained.

The PMCMV-E

The PMCMV-E is intended to supply housing to low-income[6] families organised in associations or collective housing institutions with proven experience in the area and duly qualified by the Ministry of the Cities. Among the functions of the PMCMV-E, the following stand out: Advance Purchase, which makes it possible to purchase the land and pay for a technical advisor; and the Construction or Requalification of residential buildings. Its resources come from the Social Development Fund and the general budget of the federal government.

According to the Ministry of the Cities, the PMCMV-E had as its objective 'to meet the housing needs of the low-income population in urban areas, guaranteeing access to decent housing with minimum standards of sustainability, security and habitability'.[7] It would be operated 'through the granting of funds to beneficiaries organized in an associative way by an Organizing Entity – EO (Associations, Cooperative Systems, Unions and others), with funds from the General Budget of the Federal Government directed to the Social Development Fund (FDS)'.[8] The programme could 'have a complementary offset of states, the Federal District and municipalities, by means of the provision of financial resources, goods and/or services that are economically measurable, necessary for the composition of the investment to be effected'.[9] The programme establishes three prioritisation criteria for the formation of the demand and the selection of the beneficiaries: families living in hazardous or unhealthy areas; families who have been displaced; and families with women responsible for the family unit or composed of a person with special needs. The entity responsible for the project may also define three additional criteria for the selection of families, which must be approved by a specific meeting. The programme also defines that a minimum of 3 per cent of the units should be destined to care for the elderly.

For the contract operation, the programme requires the entity/movement to create two committees: the 'Representatives' (CRE), responsible for the financial monitoring of the housing site; and the 'Construction Works Follow-up' (CAO), responsible for monitoring the technical work. These committees should have separate members and report to the beneficiary families. The formation of the committees must precede the contracting of the financing. In order to carry out the construction works, the entity can choose between four distinct construction schemes: self-management by (1) self-construction, (2) collective effort or (3) direct management, or by (4) co-management through a global work scheme to be executed by a construction company. However, the options for self-management or a global work scheme have a fundamental difference: for all options linked to self-management, there is a reduction of 8 per cent in the maximum amount of financing. Only the global work scheme option allows for the maximum amount of financing to be reached as defined by the programme. In the process of formatting the Program, the Organizing Entity undertook a leading role over PMCMV as a result of self-management requirement This leading role overburdened the Entities and obliged them to assume the structure of regular construction companies.

In the PMCMV-E, the promoting agent ends up taking over the PMCMV-FAR roles of the construction companies (feasibility, approval, work execution and regularisation of the units) and the municipalities (indicating the demand and social technical work). Among all these functions, only the role of indicating the demand was a role originally attributed to the housing movements. In the case of housing cooperatives, there is greater compatibility with the agent's[10] objectives and practices. However, when considering the PMCMV-FAR, there is doubt with regard to the compatibility of the promoting agent and the scope of the expected work in each operation. In the case of the PMCMV-E, this question becomes quite striking since it is expected that an association involved in the struggle for affordable housing is able to respond to operational issues beyond their knowledge, organisational and financial capacities. Thus, this is the main reason why only a few entities are actually able to access the programme (Rossetto Netto, 2017).

Based on day-to-day practice in executing the programme and analysing other Brazilian experiences, it is possible to identify four hold-ups and main challenges faced by the movements and their technical advisors in the operation of PMCMV-E: (1) access to well-located land at an affordable cost; (2) the replication of market solutions for housing projects of social interest; (3) the obligation of housing movements to take over functions normally performed by professional entrepreneurs (builders and developers); and (4) the shift in the historic role of entities in the fight for housing rights.

Access to land has been a real difficulty in the process of contracting housing projects, especially in cities with a very dynamic real estate market such as in the case of São Paulo, which has been intensified by the existence of credit lines and the fact that construction companies are listed on the stock exchange. The entities have experienced a constant dispute with the real estate market for the purchase of land. As a result, the properties available for purchase by the movements (entities) usually present with environmental problems, legislation restrictions or incomplete documentation for regularisation, which requires additional efforts to be carried out. Still in relation to land disputes, the values practised by the programme have created land negotiation floor values that attract not only traditional agents, but also public companies that create 'land banks' as they have a disproportionate volume of resources when compared to that of the movements. At the same time, the movements demand an active presence and attitude of the municipal governments regarding access to land, through either the donation of land, assistance in the mediation of and collaboration in the actual purchase of the land, or ensuring the utilisation of the instruments of the City Statute[11] in purchasing well-located land units.

The adoption of *market solutions* is also a problem, both due to the type of gated housing condominium communities normally used by developers to reduce the feasibility costs, and when contracting the actual construction work. The 8 per cent discount on the final value of the units for the self-management options, together with the difficulties experienced by the movements when contracting by direct management, leads to the favouring of the global work scheme in an attempt to exclude operational risks, yet it is not a guarantee of success (see Rossetto Netto, 2017: ch 2).

With the current structure of the programme, the housing movements have moved from being actors to agents, becoming responsible for functions originally intended for entrepreneurs – developers and builders – and having the additional requirement to do it more effectively since the actual margin is very small, making the entire process even more difficult. In this way, entities are being linked to builders (or fraudulent builders) who use this opportunity to set up and illegally pass on their businesses. Thus, the role played by entities in the fight for the right to housing has been transformed, with the shifting of their activism towards operational actions imposed by the programme, demanding commitment and care with management aspects that obstruct or hinder the deepening of their political activity. Furthermore, in this 'operational' process, the entities go through setbacks, such as attacks carried out by major press outlets over the practices of financial contributions by the families or of regarding political activism as a criterion for selection. Both of these scenarios are allowed by the programme either as the offset composition required by the actual operation to make the venture feasible (Camargo, 2016) or in the scores given to the families considering their participation in the activities of the entity (Jesus, 2015).

Indeed, from a quantitative point of view, according to Tables 5.1 and 5.2, the PMCMV-E has been insignificant, both in terms of the volume of resources contracted (0.51 per cent of the total programme) and the total number of units produced (less than 1.5 per cent of the

Table 5.2: PMCMV-E, July 2009 to July 2018

Contracting year	No. of housing units obtained	Amount obtained (R$)
2009	309	2,937,581
2010	7,715	73,890,623
2011	2,988	92,350,528
2012	7,751	182,608,289
2013	16,382	324,302,240
2014	18,737	484,559,011
2015	6,638	243,372,997
2016	11,776	346,780,777
2018	5,855	463,845,904
TOTAL	78,151	2,214,647,949

Source: Ministry of the Cities (2018), 2 October

total obtained). In addition, the last two years have shown insignificant contracting, with no contracts undertaken in 2017 and just under 6,000 units in 2018. Despite this far from encouraging scenario, we will consider two projects made possible by the PMCMV- E in the city of São Paulo that we consider paradigmatic: the Dandara and Maria Domitila buildings. Both projects were made possible through the partnership between the Integra technical advisory team and the Unification of the Tenements and Housing Struggles Movement (ULCM).

The São Paulo experience: self-management experience in the central area

Until 2017, the ULCM partnership was responsible for the only three projects approved in the central area of São Paulo by the PMCMV-FAR and the PMCMV-E: Iracema Eusébio and Dandara (retrofitting an existing building; see Figure 5.1) and Maria Domitila (new construction; see Figure 5.2). Among the contracted projects made in 2018, there are three[12] new projects of the requalification of existing buildings in the central area of the city that involve other movements related to housing and technical advisory services. The Iracema Eusébio and Dandara buildings, both located in the city centre in the Republic/Santa Ifigênia region, were made possible after periods of occupation by the movement of the vacant buildings, followed by long periods of negotiation. The Maria Domitila building, with works still in progress, is a new construction located on a lot in the Brás

Figure 5.1: Dandara building

Source: Juliana Lima

neighbourhood. The project is also the result of a long struggle, with several occupations and actions of repossession, the first being carried out by the movement in 2000.

Dandara building

The case study of the Dandara building seeks to elucidate and deepen the issues raised in the analysis of the PMCMV-E since this is, so far,

Figure 5.2: Maria Domitila Assembly

Source: Camila D'Ottaviano

the only project undertaken by the programme in the centre of São Paulo. The analysis focuses on the feasibility, selection, contracting and construction work of the Dandara building, with the ULCM as an organising entity and Integra as the technical advisor. The Dandara building project, located at 1225 Avenue Ipiranga and a few minutes' walk from the city's landmark at Praça da Sé, is a reform and change of use project, from commercial to residential housing in the social interest category. According to City Hall records, the project was conceived by architect Eduardo Augusto Kneese de Mello and approved in 1965, with the permit to occupy the building issued on 19 November 1969. The building was purchased by the federal government on 1 April 1970 to accommodate the Regional Labour Court of the 2nd Region, hosting the 23 Conciliation and Trial Boards of the capital,[13] and was used until the early 2000s, when the court was transferred to the Barra Funda Courthouse in the western part of the city.

The first approach to obtain the property was made in 2007, with negotiations initiated with the São Paulo State Department and its Properties in São Paulo (SPU-SP). The feasibility process began in 2009 with the donation of the property to the entity; its contracting took place in August 2014 and work began at the end of the same year. It is important to highlight that the donation was only possible after the approval of Federal Law No. 11,481 of 31 May 2007 (Provisional Measure 335 of 2006), which provides for the allocation of properties belonging to the government for housing with purposes relating to social interest. The building is constructed on land measuring 520.00 m^2 (5,597 sq ft). The construction covers 7,123.00 m^2 (76,671 sq ft) over 18 floors, composed of underground, ground floor, mezzanine, 15 floors with three types of apartments plus an attic. In total, 120 housing units were made available, with areas varying between 24.47 m^2 (263.39 sq ft) and 46.21 m^2 (497.40 sq ft).

During the contracting period, the operation received resources from the PMCMV (R$76,000 per unit) and a contribution from the state government through the Paulista House (R$20,000 per unit). As a result of the reduction of the federal funds transferred and consequent extension of the forecasted schedule, the City Hall ended up contributing with funds from Paulistana House (R$465,301.55, around R$3,900 per unit). The feasibility stage was the longest and most problematic, lasting five years in total (2009–14), as it faced the legal limitations of a retrofit project, the freezing of the area due to a proposed urban concession that did not take place and the recurrent difficulty of operating the programme with the administrator (the Ministry of the Cities), with three changes to the programme and the continuous need to pass through exceptional specifications established for all projects within the national territory. In addition, with regard to the attributions and requirements of the operating agent (CAIXA), unattainable internal regulations, team turnover and ongoing auditing procedures contributed to the process becoming a long operation with endless obstacles.

The execution stage of the construction works intensified the process of self-management by the movement since all decisions taken by the entity were backed by the technical support of Integra. Only at this stage was the financial compensation for the technical work that was carried out for the execution of the programme initiated. The major difficulty during this stage was managing the renovation works and the widespread unexpected services that came about. The entity had to deal with a fixed and non-adjustable budget and with an association that, for obvious reasons, does not have working capital to maintain the flow of the construction works. The scenario further deteriorated with the situation experienced as of mid-2015, with a limitation of the monthly measurements imposed by the programme administrator given the serious budget crisis faced by the federal government, causing the construction works, which were forecasted to last 18 months, to actually be completed over 25 months. Another factor that worsened the programme's progress was that although the construction works were completed in December 2016, the entity faced new difficulties in requesting a certificate of completion of the construction, in particular, obtaining a licence from the Fire Department. While the families should have been allowed to move to the new housing in December 2017, this actually only happened in March 2018 due to delays in the issuance of the contracts by the operating agent.

At this moment, the 120 families selected by the ULCM are adapting to the new reality of life in a condominium, with new daily challenges, such as living together in a condo, the maintenance costs of the building and waiting for the final legal documentation of their apartments. We also believe that the families will soon begin to experience pressure from the informal housing market to transfer their units, which are already worth 2.5 times more than the average amount spent on the renovation of each apartment. These challenges can only be overcome through permanent action of the entity in the maintenance of this unique example within the programme.

Maria Domitila

The Maria Domitila project is a new construction building located at 228 Rua Maria Domitila in the Brás neighbourhood, defined as a special area of social interest (ZEIS 3) by the 2002 master plan. The property accommodated warehouses and has been owned by the Social Security Department (INSS) since 1979. As far as is known, it has remained closed and unused. The first movement occupation of the ground site was in 2000, along with a number of occupations undertaken by the housing movements. After an action of repossession by the INSS, this was followed by other occupations almost every year thereafter, especially in 2004, 2007 and 2011. The feasibility process started in 2003 through the PAR, with several alterations up to 2008. At this point, a public call for builders and developers was issued by the state-owned bank CAIXA; however, the project had no interested bidder. Nonetheless, the project was never abandoned and later reappeared in 2009, under the PMCMV-FAR programme, and was contracted in the third phase of the Programme in July 2016.

The very narrow land, with 2,392.50 m² (25,752 sq ft), made it possible to construct a building with 14,608.58 m² (157,245 sq ft), with areas ranging from 11 to 17 floors, having a ground floor and three other floor types besides the attic. There are 245 units of two types: one with 41,21 m² (444 sq ft) and the other one with 41,90 m² (451 sq ft). The project was initially proposed in the PMCMV-FAR programme and was later transferred to the entities programme. During the contracting phase, the operation received resources from the PMCMV (approximately R$83,000 per unit) backed by the City Hall with resources from the Casa Paulistana (R$20,000 per unit). However, due to the fact that the state government withdrew from providing funds, in order to carry out the contracting of the construction, the families had to fund the maximum amount expected of 3 per cent of the operation (R$3,200 per unit). The construction works are scheduled to be completed by the first half of 2019 and began in January 2017.

The Maria Domitila real estate development can be considered an example of self-management in production via the PMCMV-E. Beneficiary families have actively participated in all stages of the process: project, the construction work and future post-occupation. The participative process was carried out through the partnership between ULCM and the Integra social technical advisory service, through the organisation of future residents into work groups/committees, and through the monthly meetings and periodic visits to the real estate development site.

In addition to the two commissions required by the PMCMV-F – CAO and CRE – eight participatory committees were formed by the future residents: Communication; Income Generation; Environment; Purchases and Pricing Quotes; Accounting Reporting; Control of Participation; Participative Democracy; and Understanding the Neighbourhood. The committees aim to increase the participation of the families in all instances and stages of the development, providing discussion and decision-making in an agile and horizontal way. All beneficiary families must be part of at least one committee. Participation in the committees reflects a process of discussion and learning as the families take ownership of the project and strengthen their relationship with their future neighbours.

Through participatory committees, it is possible to bring future residents closer to the process of obtaining their housing, thus building a bond and a sense of ownership in relation to the real estate development. Taking as an example other participatory processes of other programmes and the experience in the Dandara building, it is possible to state that the bond between the families and the development as a whole creates a greater appraisal of the achievement of their own houses. The residents come to realise that their houses are a result of a real and daily struggle. The committees also promote the strengthening of bonds of friendship among the residents themselves, contributing to the future coexistence of condominiums, as well as reaffirming the equal importance of the members of the building. The work developed by each of the committees and the subsequent exchange of knowledge between them provides the training and capacity development of the people involved as managers of their own housing. Living in a condominium and the management of the common areas of the apartment building are processes facilitated by this formation, which can normally be carried out in a quiet and collective manner. This issue becomes quite relevant when considering that one of the most recurrent problems in social housing developments is the degradation of common areas since they are often considered areas over which residents do not feel or take ownership, and can sometimes intensify conflicts among the neighbours.

Conclusion

We have reached 2018 with the National Housing Plan (PLANHAB) complete, with more than 5 million new housing units obtained by the PMCMV and with the city's land-use master plan only partially implemented, with their urban tools underutilised or misused. Despite the large number of new units produced, the national housing deficit remained at over 6 million units (Fundacão João Pinheiro, 2016). Despite the presence of urban instruments such as the social function of property, compulsory instalment plan and progressive urban land and territorial tax, normative advances were not accompanied by real advances in the appropriation of urban property in Brazil, even in cases of vacant or underutilised buildings. Access to land for the low-income population continues to occur almost exclusively through self-built or rented housing in precarious settlements, slums or tenements. In recent years, we have witnessed attempts by public authorities to use vacant real estate in central areas; however, the lack of recognition of judicial power with regard to the prevalence of the social function of property over the right to property has prevented the advancement of broader programmes. At the same time, there are an increasing number of invasions of vacant buildings by organised housing movements in the central areas of large Brazilian cities – São Paulo, Rio de Janeiro, Porto Alegre, Belo Horizonte and Recife (Prefeitura da Cidade de São Paulo, 2013). In October 2016, the then Secretary of the Housing Department of São Paulo estimated that the number of buildings occupied in the central region of the cities was close to 50 (*Folha de São Paulo*, 2016), against 31 buildings occupied in January 2013 (*Folha de São Paulo*, 2013). By 2018, this number had already reached 72 occupied properties (*Folha de São Paulo*, 2018).

As Maricato (2008) points out, land is still the 'knot': 'Whether in the countryside or in the city, land ownership continues to be a knot in the Brazilian society.... In the cities, the difficulty to access land for housing is responsible for the explosive growth of favelas and illegal settlements.' This same issue is reinforced by the promotion programmes themselves since land provision or land regularisation programmes for the low-income population have access to private property as pretty much the only form of access to social housing. Over the last few decades, only two housing programmes did not contemplate private property as a form of access to housing: the federal government's PAR and the Social Rental Programme of the city of São Paulo. In the case of the city of São Paulo, of all the projects approved under the PMCMV, only the renovation of the Dandara building, property belonging to the federal government, accesses the housing site not through private property, but rather by a permit of use (Rossetto Netto, 2017). In this sense, it is important that the allocation of properties belonging to the federal government for housing of social interest, as provided by Federal Law No. 11,481 of 2007, is maintained and extended, in particular, in the various cases of vacant and unused real estate spread throughout various Brazilian cities, especially in central areas.

We believe that providing housing in the city centre, aimed at low-income families, is an adequate and efficient way to face spatial segregation and social disparity through a single action. It is a guarantee of rights that is only possible through a public policy that provides quality, affordable and well-located housing, and a more democratic city, where inequality is not abysmal and living with dignity gives more meaning to life than the mere focus on survival. In this sense, the PMCMV and especially the PMCMV-E are analysed as available instruments for city centre areas; however, the viability logic for lower-income families (large housing and peripheral and standardised projects) goes in the opposite direction of an inclusive policy. This logic, provided by the programme itself in its form and structure (a housing-based 'economic programme'), relies heavily on large financial subsidies as the only solution to the very diverse range of housing needs that exist across the country, as well as to different income ranges, based exclusively on the private agent, replicating the market logic in public action. As an alternative, it is up to the municipal government to structure housing policy for the centre, articulated with the other spheres of government and also with private agents, using the PMCMV as a support to make construction or renovation works feasible and thus guaranteeing access to housing.

In the case of the Dandara building, even with the property carrying zero cost to the operation and with the construction work itself having no profit interest, once the entity became interested in the viability of housing and its value of use, the feasibility of the real estate development and the completion of the construction works depended heavily on the political strategy and activism of the ULCM and Integra, the funds of the families that benefited from the programme, and the raising of additional resources from City Hall. Even with the small number of units obtained by the PMCMV-E, we believe that experiences such as those of the Dandara and Maria Domitila buildings show that there are ways of producing well-located quality housing for the low-income population that can adapt to the models of the public housing programmes. In this sense, in addition to maintaining programmes such as PMCMV-E, it is necessary to value and encourage existing partnerships between technical advisory services and housing movements as these are essential for this special type of housing provision.

Notes

[1] The research was developed with the support of the São Paulo Research Foundation (FAPESP).
[2] For more details on the programme, see Chapter 2.
[3] The Programme of Social Interest for Housing Subsidy of 2001 offered a subsidy for the acquisition and/or production of housing units for the low-income population; however, it operated under an auction model and with resources intended for municipalities/housing companies.
[4] Source: Ministry of Cities/Transparency Portal, October 2nd 2018) , 02 de outubro de 2018.
[5] Source: Ministry of Cities/Transparency Portal, October 2nd 2018., 02 de outubro de 2018.
[6] The established parameter is the maximum gross income limit of families, which has been updated for each edition of the programme. In PMCMV-1, the income was R$1,395.00 (US$697.50); for PMCMV-2, the limit was of R$1,600.00

(US$993.80); and for PMCMV-3, it reached R$1.800.00 (US$497.20) (conversions to the dollar based on the exchange rate on the day of the launching of the programme editions [source: UOL Economia]). During the implementation period of the PMCMV (2009–16), the Brazilian currency (*real*) first entered an appreciation cycle against the US dollar (2011/12) followed by a continuous process of depreciation since then. However, if we only consider the value of the financing in *reais*, there was a nominal increase over the period.

[7] See: www.cidades.gov.br
[8] See: www.cidades.gov.br
[9] See: www.cidades.gov.br
[10] The housing movement is a social movement, organised after the demand for housing, that demands housing public policies. Cooperatives, on the other hand, are a productive agent, a association of families for the production of their homes, and may or may not work through a Housing Program.
[11] As Progressive Municipal Tax, Pre-emptive right (preferential right of purchase by the State itself), Compulsory Parcelling and Building, Expropriation with public debt securities, and Social Function of Property effectiveness..
[12] Projects of renovation of Hotel Cambridge, Hotel Lord and the Prestes Maia Building.
[13] See: www.trtsp.jus.br/acessibilidade/232-institucional/gestao-documental/17947-historico-da-justica-do-trabalho-e-trt-da-2-regiao

References

Azevedo, S. and Andrade, L.A. (1981) *Habitação e Poder. Da Fundação da Casa Popular ao Banco Nacional de Habitação* [*Housing and Power. From the Popular House Foundation to the National Housing Bank*], Rio de Janeiro: Zahar.

Camargo, C.M. (2016) 'Minha Casa Minha Vida: entre os direitos, as urgências, e os negócios' ['My House, My Life: between rights, urgencies and business'], PhD thesis, IAU-USP, São Carlos.

Dallari, A.A. and Ferraz, S. (eds) (2006) *Estatuto da Cidade. Comentários à Lei Federal no 10.257/2001* [*Statute of the City. Comments on Federal Law no. 10,257/2001*], São Paulo: Malheiros Editores.

D'Ottaviano, C. and Quaglia-Silva, S.L. (2010) 'Regularização Fundiária No Brasil: velhas e novas questões. Revista Planejamento e Políticas Públicas' ['Land regularisation in Brazil: old and new issues. Planning and public policy magazine'], *PPP IPEA*, 34: 57–84.

D'Ottaviano, C. and Rossetto Netto, A. (forthcoming) 'Programa Minha Casa Minha Vida – Entidades. Edifício Dandara – moradia de interesse social de qualidade na área central São Paulo' [My Home My Life Programme – Entities. Dandara building – quality housing of social interest in the central area of São Paulo'], in F. Córdova Canela, V. Livier Díaz Núñez and T. Antonio Moreira (eds) *Miradas Cruzadas de Vivienda Social Brasil-México*, Guadalajara: Universidad de Guadalajara.

Folha de São Paulo (2013) 'Centro tem 31 prédios invadidos por sem-teto' ['City center has 31 buildings invaded by the homeless'], Caderno Cotidiano [Daily Section], 15 January.

Folha de São Paulo (2016) 'São Paulo Ocupada' ['São Paulo Occupied'], Caderno Poder [Political Power Section], 7 May.

Folha de São Paulo (2018) '20 O que já se sabe sobre o desabamento do prédio em São Paulo?' ['What do we already know about the collapse of the building in São Paulo?'], Caderno Codiano [Daily Section], 1 May.

Fundacão João Pinheiro (2016) *Déficit Habitacional no Brasil, 2013–2014* [*Housing Deficit in Brazil, 2013–2014*], Belo Horizonte: Fundação João Pinheiro.

Jesus, P.M. (2015) 'O Programa Minha Casa Minha Vida Entidades no Município de São Paulo' ['The My House, My Life Entities Programme in the city of São Paulo'], PhD thesis, FFLCH-USP, São Paulo.

Maricato, E. (2008) 'O Nó da Terra' ['The land knot'], *Revista Piauí Magazine*, 21 June.

Ministry of the Cities (2018) 'Transparency portal', www.portaltransparencia.gov.br/

Moreira, F.A. (2009) 'O lugar da autogestão no Governo Lula' ['The place of self-management in the Lula government'], PhD thesis, FAUUSP, São Paulo.

Pasternak, S. and D'Ottaviano, C. (2014) 'Half a century of self-help in Brazil', in J. Bredennoord, P. van Lindert and P. Smets (eds) *Affordable Housing in the Urban Global South*, London: Routledge, pp 241–55.

Prefeitura da Cidade de São Paulo (2013) 'Prefeitura mapeia 42 prédios ocupados no Centro' ['City Hall maps out 42 buildings occupied in the Centre'], web portal of the city of Cidade de São Paulo, 16 May.

Rossetto Netto, A. (2017) 'Habitação Central. Produção Habitacional no Centro de São Paulo, no âmbito do Programa Minha Casa Minha Vida' ['Central housing. Housing production in the center of São Paulo, under the My House, My Life Programme'], master's dissertation, FAUUSP, São Paulo.

6

The Solano Trindade housing occupation as an urban self-management project in metropolitan Rio de Janeiro

Luciana Corrêa do Lago, Fernanda Petrus and Irene de Queiroz e Mello

Introduction

The objective of this chapter is to present an experience of self-managed housing and work struggle led by an urban social movement, and to analyse the challenges that this movement has faced in the process of constructing and carrying out its project. The case study is a housing occupation on public land, named after Solano Trindade,[1] organised by the Movimento Nacional de Luta pela Moradia (National Movement for Housing Rights in Brazil [MNLM])[2] in Duque de Caxias, a city on the periphery of the Rio de Janeiro metropolitan area. This project's main innovation is its development of a partnership between the social movement and the Federal University of Rio de Janeiro (UFRJ) for the collective construction of technical and political training associating housing to emancipated labour.[3] This training is constructed through processes of building housing units, as well as through urbanisation, urban services and agro-ecological products developed with alternative technologies. We will try to highlight the tension between scientific and popular knowledge in the process of constructing this alternative city project. The partnerships between social movements and their technical advisers have shown themselves to be strategically advantageous for expanding innovative possibilities through horizontal exchanges of knowledge. In this relationship, distinct ideals of urban well-being and cultural values are constantly at play. Private versus collective property, fenced versus open lots, allotments versus condominiums, high versus low density, single family houses versus multifamily buildings, and private versus collective kitchens and laundries are some of the tensions present throughout the development of the project.

Our intention is to examine the transformative potential of certain collective practices carried out by social organisations under the banner of decommodifying the city. We will analyse an experience of low-income habitat production based on the material and symbolic necessities of those who use the city in their everyday lives. In this sense, we examine insurgent practices that confront the neoliberal project imposed through violence and ideology. These practices question the parameters of urban well-being created by a mercantile rationality, seeking to develop an alternative project for the city by means of technological experimentation and democratic management.

The struggle to decommodify the city and to transform it into a common good – especially when unified with the struggle to decommodify labour – is a powerful path towards constructing an egalitarian, democratic society. The working class, fragmented by cultures and by different forms of labour, is the agent of urban insurgencies, some of which are politically organised. We know of the difficulties that popular urban associations face in moving beyond 'community consciousness' and developing a 'class consciousness' (Harvey, 1982).[4] In this case, class consciousness is forged not on the factory floor, but rather in the experiences of collective work for the 'broader reproduction of life' (Coraggio, 1999); in other words, experiences that provoke the elevation of the standards of basic social necessities. In this sense, we aim to evaluate the insurgent urban practices of the Solano Trindade occupation by emphasising both their transforming power and their contradictions. We do so within the political and economic context of the past 15 years in Brazil as it relates to the production of cities.

Cities in Latin America are immersed in a political and economic context marked by both new and old contradictions. Since the 1990s, we have watched the growing power of financial agents in determining and controlling the living conditions in our cities, especially in terms of access to housing and public services. In the 1990s, the focus was on the privatisation policies that altered the distribution of public funds in favour of large international corporations; in the next decade, real estate capital – which was inserted in circuits of international finance – began to take on a privileged position in the dispute for public funds. The consequence has been the large-scale production of large public housing projects on the peripheries of major cities; these have been built with significant public funds, during which time city centres have become objects of requalification and real estate appreciation by means of public–private partnerships that legitimate policies of evicting low-income families from their places of residence. Brazil can be seen as having one of the most thorough realisations of this process. The housing policy implemented in 2009 placed homeownership as a primary and urgent necessity. In order to address this so-called 'housing deficit' – a legitimising instrument of the merely quantitative character of these policies – hundreds of thousands of houses were constructed on or beyond the limits of major cities. We cannot identify any principle of well-being from these building activities led by major construction firms; instead, we identify them as the active negation of the city, albeit in a paradoxical context. The elevation of the consumer power of much of the Brazilian working class – whether through real increases in the minimum wage or through easier access to credit – guaranteed that, until 2015, families experienced significant improvements in terms of access to food, durable goods, leisure activities, healthy houses and so on. This was a question not merely of integrating workers *into* the market, but rather of integrating them *through* the market as consumers (Do Lago, 2016).

However, in the coalition government led by the Workers' Party (PT) between 2003 and 2016, a certain space for negotiation existed for workers' organisations and social movements engaged in the struggle for redistributing public resources, including state-owned properties. Such was the case with national movements for housing rights, organised in the National Forum for Urban Reform (FNRU),[5] which had some opportunities for negotiation with the federal government from 2003 onward. In return, they received the possibility of direct financing for social organisation, which was to be used in the self-administered production of living spaces. As a result, Brazil now has a number of different experiences in producing housing, especially through federal programmes like Crédito Solidário (Solidarity Credit) and Minha Casa Minha Vida Entidades (My House, My Life Programme –Entities [PMCMV-E]). The former was implemented in 2005 and substituted by the latter in 2009. These programmes were not intended as policies for fomenting innovative experimentation or as alternatives to the mass-produced housing of construction companies. Instead, they were skewed responses to the demands of housing rights movements that have fought for the democratic distribution of national funds for financing public housing since Brazil's new constitution was approved in 1988. In this sense, the successes of social movements in gaining access to public funds for the collective production of housing was not accompanied by a change in the correlation of forces behind the norms and principles that regulate the use of these resources, much less by the redistribution of public lands.

Between 2005 and 2015, Brazil accumulated almost 90,000 housing units financed by the aforementioned programmes that make collective forms of production viable. Yet, this production is a marginal gain when compared to the more than 2 million commercially constructed units guaranteed by public resources. However, this meagre portion of direct financing for social movements, community associations and housing cooperatives has, until now, led to an expressive set of housing production experiences resulting from experimental collective practices. Housing rights movements that have acted in and across spheres of power since the 1980s, demanding the right to the city (and the right to produce another kind of city), have amplified the nature of their actions by taking over the production of housing developments with state financing.

As productive agents, housing rights movements take on new conflicts, especially with those public institutions involved directly in managing housing policy. The principal aim of these movements has been to invert the dominant rationale of real estate production, that is, to produce housing for the use of workers, rather than for market value.[6] This aim demands a variety of different innovations and insurgencies, beginning with the reaction to norms – imposed by the Ministry of Cities and by Caixa Econômica Federal public bank – based on principles of efficiency in accordance with a mercantile logic and profitability (risk reduction).

Many differences exist between Brazilian regions and between social organisations in the forms of the management and production of housing developments. However, the accumulated experiences have heightened the parameters of urban well-being by questioning the pattern of living that has been instituted and morally accepted for low-income families. The relationship between social movements and technical advisors has been fundamental to amplifying the possibilities of innovation. The construction of this relationship – when sustained through horizontal exchanges of knowledge – has been a permanent challenge since distinct ideals of urban well-being are at play. When we encounter innovations in housing developments, we also encounter an accumulation of practices of mutual convincing (which is to say, democratic practices) among cooperating partners and their advisers. This learning process has been motivated by social movements' struggle for the appropriation of the city so as to transform it into a commonly held good.

Thus, we would like to emphasise that as a social construction, the notion of urban well-being is an object in dispute and it is on the agenda of social movements. The experience of self-management that we present in this article joins together practices that feed this dispute, confirming the idea of self-management as a pedagogical process for all involved. We will begin the analysis with a short history of the Solano Trindade occupation, of the social movement at the centre of this action and of the technical advisory team at the UFRJ. Thereafter, we will present the analysis of three work fronts that have been developed – the elaboration of the master plan, the construction of the housing requalification project and the agro-ecological front – trying to show the innovations, the tensions and the learning processes accumulated in each activity up to now.

The Solano Trindade occupation and university technical advice: a short history

The Solano Trindade occupation was organised in 2014 by the MNLM in Duque de Caxias, a municipality in the Rio de Janeiro metropolitan region. It is located in a 48,000 square metre property owned by the Brazilian federal government[7] that had been abandoned for more than 15 years. It is located five kilometres from the Duque de Caxias city centre in an area with precarious urban infrastructure and public services, and with scant local commerce.

The MNLM was formed from the urban struggles of the 1980s, the period of formation of national housing movements. At the time, a number of housing occupations occurred in the large- and medium-sized cities as a result of economic crises and the absence of social housing policy. Leaders from local movements, who fought for the regularisation and urbanisation of occupied properties, and who developed the terms of discussion regarding the rights to urban land and to property, received support from the Catholic Church and from the national PT. In this sense, the motto of the MNLM was, and continues to be, reaching 'solidarity through urban space' by means of a struggle for the right to the city, to urban land and to housing in an 'organic and unified struggle, together with the Landless Rural Workers Movement (MST)' (MNLM-RS, 2007). As such, they understand that in order to access these rights, movements must be focused on the decommodification of housing and on housing policy that includes low-income families, guaranteeing the social function of property. In order to accomplish this, the occupation of empty properties makes strategic sense for the movement inasmuch as it highlights the lack of social function of these properties while, at the same time, making better-located housing more viable. Through its occupations, the movement[8] – in addition to articulating institutional struggles – places itself in clear opposition to the city capitalist production system by means of spatial and collective self-management practices (De Queiroz e Mello, 2015).

In Rio de Janeiro, MNLM coordinates four self-managed occupations,[9] of which the Solano Trindade occupation analysed here is one. It is interesting to note that movement leaders differentiate the territory within this occupation into three distinct categories. The first is relative to living space – in other words, housing units – to be maintained as private, individual property. The second category comprises streets and squares falling under the category of public property, which movement leaders understand as the responsibility of the state, or, in this case, the municipal government. Leaders refer to the third category as comprising 'housing movement spaces' or 'residents' association spaces', which correspond to space for collective use, whether open-air or constructed. These spaces do not fit neatly into the parameters of either public (state-owned) or private property. Free spaces for collective use are destined for planting crops through agro-ecological techniques, as well as for composting organic residue and urban infrastructure, in this case, an evaporation-transpiration basin (BET) (an ecological sanitation solution that results in the production of bananas). Meanwhile, the constructed space[10] for collective use includes a collective kitchen and agro-ecological restaurant, a library, lavatories, a laundry room, and an auditorium for political and technical training activities (see Figure 6.1).

Therefore, we can perceive that the majority of the spaces designated as 'movement spaces' are destined for training and collective work – they are spaces for cooperation and reciprocity – as such, they are connected to the movement's project for sustainable economics. Faced with the poverty conditions in which the occupation's residents live, movement leaders understand that the right to the city cannot be dissociated from the right to work and to income, so as to guarantee decent living conditions in the long term. It was this principle of urban sustainability as connected to economic sustainability for the movement's families on which the partnership between MNLM and UFRJ was created. This partnership is focused on experimentation with social technologies; in other words, technologies that produce the goods necessary for their producers in the areas of construction, urban infrastructure and agro-ecology by means of technical and political training for movement families and leaders, as well as for university students, professors and staff. The social technologies that have been developed rely on collective, self-managed work at all levels, as will be analysed further later.

Figure 6.1: Solano Trindade map

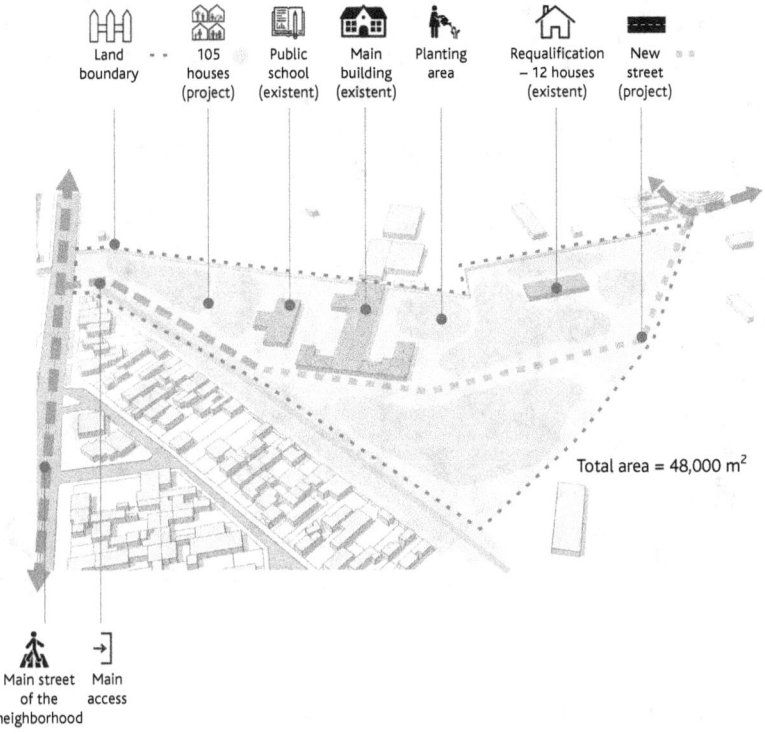

Source: Fernanda Petrus

In order to respond to projects that, since 2014, have been elaborated through this partnership between the social movement and university, the UFRJ technical advisory team took on new members over time, including students, professors and staff. Today, the group includes members of a wide variety of laboratories and research groups in architecture, urbanism, environmental sanitation, social technology, economic solidarity, agro-ecology, constructive technology and urban planning. University outreach projects comprise institutional forms of making the partnership viable – which will be explored in further detail later – as well as certain undergraduate and graduate courses. Seven courses for undergraduate and master's degree students have been based on the theoretical and practical study of the Solano Trindade occupation. Six of these were taught by professors from the undergraduate programme in architecture and urbanism. Some were divided equally between theoretic and practical modules, whereas others were predominantly practical; these took place on Saturdays so that students could take part in collective work and construction projects together with residents (see Figure 6.2).

Figure 6.2: Timber roof design course

Source: Fernanda Petrus

Self-management, university advice and the confrontation of values and knowledge

The technical advice carried out in the context of university outreach projects offers general possibilities of re-evaluating and extending academic knowledge when we move beyond the walls of the university and seek to use this knowledge in everyday struggles for the common good. We know that knowledge intended to transform social reality cannot be destined for a passive public that merely receives information. Extending critical knowledge to the non-academic community implies moving beyond the diffusion of knowledge through training and advice. It implies questioning knowledge at the moment of interacting with the 'other', thereby provoking a reaction. Next, we will report on three university advisory activities carried out together with the families of the Solano Trindade occupation, highlighting the interactions between the agents, especially the reactions of the families to the technological innovations and proposed urban project, and the incorporation of the knowledge and proposals of the families themselves into the projects and productive activities.

The dialogic process of elaborating the master plan and the project of new housing with the families

Throughout the process of elaborating a master plan, beginning in 2015, six months after the Solano Trindade property was first occupied, meetings were held between the residents' group and the technical advisory team. In these meetings, possible projects of city, neighbourhood, street, lot and house were discussed. The technical team aimed to increase the repertoire of possibilities based on other experiences in Brazil and throughout Latin America. The examples that they chose for discussion highlighted different self-managed collectives so that the occupation's families could familiarise themselves with the successes of other popular housing rights movements, and innovate in forms of housing, construction technology and implementation, among other aspects.

However, the possibilities for innovation and the alternatives to the hegemonic model of production discussed during meetings were not, by and large, incorporated into the final urbanistic or architectural projects for new housing. Among the possible causes of this fact, we identify certain challenges that arose throughout the process. The primary challenge is related to the movement's decision, in 2016, to prioritise funding from the My House, My Life Programme – Entities (PMCMV-E)[11] as a primary strategy in order to guarantee the maintenance of the land. Within this context, PMCMV-E represents the only state-sponsored opportunity to gain access to the resources necessary for the self-managed construction of the 105 housing units projected in the master plan. For these reasons, the movement's coordinators – together with the advisory team, which agreed to these demands – decided to 'accelerate' or bypass certain stages of the collective elaboration of projects that had been developed together with families in order to make viable the delivery of the necessary documents and architectural plans within the government-stipulated deadline.

In this sense, the focus of the activities developed by the technical team became the preparation of architectural and urbanistic projects (at the level of detailing required) and other technical documents required by the Caixa Econômica Federal bank (CEF), the public bank responsible for the projects' financing. This shift in priorities occurred to the detriment of project discussions and participatory planning.

Therefore, there was not a sufficient accumulation of practices of mutual convincing (or democratic practices) between the families and the technical team – practices that we have already indicated as being fundamental to the innovative process – so as to allow the final result of the projects to reflect the movement's struggles and collective discussions regarding the city as a commonly held good. When this accumulation is constructed, the possibilities for innovation grow, as do alternatives to hegemonic strategies and techniques of housing production.

Aside from this, the PMCMV-E's rules dictate a series of limitations related not only to possibilities for urban design, but also to the technologies that can be adopted and financed by the state. Many of the construction technologies discussed during meetings realised by the technical advisory team with the occupation's families as part of the architecture participatory project could not be financed according to the programme's norms. Bio-construction techniques using earth, for example, were not accepted by funding agent rules. However, current national and local political and economic realities remove any possibility of public resources for new housing units at the Solano Trindade occupation, or even predictions of when these might be available in the future. Paradoxically, this has not only freed the project from the programme's restrictive rules regarding construction technologies, urban design and time frames; it has also allowed the social movement and the advisory team to dedicate more time to discussions and practical experimentation with other forms of producing urban space.

The introduction – through practical workshops in the occupation – of alternative technologies, such as earth structures, alternative masonry and mortars, among other things – opens a new horizon of possibilities for the future local production of elements that might be utilised in constructing new housing units by means of contributing to the reduction of costs borne by families and to the quality of the constructed environment. Initially, the residents' group was quite resistant to experimenting with alternative construction techniques. However, after our practical workshops, most participants showed themselves to be very enthusiastic about these possibilities. The building components that resulted from these workshops have been incorporated into the construction of spaces for collective use in the occupation, such as a henhouse and a lavatory. These construction experiences can be seen as alternative technologies to those used by capitalist real estate production, whose logic is to build on a large scale in the shortest time possible. Many of these innovations will also be applicable to fields beyond housing, as we relate further later.

The construction of the project for requalifying 12 housing units

Faced with Brazil's current political context – in which no access to state resources is immediately predictable due to the emptying of the

Figure 6.3: Participatory project: families and the technical advisory team

Source: Fernanda Petrus

PMCMV-E budget – groups from UFRJ have concentrated their efforts over the last few years on searching for other financing possibilities.[12] Through parliamentary redress, the collective gained 340,000 Brazilian *reais* to be used towards the reform of one of the occupation's existing buildings, using alternative technologies for collective infrastructures such as sanitation, electricity, street paving and so on. This renovation, currently in its beginning phase, will transform the building into 12 new housing units for resident families. The collective will implement systems of ecological sanitation, as well as a 'green roof' and rainwater collection system, in addition to other innovative technologies. The proposal of recuperating the building has existed since the occupation's first year, yet its future has been debated and altered over time. The first participatory project developed for transforming the building into housing units took place in 2015; at the time, this was the subject of much debate among future residents and the advisory team (see Figure 6.3).

The main debate dealt with the ventilation of the lavatories. Faced with the challenge of adapting a building for residential use in which each unit would have only seven front-facing metres for ventilation and illumination, all of the alternatives initially proposed by the technical advising team localised the bathroom in the back of the unit, with no natural ventilation, so as to prioritise ventilation for the living room, kitchen and bedroom. This provoked significant reactions from residents, who said that they would not accept a lavatory without natural ventilation under any circumstances. This reaction led to an exhaustive exercise on the part of the technical team, which managed to propose an alternative plan in which all of the rooms would receive adequate lighting and natural ventilation, though the window in the bedroom would not be as large as in the first proposals. Ventilation for the lavatory was made possible through a differentiation in the height of the existing ceiling. The final project was the result of a long debate in which alternative plans were designed on the floor of the building so that families could experience the space. The lavatory ventilation debate reflects negotiation based on criteria of well-being and cultural values that differed between the residents and the technical team.

In the context of a real expectation of resources to improve the building, one relevant conflict that revealed itself over the course of 2018 was the question of the forms of property of the units scheduled for construction. This theme highlighted previously existent contradictions in the relationship among (non-resident) leaders and residents in the Solano Trindade occupation. The residents want private, individual properties in which they will be able to invest personal resources for improvement given that the parliamentary resources will not be sufficient to complete construction. At the same time, movement leaders have decided that these units should be temporary. For them, the units should be temporary since the main struggle is to finance the construction of new housing.

This decision by the movement's leaders also resulted in other consequences that have an impact on families' desires. The first is related to the differentiation of housing units through the development of different types adapted to the specific characteristics of each family. Another limit imposed by the leaderships is related to the plan for expanded areas in certain units. An agreement existed among residents that families with the largest numbers of members would receive units featuring an area planned for expansion. However, the occupation's leaders did not approve this plan, basing their decision on the temporary character of the housing, and claiming the use of annex space for the allocation of more temporary accommodation.

The agro-ecological front and the learning process

The housing plot of the Solano Trindade occupation presents certain physical peculiarities. First, it is located at the margins of São Bento Environmental Protection Area (APA), the first environmental protection area in Rio de Janeiro state's Baixada Fluminense region. The plot also has a significant quantity of green areas and open spaces: it is approximately 4.5 hectares but currently only three constructed buildings occupy roughly 10 per cent of the total area. These characteristics, in addition to the region's frequent flooding, justify the option of a low-density urban project with 105 new housing units.

Thus, the reality of the Solano Trindade occupation is entirely distinct from most occupations in the central area of the city, which are often located in abandoned buildings or small and unused lots. In this sense, by considering strategies for economic sustainability, both the movement and the university have wagered on the potential for producing foods and other agro-ecological activities as possible sources of work and income generation.

In this context, Mutirão de Agroecologia da UFRJ (MUDA UFRJ)[13] was invited to contribute to issues related to food production (and its processing), organic waste composting and ecological sanitation (the region does not have a sewage network). The format of activities was created collectively during the first meeting of the groups. It was decided to carry out activities at the occupation called 'Agro-ecological Exchanges', lasting 48 hours from Friday to Sunday, during which time participants camped in the main building's garden. Since the beginning of this partnership in the final months of 2016, eight of these activities have already been held, mobilising more than one hundred participants, including students and residents from the occupation and from the surrounding neighbourhood. The group's actions sought to question the mode in which we live and to insert socio-environmental dimensions into our discussions of territory, in addition to contributing to local demands. During these eight exchanges, all of the agro-ecological activities that currently exist at the occupation were implemented, as related in detail in the following.

In the minds of the Solano Trindade occupation's residents, an agricultural *mandala* had always existed. One resident who participated in founding the occupation – and who later became one of MNLM's leaders – always made clear his desire for an area for growing food, organised in concentric circles, based on his earlier experiences in North-Eastern Brazil. The first images generated by the technical advisory team and utilised to claim the use of land in negotiations with the state (three months after the occupation's beginning) brought the *mandala* to the place where it stands today: in a sort of patio at the back of the main building where the occupation's families live.

The *mandala* was finally constructed at the start of 2017, when work began during the first Agro-ecological Exchange. MUDA members had never implemented an Agro-Forest System (SAF) in the form of a *mandala* (a common familial technique in North-Eastern Brazil). For their part, Solano Trindade residents did not have experience in planting mixed agricultural crops – a characteristic of SAF agriculture – or without the use of chemical pesticides. After a series of discussions, and through a combination of techniques utilised by both groups, the first agro-ecological *mandala* took shape. Currently, the space for planting occupies an area of approximately 450 square metres, which is still in constant expansion and reconfiguration, featuring more than 50 different crops.

Based on this experience, the occupation began other forms of agro-ecological work. Residents created a patio for composting organic waste from individual and collective kitchens; this compost can either be commercialised or utilised in the occupation's community garden. The residents took longer to appropriate composting techniques than to grow crops, perhaps because it was an initiative led by MUDA rather than a local demand. However, through the exchanges, residents recognised the importance of this technology in producing the organic compost on which the community garden depends, and to significantly reduce the rubbish generated by the occupation. Gradually, residents began tending to the compost bins as part of their daily tasks, instead of exclusively during exchanges, and a resident taught the final composting workshop for UFRJ students.

Another technological form implemented during these exchanges was the BET[14] and the circle of banana trees for the treatment of effluent from one of the collective bathrooms. BET is a low-cost sanitation technology for treating black water; it is a closed system (meaning that it does not contaminate the soil, superficial waters or the water table); it is decentralised (independent from public sewage networks); and in addition to treating sewage, it produces food, based on its use of banana trees for the water evaporation process. In the case of the Solano Trindade occupation, the BET system was implemented together with a circle of banana trees for grey water treatment (see Figure 6.4).

Figure 6.4: BET construction process

Source: Fernanda Petrus

Finally, another important transformation that began as part of the exchanges was the creation of the agro-ecological kitchen. Initially intended to produce meals for internal consumption, the kitchen was transformed into a space for generating work and income for the occupation's women's collective. The space functions during social

Figure 6.5: Vegetarian cookery course

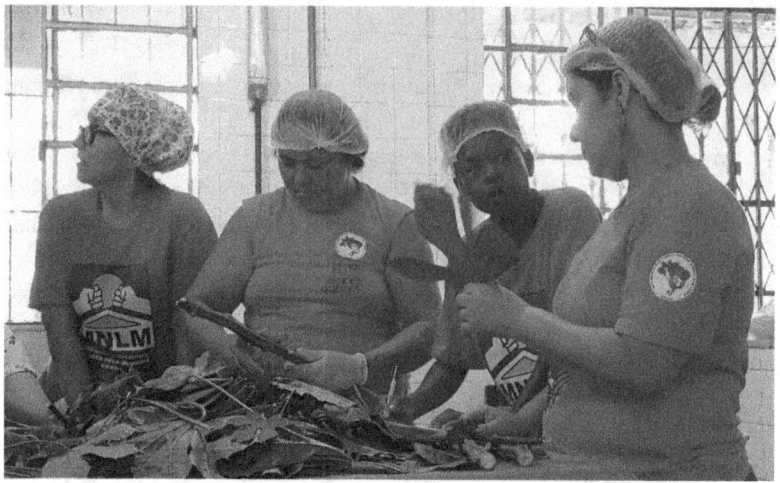

Source: Fernanda Petrus

events but it has also become an important space for training and for exchanging techniques and popular knowledge as part of the MUDA–Solano partnership. The improvement of the quality of food produced in the collective kitchen – and in certain individual kitchens – is notable; once rich in carbohydrates and fats, the occupation's cuisine is now more balanced, with greater nutritional value and ample use of resources available at the occupation (see Figure 6.5).

Conclusion

The practices related here show both the potential and the challenges of an urban self-managed experience based on exchanges of popular and scientific knowledge. Learning and knowledge advancement for everyone involved have been the result of collective practices of discussion and production.

At first, MNLM did not prioritise innovations and experimentations; therefore, they did not reflect on architectural and urbanistic projects developed by the technical team for new housing to be financed by the state. However, the current combination of economic and political crises in Brazil has led every group involved in the project to search for alternative means of financing, which makes technological experimentation and democratic negotiating practices viable. In this stage, new tensions have arisen around the requalification of the abandoned building for housing purposes. Debates regarding the forms of property –whether private or collective – have interfered in discussions regarding the project for houses and possible project-based and technological innovations.

As they demand less financial resources, we have seen that the activities in the field of agro-ecology have caused more significant transformations in the quality of life and in the culture of the residents than those related to the production of housing units. The collective production of healthy food and environmental infrastructure – among other actions in this field – foment multidisciplinary practices that complement the self-management of decent housing. It is a promising path towards the production of popular spaces oriented by urban self-management, economic solidarity and socio-environmental sustainability.

Lastly, concrete practices of urban social movements beyond the collective production of housing are inputs to expand the urban reform agenda. Decommodification of the city requires production strategies that combine the various dimensions of urban life, such as housing and decent work. In this sense, self-managed production is a permanent strategy fuelled by the everyday experiences of social movements. The experiences accumulated in several Brazilian cities show the elevation of the parameters of urban well-being and necessities for a decent life; consequently, there is a significant expansion of the social movements' demands in this field. The decommodification agenda is demanded from social movements' innovations and insurgencies of various types, such as the non-acceptance of norms imposed by the state for housing production, which are based on principles of financial profitability. We can say that self-managed experiences reaffirm the comprehension of the city as a product and producer of social conflict.

Notes

[1] A poet, painter, theatre artist and communist activist of Afro-Brazilian descent.

[2] The MNLM is one of four national urban social movements that have been organised in Brazil since the 1980s, being active in 16 of the country's 27 states. Beginning in 2003, these movements have participated in public spheres of negotiation regarding urban policy.

[3] The university's technical advice is being carried out by a team of professors, students and associate professionals in the areas of urban planning, architecture, environmental engineering and solidarity economy. The authors of this chapter are members of the team.

[4] 'Class consciousness' is the first condition for workers 'struggling against all forms of exploitation, whether they be in the workplace or the living-place' (Harvey, 1982: 22).

[5] The FNRU originated through popular movements, non-governmental organisations (NGOs), working-class collectives and academic institutions, with the objective of elaborating a proposal for a People's Amendment for Urban Reform in the 1988 Constitution. One central principle of urban reform is breaking with

the logic of the mercantile production of the city, prioritising its value for use instead. Other principles include: the social function of property and of the city; redistributive urban policy; and the democratic and participatory management of cities (Ferreira, 2018).

6. For a discussion on the tension between use value and commercial value, see Chapter 1.
7. After negotiations between the MNLM and the Secretary of National Patrimony (SPU) – and with strong participation of the UFRJ technical advisory team involved with the squat – the SPU declared the area to be of interest to public service for social housing, which, in turn, has contributed to making the occupation's continued existence viable in recent years.
8. The MNLM is organised into three levels of coordination (national, state and municipal) and coordinators are elected at the triennial meetings by the families that make up the movement. All levels must follow the movement's general political guidelines but each municipal core (like that of Duque de Caxias) has the power to make decisions that do not come up against national guidelines. This vertical structure differs from that of other housing movements, characterised by the aggregation of local organisations with greater autonomy.
9. The Manoel Congo and Mariana Crioula occupations in downtown Rio de Janeiro; the Nove de Novembro occupation on the periphery of the city of Volta Redonda; and Solano Trindade on the periphery of Duque de Caxias.
10. The occupied property consists of two abandoned buildings, both of which were fit to be renovated and utilised.
11. Brazil's federal government created the Minha Casa Minha Vida (My House, My Life Programme [PMCMV]) in 2009 as a preventive action in response to the worldwide financial crisis, as well as in response to commercial demands from the construction sector. In spite of large-scale investments for building housing, the programme also presented a certain backward progress inasmuch as it focused on the quantity of housing units rather than the quality of their construction and their integration into the city. Social movements were dissatisfied with the logic of PMCMV but they understood that they would only have access to funding for self-managed programmes if they followed the government's directions. As such, they pressured the government and were given a small part of the programme's funding (only 3 per cent) for PMCMV-E, an offshoot for self-managed production; in other words, a portion of the budget that is controlled by civil society organisations.
12. The group attempted to access funding through national and foreign grant opportunities, crowd-funding campaigns, and parliamentary amendments, among other possibilities.
13. MUDA UFRJ was created in 2009 through an initiative led by environmental engineering students. As a university outreach project that also articulates teaching and research activities, the group carries out experiences in agro-ecology and perma-culture, aiming to generate knowledge through an exchange of technical and popular techniques.
14. BET – *Bacia de Evapotranspiração* in Portuguese.

References

Coraggio, J.L. (1999) *Política social y economía del trabajo. Alternativas a la política neoliberal para la ciudad*, Buenos Aires: UNGS/Miño y Dávila Editores.

De Queiroz e Mello, I. (2015) *Trajetórias, cotidiano e utopias de uma ocupação no centro do Rio de Janeiro*, Rio de Janeiro: Letra Capital.

Do Lago, L.C. (2016) 'A produção autogestionária do habitat popular e a requalificação da vida urbana', in *Vinte e dois anos de política habitacional no Brasil: da euforia à crise*, Rio de Janeiro: Letra Capital, pp 129–50.

Ferreira, R. (2018) 'Movimentos de moradia, autogestão e política habitacional no Brasil: do acesso à moradia ao direito à cidade', http://agburbana.files.wordpress.com/2013/12/texto_isa_reginaferreira_port.pdf

Harvey, D. (1982) 'O trabalho, o capital e o conflito de classes em torno do ambiente construído nas sociedades capitalistas avançadas', *Espaço & Debates*, 6(June/September): 6–35.

Movimento Nacional de Luta pela Moradia – Santa Maria (2007). Por que tanta gente do Km3, participava das ocupações do MNLM nos prédio federais durante a realização das edições do Fórum Social Mundial. Blog MNLM – SM. Rio Grande, 05 jun 2007. Available on: http://mnlmsm.blogspot.com/2007/06/reforma-urbana-j-destinao-de-imoveis-da.html.

7

Self-management and the production of habitat: a case study of the Alianza Solidaria Housing Cooperative in Quito

Hernán Espinoza Riera, Andrés Cevallos Serrano, Bernardo Rosero, Irina Godoy and Janaina Marx

Introduction

An intense migration from the rural areas to the emerging urban settings of Ecuador took place during the second half of the 20th century. Most of the population concentrated in Quito and Guayaquil. This spawned high demand for housing units and, ultimately, because of the government's lack of response, a great housing deficit. Therefore, working-class groups found answers and solutions through self-building and self-management practices. Such experiences included housing committees and cooperatives. The latter were highly studied in Chile and Uruguay, but the same attention has not been paid to the Ecuadorian cooperatives. However, these organisations promoted a significant growth in the urban footprint of Quito, especially in low-cost land at the peripheral areas, where working-class solutions for habitat took place.

This chapter presents the experience of the Alianza Solidaria Housing Cooperative, which undertook the construction of houses and a sustainable environment through self-management, prompting a shift in their relationship with their territory.[1] This chapter is organised in three sections. First, a historic review of both Quito's urbanisation process and national housing policies is presented, through a simultaneous narrative of urban growth, the construction of public policies and the pro-housing struggle. The second section is focused on the cooperative movement of Ecuador, providing context for the formation of housing cooperatives in Quito aimed mainly at the working class. Lastly, the third section presents the experience of the

Alianza Solidaria Housing Cooperative, where solidarity economy and self-management shaped not only the production of habitat, but also the edification of participative and aware communities. Such efforts are revealed in the population and their lively and healthy territory.

Historical context of urbanisation and housing policies in Quito, Ecuador

The concept of habitat is understood in Ecuador as the built and integral space in which the population settles and develops its activities; therefore, it is necessary to achieve environmental quality in order to offer secure conditions for its inhabitants (SENPLADES, 2013). The Constitution of Ecuador (2008) requires all government levels to provide appropriate habitat and housing based on the principles of universality, equality, equity, progressiveness, interculturality, solidarity and no discrimination. Nevertheless, the human right to the habitat approved in the Constitution needs to be understood as a social struggle of the poor for housing, habitat and, ultimately, the right to the city. Since 2015, more than 60 per cent of the Ecuadorian population is settled in urban areas (Programa de las Naciones Unidas para los Asentamientos Humanos, 2012). This urban explosion derives from a development model that promotes the uncontrolled growth of the urban footprint in a way that exacerbates spatial segregation. In the case of Ecuadorian cities, inequality and poverty translated into limited access to serviced urban land, resulting in the proliferation of precarious settlements, often located in areas of risk. Up to 25 per cent of Ecuadorian households (703,000 families) live under precarious conditions, of which 500,000 are in urban areas (HABITAT III, 2016).

The territorial structure of Ecuador, similarly to many Latin American countries, is a result of its colonial legacy. The breakup of the pre-capitalist system triggered an agro-export model that resulted in the concentration of wealth in the main cities: Quito and Guayaquil. This new bipolar structure was the basis for regional asymmetries within the country. While Quito became the centre of political and administrative power, Guayaquil gained momentum as a port city and the country's financial engine (SENPLADES, 2009; Carrión and Erazo, 2012; Larrea, 2012). Such polarisation deepened throughout the 20th century through the three important economic cycles of cocoa, banana and oil booms, pushing a process of urbanisation concentrated in the big cities.[2]

Since 1950, the incipient urban areas started to develop by absorbing rural populations searching for better livelihood conditions. This rural–urban migration intensified, most notably, during the 1970s' 'oil boom', resulting in a problematic process of urbanisation with lasting consequences in current urban areas. The proper access to habitat became a national structural problem marked by social precariousness, limited access to housing with basic urban services and deficient public sector management. In the case of Quito, the geographical setting of the historic colonial core resulted in a high-density concentric urban space.[3] As the first half of the 20th century went by, the role of the capital city in the national context, along with emerging industrialisation and important infrastructure projects, translated into the longitudinal growth of the city, which occurred in a stratified fashion: the wealthiest settled in northern areas; the central area became overpopulated by the marginalised; and the south consolidated as a space for the railway and industrial working class. A significant process of valuation and commoditisation of urban land occurred thanks to the development of expansion areas fostered by an emerging landlord class that influenced the development of the city in the following years (Carrión and Erazo, 2012).

The unrestricted commercialisation of urban unused land provoked significant urban problems and forced the municipality to bear the heavy financial burden of new infrastructure. These social contradictions allowed for the rise of urban movements of resistance, including the pro-housing struggle. This moment was the breeding ground for the first self-management social organisations in relation to habitat, such as the Liga dos Inquilinos (League of Tenants)[4] in 1930, created to protect the right to habitat of the marginalised that were renting apartments in the historic urban core of Quito. In the face of the widespread social precariousness of numerous Ecuadorian cities, the state proceeded to take part in housing production directly. The national state undertook the role of reducing the housing deficit in what Acosta (2009) considers two different stages: the first one, from 1930 to 1997, is the state as a 'maker/giver'; and the second one, from 1997 to the present day, is the state as a 'facilitator'. During the first stage, the main objective was the consolidation and control of the housing supply through the purchase of land and the direct construction of houses. This moment is characterised by the creation of the first development plans, which tackled the housing production problem along with many of the other country's issues and included the creation of key public institutions such as the Ecuadorian Housing Bank (BEV) in 1961 (Superintendencia de Bancos, 1961) and the National Housing Board (JNV) in 1973. Nevertheless, built units and loans were mostly granted to the middle class, considered creditworthy at the time.

The discourse of the need for urban growth control and land market regulation was reasserted at the city scale through the implementation of Quito's Regulatory Plan in 1949, elaborated and conceived by the Uruguayan urbanist Jones Odriozola. The plan's zoning concentrated different urban amenities according to the working profiles of the population (Odriozola, 1945). Its segregational nature consolidated a historically exclusionist organisation of space by designating the northern areas as the space for middle- and high-income citizens, and the southern neighbourhoods as the place for the working class (Narváez, 2017). This configuration allowed for the development of social housing projects on peripheral neighbourhoods, such as *La Magdalena*, *Villaflora* and *Solanda* in the south, and *Comité del Pueblo*, *Carcelén* and *Carapungo* in the north, an indication that the municipal policy was for the peripheralisation of the poor. During the 1960s, economic development fostered a newer urban rearrangement of Quito, as observed in the city centre's obsolescence, the formation of new peripheral neighbourhoods, the relocation of industry, retail and management activities, and an increase in the number of vehicles.[5] These articulated processes of expansion and renewal consolidated a new metropolitan scale and the centre–periphery configuration.

By the 1970s, the state played the role of housing planner and producer through the JNV, the Social Security Institute and the Mutualist System. In Quito, there were land reserves for governmental public housing developments, and peripheral land for private plotting projects by cooperatives and mutualists. Mutualists were private financial institutions with social objectives, whose core business was fundraising from their contributors in order to finance house purchases, construction and household welfare. Initially, they were created to channel external credit that targeted the housing demands of marginalised citizens (Murillo, 2012: 182). Nonetheless, since the 1990s, after the issuing of the General Law of Financial System Institutions, mutualists became the only private entities in Ecuador that specialised in housing, and they started to exclusively meet the demands of the middle- and high-income class, undermining their social nature. Many *ciudadelas*[6] built in planned and legal zones of Quito were aimed at middle-income families (Narváez, 2017), whereas low-income citizens had their options limited to the periphery, where self-organisation and self-building through cooperatives and committees were prevalent. These peripheral developments were mostly established through the speculative plotting of land, where landowners illegally sold plots to low-income families (Godard, 1987).

Since 1977, cooperatives turned into the legal means of access to credit for pro-housing organisations. Thanks to its own regulations, the BEV started to 'grant loans for the purchase of land, urbanization and house construction to cooperatives with the objective of providing social housing to their associates' and 'for urbanization and house construction to similar cooperatives that own land, as long as the cost of houses does not exceed the maximum values' (JNV-BEV, 1984: **102**). This initiated a process of exponential growth in cooperative experiences, which constitute the breeding ground for many of the now-consolidated peripheral neighbourhoods of Quito, such as *La Ecuatoriana* and *Lucha de los Pobres* (Argüello et al, 1985). During the 1990s, amid the rise of neoliberalism, the cooperative movement lost momentum and many cooperative institutions vanished. The marginalised sectors of society with no access to cooperative institutions found another means in the struggle for housing: committees.[7] Such citizen organisations were commanded by political or religious leaders who knew how to put the government under pressure for the construction of social housing programmes. Research carried by the JNV found that Quito had 80 pro-housing grass-roots organisations in 1983: 45 pro-services committees, 35 neighbourhood committees, four neighbourhood associations and ten other various associations. Although many committees could not gain momentum, some emblematic examples, such as Comité del Pueblo (CDP)[8] in 1971, gathered up to 5,000 associates (JNV-BEV, 1984: 104).

However, it is necessary to consider that although self-management and self-construction are linked to citizen organisation, these processes derived from the population's vulnerability and the need to obtain a house for the development of life. These collective forces, though not always institutionalised, were one of the driving forces of urban expansion at the time (Godard, 1987), fostering poorly serviced settlements in peri-urban areas since most of the cooperatives operated with no regard for infrastructure, basic services or legal tenure.

As a counterpoint to the precarious social strategies, some attempts to solve social housing demands were made by the national government during the 1980s. For instance, the Solanda plan[9] was implemented in 1980 by the JNV and the municipality of Quito. These two entities collaborated to provide an official response to social demands, integrating urban attributes into social housing. Nonetheless, the biggest quantum leap occurred with the creation of the Quitumbe plan by the municipality of Quito in 1991. By establishing a new role for the south of Quito, for the first time an official plan disassociated the recurrent relation between industry and working-class neighbourhoods previously reaffirmed in Jones Odriozola's plan of 1949. The Quitumbe plan took into account the then housing deficit index of around 1 million units nationwide. In Quito, the index was built upon the quality and precariousness of the existing houses that resulted from numerous informal land occupations (Municipio de Quito, 1991).[10] Also, the plan sought to incorporate new land uses in the southern area in an attempt to overcome the noticeable lack of sufficient amenities dedicated to education, culture, recreation, government agencies, health care and social welfare. Thus, the plan aimed to create a new centre to 'decentralize the functions and amenities through the complete or partial transferring of activities related to public administration, services, finance, management agencies and informal market' (Municipio de Quito, 1991: 19). However, the plan was only implemented in 2004 through a special municipal ordinance named 'Ciudad Quitumbe 2005'.

The emergence of real estate developers and construction industries[11] gave rise to a new housing market segment. Private banking institutions became credit entities that targeted housing supply mostly at middle- and high-income households, which was a market segment that grew exponentially until getting hit by the deep economic crisis in 1998. Subsequent events, such as dollarisation, the growth in family remittances from migrants and mistrust of private banks, provoked an increase in housing demand and the strengthening of real estate companies. Regarding the public sector, solutions followed the neoliberal path of reducing state functions, privatising public services and state corporations, and welcoming foreign investment, directly affecting the housing supply. During the late 1990s, the national state turned into a 'facilitator' by subsidising the demand and partnering with real estate and construction companies, non-governmental organisations (NGOs) and cooperatives. A new housing policy was consolidated during this second stage, aided by the creation of the Housing and Urban Development Ministry (MIDUVI), which, along with the Inter-American Development Bank (IBD), developed the Housing Incentive System (SIV) that was responsible for delivering various housing bonds[12] for low-income families.

Over the years, the SIV suffered multiple changes, including the creation of new types of bonds that diversified the options available to the population. Between 2007 and 2015, MIDUVI delivered more than 330,000 bonds to financially support rural and urban households, amounting to approximately 1.371 million dollars of investment (MIDUVI, 2015). State support and financing policies, either through the housing bond or low-interest mortgage loans from the Ecuadorian

Institute of Social Security (IESS), increased the options available for the private sector in terms of housing production for medium- and low-income segments. In 2008, IESS granted up to 43 per cent of housing credit, followed by private banks (39 per cent), mutualists (11 per cent), cooperatives (7 per cent) and financial stock companies (0.1 per cent) (MIDUVI, 2015). With the goal of scaling up the credit system, and thus reaching population demands more easily, the national state created the Bank of the Ecuadorian Institute of Social Security (BIESS). Between 2009 and 2010, BIESS had granted up to 105,000 loans, amounting to around 4,000 million dollars, for purchasing land, house purchase, house building, refurbishment and/or house enlargement (MIDUVI, 2015).

Under such a scenario of the public funding of private housing production, a sophisticated case of self-management for habitat took place in the city of Quito: the Alianza Solidaria Housing Cooperative. The project, located in the southern area of the city, was developed in 2005 and supported by the re-launching of the Quitumbe plan, which defined urban parameters for block typologies, green spaces, *quebradas*[13] and the location of public amenities that were built later. The discourse of decentralisation presented in the Quitumbe plan led to the construction of major infrastructure works during the following years, such as Las Cuadras Park in 2007, Quitumbe Bus Terminal in 2008 and the Governmental Platform of Social Development in 2018. Thereby, social housing came to be included within the city, offering the low-income classes the right to the city.

Cooperativism as an alternative for housing in Ecuador

The cooperative movement arrived in Latin America during the 19th century, mostly inspired by European experiences developed by the followers of Robert Owen[14] and by the creation of social banks and rural savings banks in Germany. By the end of the 19th century, saving banks had started to emerge in Ecuador. These entities had the purpose of contributing to the social, moral and intellectual betterment of their associates, based upon a culture of saving and mutual aid (Da Ros, 2007). Benefiting from a significant monetary input derived from the so-called 'cocoa boom', saving banks became an alternative for the sectors who looked for more flexible financial models than those offered by traditional banks. In the global context, the rise of the Soviet Union (from 1917) and the advancement of social awareness contributed to the ascent of the socialist ideals that triggered the Juliana Revolution[15] of 1925 in Ecuador. The strengthening of the state and the enactment of nationalist social laws came along with the foundation of the Central Bank of Ecuador and the institutionalisation of savings and credit cooperatives through the issuing of the first Cooperatives Law of 1937 (Ramón, 2004; Paz y Miño, 2013). Nonetheless, the law cannot be considered a social gain for the poor since it was enacted on the basis of satisfying the speculative interests of the middle class regarding the appropriation of empty land and the fiscal benefits that came with it (Da Ros, 2007).

Since the 1960s, the proliferation of savings and credit cooperatives can be attributed mainly to the 'investment' that the US government made in Latin America through its *Alianza para el Progreso*[16] programme. During this decade, cooperatives engaged in civil construction projects dedicated to social housing, which enabled them to expand their credit portfolio. Furthermore, the number of cooperatives that specialised in housing credit increased exponentially, supported by an increasing demand from low-income sectors with no access to the main urban housing markets. Simultaneously, the BEV was founded in 1961, aiming to solve the urban and rural housing crisis by means of the accumulation and provision of funds for the construction and improvement of houses. In 1964, the Federation of Housing Cooperatives (FECOVI) was founded. It assembled 83 cooperative organisations with approximately 8,000 associates mainly from the provinces of Pichincha (50 per cent), Tungurahua (10 per cent) and Guayas (10 per cent) (JNV-BEV, 1984).[17] Although the cooperative movement flourished during those years, factors such as substandard financial management and leaders' politicisation prevented the housing cooperative movement from gaining organisational strength (JNV-BEV, 1984).

During the 1970s, the economic changes that derived from the oil boom provoked significant growth of the informal urban sector and the housing deficit. Therefore, a wave of social struggle unfolded in Quito and Guayaquil. Along with the creation of the JNV in1973 and the BEV in 1961, the government introduced regulation for investments and loans for the purchase of land, urbanisations and housing construction. This regulation specified the granting of 'loans for cooperatives with the purpose of delivering social housing projects to its associates' (JNV-BEV, 1984: 101). In a survey to 85 housing cooperatives, the JNV found that 78 per cent of them had solved landownership conflicts, and those that were in the process of purchase and tenure amounted to 22 per cent (JNV-BEV, 1984). This sample revealed that cooperative organisations had the capacity to directly access public credit.

During the neoliberal period of the 1990s, a capital accumulation phenomenon promoted the growth of major companies to the detriment of small and medium enterprises. Also, the issuing of the General Law for the Institutions of the Financial System of 1994 stimulated the participation of the private sector in the financial market, which allowed for the proliferation of new cooperative organisations. However, many of these organisations lacked the strength required for their sustainability, resulting in a process of fragmentation and eventually in the crisis of the cooperative system in Ecuador (Miño, 2013). In response to the state's limitations, land occupations became more frequent in peripheral areas in order to provide proper housing for the poor. In defence of property rights, these families suffered violent oppression by public forces. In 1991, a dreadful attack by the police against 1,000 families occupying a plot in the south of Quito sparked the creation of one of the most important organisations for the right of housing in the city: the 'Reina del Cinto'[18] cooperative. This organisation later began the Alianza Solidaria Housing Cooperative (COOVIAS, 2012a).

COOVIAS: self-management in the Andean context

> First, it was the struggle for a piece of land and urbanization works in order for every associate to be able to build their own house, according to their own needs and possibilities. This led to the consolidation of neighbourhoods with deeply unequal levels of development, and the generation of lots of issues, such as a large number of abandoned plots of land, plot subdivisions, illegal land transfers, clutter, neglect and lack of hygiene. From this experience we learned that obtaining land, even when it is urbanized, will not solve the housing problem nor, even worse, it would be a contribution to community building. (Melo, no date [a])

Several attempts were undertaken by pro-housing social organisations in the search of alternatives that respond to the social context and government requirements. In 1992, nine cooperatives of various lines of work on the south side of the capital city assembled to create the Association of Multiple Cooperatives of Quito (ACMQ). These cooperatives had autonomy but were organised under a coordination umbrella that managed and solved common issues.

Based upon this support and exchange network, the ACMQ decided to undertake a community development programme named '*La Solidaridad*', focused on rescuing environmental and cultural values. This programme fostered the '*Villa Solidaridad*'[19] social housing project, located in the south of Quito, with the proposal to create:

> a new way of life, with a participative, conscious and solidary community, located in a properly planned territory, with forms of power and control that lead to the constitution of a social force with its own identity, based upon work, respect to diversity, democracy, individual and collective initiative, mutual help and self-management. (COOVIAS, 2012b)

Although the outcome of this project was not what they expected, the experience itself led to the creation of COOVIAS. In 2000, the cooperative purchased a plot of land of roughly six hectares in the south of the city, were they built the 'Solidaridad Quitumbe' social housing project 'dedicated to the construction of habitat, housing and community through cooperative, self-managemental and solidarity economy like ways for good living' (Melo, no date[b]; see also López, 2014: 44). The plot was located in the 'Ciudad Quitumbe' plan, enclosed by the Ortega and El Carmen *quebradas* (both ravines are shown in Figure 7.1), which became the symbol of the project (COOVIAS, 2012a). Once the plot of land was purchased, a participatory process to define the project's guidelines started. Along the course of the project development, many training and sensibilisation activities that were undertaken allowed for the critical positioning of the associates. They began to understand that 'the housing problem is not only about building houses: the natural environment that surrounds the houses must be taken into account ... thus, it is necessary to discuss about habitat' (Melo, no date[b]). As a result, for instance, *quebradas* are considered for recovery and protection projects, and the maximal densification of the plot is avoided.

Self-management and the cooperative model were essential to the urbanisation process. COOVIAS divided the land in big plots as neighbourhoods, moving away from the individual plot approach. This co-ownership[20] model successfully facilitated several agreements between the cooperative and public institutions for the implementation of water supply, sewage systems and paving works by the respective municipal companies. Such agreements stipulated joint responsibility for the costs of the public works, which were partly subsidised by the municipal company and partly financed by the families once they received their property deeds. Acquiring such title deeds and thus gaining access to loans from the BEV required the support of the municipality of Quito in terms of the approval of the urbanisation ordinance over the cooperative's land (COOVIAS, 2012b). This experience demonstrates that citizen organisation has the capacity to influence decision-making at the public level (Melo, no date[a]).

Site planning, architectural designs, infrastructure plans and construction projects were entrusted to the Andino & Asociados architecture office. This private company, appointed by the cooperative as a technical consultant, worked under the coordination of the 'management unit'. This unit, composed of the cooperative's associates and professionals from the company, undertook the task of 'defining, applying and evaluating planning, construction, financing and housing organization processes' (COOVIAS, 2012a: 43). Through this modus operandi, COOVIAS ensured the establishment of a permanent decision-making group.

The first neighbourhood housed 60 families. The second and third neighbourhoods were built from 2003 to 2005. By 2007, the cooperative completed the construction of all the houses, benefiting 600 working-class families (COOVIAS, 2012a). As advised by the management unit, only one type of house was built (single-family and semi-detached), aiming to facilitate management and reduce the

Figure 7.1: 'Solidaridad Quitumbe' social housing project is located in the south of the city of Quito, enclosed by the Ortega and El Carmen *quebradas* (5 November 2018)

Source: Authors

construction costs. The incremental housing scheme[21] allowed house extensions according to each family's ability to pay. The company–cooperative partnership resulted in the application of good technical solutions, for example, the three-meter rear setback, prioritising environmental comfort over densification since 'it was not about building houses for the poor, uncomfortable and without design' (COOVIAS, 2012a: 47).

Although the initial idea was to build the houses with alternative materials (adobe, wood, steel), the houses ended up being built in concrete, the most common technology in the country, since there were no precedents in the public financing of other types of construction systems. As a following step, COOVIAS conducted training sessions for some of the associates to become part of the construction workers. Two motivations were behind this decision: first, many families were unemployed as a result of the political and economic crisis; and, second, there was a preference for local labour in construction and management tasks. Fabián Melo (no date[a]), one of the founding members, considers that self-organisation and self-management were the fundamental pillars of this experience, which enabled people to become protagonists in their own history. A cooperative is a non-profit organisation driven by the savings of its associates. Looking to warrant access to housing for every associate, especially the most vulnerable families, a 'solidarity savings' structure was implemented. Under this system, families that were randomly drawn to inhabit the same neighbourhood started to save collectively, according to their own possibilities. The collective funds were invested in the construction of the first stages, until its associates obtained their housing bond. In the event that a family could not pay the monthly instalment, they were relocated to a more affordable housing project or one with longer delivery times. Cooperative financing, based on the social solidarity economy, developed under different principles to those from the standard housing market. Although the construction process was slightly delayed (two to four years), it observed the dynamics of the community (COOVIAS, 2012a).

Since it was founded, COOVIAS acknowledged the value of creating a culture of education to build participative, conscious, solidary and self-managed communities, where families are educated through cooperative values. Inspired by the experiences of the Brazilian educator Paulo Freire,[22] they sought to promote personal transformation through beliefs, attitudes, paradigms and ways of thinking beyond the mere knowledge transfer. In order to promote critical thinking and conscious positioning in the face of the coming challenges, the training workshops addressed the concepts of good living, community, healthy habitat, neighbourhood interrelationships, community safety, conflict management and conversation culture (López, 2014). An additional strategy that contributed to strengthening the group was bringing back community work through the *minga*.[23] Traditionally, the *minga* is a powerful collective ceremony that summons communities, thus constituting a platform for the exchange of social and cultural norms (Acosta, 2012). Also, it highlights the value of work in Andean culture as a fundamental pillar for individual, family and collective well-being. Ancient values, still relevant in today's culture, were the force that enabled the community to ecologically restore the Ortega and El Carmen *quebradas* (ravines), through reciprocal and solidary actions. *Mingas* were carried out every Sunday, without the hierarchy of the organisation that goes from the director to the newly associated member. Such dynamics strengthened the horizontal relationship among the members, creating solidary ties that set this experience apart from the rest (COOVIAS, 2012a). Along the process, people got involved, understood their social situation and grew politically in a 'hard and sacrificed but rich and enlightening experience' (Melo, no date[c]).

Both of the surrounding *quebradas* (ravines) provoked great disappointment for the associates during the first field survey. In the popular imagination, such land features are considered waste deposits and sewage dumps, and historically only the poorest were condemned to settle next to them. These beliefs, which originate from colonial times, are indicators of discrimination, contempt and fear of nature (Melo, no date[c]). In Quito, it was a common practice for inhabitants to fill up any ravine. Nevertheless, this community favoured their restoration by implementing an ecological park. As Sandra López explains, the challenge of provoking collective action and the commitment to deliver manual labour demanded constant effort to both communicate a vision for the future of this neglected space and convince people that every collective action is important (López Giler, 2018). However, all the training and conversation cultivated by COOVIAS provoked a change of mindset that transformed the issue into an opportunity, which is an indication of how important it is 'to promote shifts in cultural patterns of communities' (López, 2014: 50). The development of the ecological park lasted for ten years, and it was achieved in three stages: (1) cleansing, (2) recovery and (3) construction. During the first three years, dwellers removed roughly 10 tons of waste (Melo, no date[c]). It was in this stage that early social organisation methodologies emerged, such as the 'tools bank', created with the purpose of facilitating labour during the *mingas* and thus reducing transportation inconveniences. The associates donated several tools to the cooperative that were stored in a collective warehouse. The tools bank still exists, and it supports the maintenance of the park and other minor works in the neighbourhoods.

Mingas kept being undertaken in the recovery stage, and the ravines were quickly transformed from polluted spaces into clean and high-quality spaces for the city. This restoration process did not follow environmental or geological standards since it was solely based on the skills and knowledge of the cooperative's associates. However, this collective action generated urban green corridors, protected water springs and avoided floods. Later, in 2002, the municipality of Quito acknowledged the work of the COOVIAS cooperative and supported their initiative through the Municipal Corporation of Environmental Health 'Vida para Quito'.[24] An agreement was made to support the cooperative in the process of water decontamination, the reforestation of native plants with educational purposes, landscaping, the development of a water treatment zone and the construction of recreation and sports community areas (COOVIAS, 2012a). These actions were intended to foster citizen awareness about environmental conservation. During the construction stage, the cooperative built 6 kilometres of cycle lanes, kiosks, green areas, orchards, cultivation terraces, ecological trails, playgrounds and bridges (Melo, no date[c]). The overall reforestation was made with the support of local high school students, planting around 4,000 trees. The nearly 800 meters of ecological trails and the water protection areas also function for educational purposes. All these experiences turned the COOVIAS organisation into a technical advisor for other cooperatives, inspiring some public initiatives along the way. In 2004, the municipality developed Linear Park along the Machángara River, consisting of 30 kilometres dedicated to the preservation and protection of the *quebradas* (ravines) along this river. In 2008, the city officially implemented a policy to protect and recover ravines, which represents a significant step forward in terms of environmental ecology.

Nowadays, the work of COOVIAS goes on, extending their field of action to the entire Quitumbe zone. In recent years, several community-bonding events have taken place, for example, the Latin American Meeting of Solidarity and Social Economy Actors, Citizen Participation Forum of Quitumbe and Urban Environment Forum of Quitumbe. Additionally, the organisation created the Environmental Interpretation Centre of Quitumbe dedicated to social education and environmental training (Melo, no date[c]). In recognition of their persistent management of environmental issues and a strong commitment to citizen education, the municipality awarded COOVIAS with the Metropolitan Environment Distinction 'Quito Sostenible' (Secretaría de Ambiente Municipal de Quito, 2017).

Despite the outstanding contributions to municipal policies that this process has provided, it remains a challenge to obtain direct support from the public sector. Although the academic sector and some NGOs have assisted the cooperative, the logic behind this kind of production of habitat is yet to be embraced by the government and the municipality (López Giler, 2018). Legal reforms that took place, along with the issuing of the Constitution of 2008, limited many cooperatives to only delivering housing projects, thus blocking the chance of providing other services, which deteriorated their capacity to attract associates. The government's 'discipline and punish' approach, instead of coordination and promotion, threatens this process. Fortunately, this has not undermined the collective course of action or the proposition of new ideas under the self-management framework. Sandra López explains that the cooperative is shaping the project for a new stage of housing development, but including mixed-use as a response to the new local transit infrastructures. Furthermore, they keep working to materialise the idea of an integrated system for the protection and activation of the *quebradas* (ravines) as an extensive city-scale urban park that articulates tourism, art and local business, all of these through a solidary economy under a cooperative vision (López Giler, 2018).

Conclusion

The urbanisation process in Quito unfolded in an incomplete and stratified fashion: incomplete since a great part of the population still has no access to housing or basic services; and stratified due to the spatial organisation of the different social classes, initially motivated by the environmental factors and then ratified by urban plans. Thus, historically, the upper classes have opted for the north as their preferred choice, while low-income classes settled first in the south and later in the peripheries. Although different government levels promoted plans to overcome the growing housing shortage, these proved to be insufficient, forcing the low-income classes to look for alternatives based on self-management and self-building to solve the housing gap.

In 1991, the municipality of Quito overcame the historical social-spatial division for the first time when conceiving the Quitumbe plan. The plan defined a new urban centre in the south of the capital city, through the implementation of amenities, services, public institutions and housing. However, due to the national economic and political context, the plan only took effect more than a decade later, when COOVIAS put the 'Solidaridad Quitumbe' social housing project into place.

There were several attempts by working-class groups to attain decent housing conditions, including self-organisation through committees and cooperatives. Despite its successes and failures, the cooperative model was one of the main instruments by which those organised groups could legitimate their struggle and regularise their housing situation. As a result, there are a significant amount of peripheral neighbourhoods in Quito that are currently named after the cooperatives that founded them. This model enabled the conversation between working-class groups and public institutions, accelerating the urbanisation process at the peripheries, especially after the issuing of the decree that allowed cooperatives to access government housing credit for social housing. On the one hand, this caused dramatic urban sprawl without due consideration for planning. On the other hand, such a scenario allowed for the development of experiences such as that of COOVIAS. This provides evidence that the cooperative model can be applied to the production of housing and sustainable surroundings as an alternative to the current individual housing-credit system adopted by the Ecuadorian government.

COOVIAS is the outcome of both the extensive learning process of the cooperative movement and the struggle for housing that started in the 1960s. The 'Solidaridad Quitumbe' housing project is the result of this accumulation of experiences reflected in the vision of generating an integral habitat, housing and community. In other words, the cooperative found a way to develop a serviced neighbourhood, with adequate infrastructure, amenities, green areas and public spaces, through self-management and a solidary economy. They overcame the individual-plot sale approach, frequently implemented by social housing programmes. The cooperative model granted the community notable recognition by the government, allowing for access to mortgage credits for housing and the subscription of agreements with municipal departments for infrastructure provision. Furthermore, community organisation enabled the undertaking of *mingas* for the development of the ecological park and ravine restoration. Both events provide evidence for how the cooperative model adds value to properties. The 'Solidaridad Quitumbe' housing project demonstrates that quality habitat can be achieved through self-management, solidary savings, community work and cooperativism, disproving the idea that low-income families are condemned to settle in poorly serviced, peripheral, low-value neighbourhoods.

Assemblies, trainings and workshops carried along the process, fostered the exchange of knowledge and the construction of critical thinking, and transformed the associates' perspective. Eventually, the idea of a 'life project' rather than a housing project gained ground. Participation allowed associates to prefer quality of habitat to common practices and financial instincts, which can be observed, for instance, in the decision to create an ecological park of the restored ravines, and the prioritisation of environmental comfort instead of densification. Such elements added social and cultural meaning to property: social since the houses materialise the result of a decades-long struggle for the integration of dwellings to a serviced city; and cultural because the development of a neighbourhood with distinguishable environmental quality became an expression of both an organisation sense and the building of solidarity networks.

Lastly, this case study demonstrates the capacity that communities have to organise themselves in order to build an integral vision of the concept of habitat. COOVIAS was able to change social paradigms, setting an example for other organised communities and influencing public policies. As Fabian Melo (no date[a]), the president of COOVIAS, expresses it, this experience contributes to the city and the nation because it is built from the social and community organisation, which is the basis of a conscious, organised, proactive, co-responsible and democratic society.

Notes

[1] We gratefully acknowledge our collaborators students, Roberto Farinango, Alejandra Páez and Sofía Ponce, for their great contributions in data collection. Our gratitude also goes to the Alianza Solidaria Housing Cooperative, especially to Fabián Melo and Sandra López, for their wholehearted support in the achievement of this chapter. Our greatest appreciation to the Universidad Central del Ecuador for the funding of our research and its Faculty of Architecture and Urbanism for the valuable institutional support.

[2] A total of 41 per cent of the national population was concentrated in Quito and Guayaquil (INEC, 2010).

[3] In 1910, Quito reached a density of 276 people per hectare (Carrión and Erazo, 2012).

[4] The Liga Central Pro Inquilinato was created in July 1930 in Quito, demanding clean apartments, public amenities in the neighbourhood, the creation of neighbourhoods for the working class and a right to free transit (Baquero, 2011).

[5] For more information, see Carrión and Erazo (2012).

[6] *Ciudadelas* are urban units that, in the context of Quito, constitute a sort of small planned neighbourhood usually for middle- and high-income families. These units differ from gated communities since they tend to become integrated into their urban surroundings.

[7] A word of Latin origin meaning 'community' or 'to gather'.

8   CDP is a working-class neighbourhood in Quito's northern periphery, originated during the 1970s. It was developed through a partnership between a social organisation (CPP), a Far Left party (PCMLE) and a public faculty of architecture (FAU-UCE) (Testori, 2016).
9   The Solanda housing plan was a model neighbourhood of progressive housing for the south of the capital built under a partnership between the BEV, the US Agency for International Development and the municipality of Quito (Fabianokueva.net, 2018).
10 The *Quitumbe* Plan estimated the demand for 21.151 housing units until year 1992, and 94.737 until year 2000. At the same time, it described the increasing cost of urbanization along with the rise of occupations and self-building. (Municipio de Quito, 1991).
11 Carrión and Erazo (2012: p. 512) argue that the emergence of these segments is related to the early 1970s 'under the political and economic framework of the Alliance for Progress, where the capital of the United States financed mutualism institutions, the private banking system and state institutions for to housing supply'.
12 The housing bond is a state's monetary incentive, targeted at the population whose income is no higher than three times the unified basic wage; it was created after the first IBD loan of 1997. Many types of bond were issued: house purchasing, construction on own land, house improvements, property title and so on. In order to access the bonds, beneficiaries needed to demonstrate their financial commitment to minimal savings and having a bank loan that covered the remaining cost.
13 *Quebradas* are a type of ravine or land incision that, in the case of Quito, are the result of the last geological de-glaciation and form an extensive network (Peltre, 1989).
14 Owen, considered the 'father of cooperativism', was a textile manufacturer known for conducting socialist experiments for the betterment of the labour conditions of his workers.
15 A military coup took place on 9 July 1925, carried out by young Ecuadorian army officials against the oligarchs and the banking hegemony of the time (Paz y Miño,, 2002).
16 The *Alianza para el Progreso* programme was created by US president John F. Kennedy (1961–63) to 'support' Latin America to end 'underdevelopment'. North American interference was a response to the Cuban Revolution (of 1959) and its probable influence over South America, in the context of the Cold War.
17 Quito is also the capital of the province of Pichincha, and Guayaquil is the capital of the province of Guayas.
18 'Reina del Cinto' was institutionalised through Ministerial Agreement Number 002578 on 22 May 1992. Eight years later, in April 2000, the cooperative changed its business name to 'Cooperativa de Vivienda Alianza Solidaria' (López, 2014: 43).
19 This project was developed by 11 housing cooperatives to provide housing for 3,000 families (COOVIAS, 2012a).
20 Co-ownership distributes the property rights in equal parts for every associate, eventually resulting in a sort of condominium.
21 In 2001, COOVIAS, in partnership with the technical consultant company, adopted the incremental housing scheme. For a 65 m2 house, the construction started as a 36 m2 building, then it could be extended to 42 m2, before reaching the full size. Other alternate sizes were also included: 74 m2 and 83 m2 (COOVIAS, 2012a).
22 Paulo Freire (1921–97) was a Brazilian educator known worldwide for his pedagogical methods for literacy. He condemned the orthodox ways of most educational institutions, labelling them as exclusionary and elitist. For him, a student is not a mere knowledge receiver (banking education); rather, students need to

[23] In Ecuador, *minga* ('*minka*' from the kichwa language) is an ancient tradition still practised in present days. It is a way of organising community works of social utility from which territorial interventions are undertaken.

[24] This corporation was part of the municipality of Quito dedicated to the city's environmental affairs. It was financed through a portion of Quito's overall income tax.

References

Acosta, A. (2012) 'O Buen Vivir: uma oportunidade de imaginar outro mundo', in Heinrich Böll Foundation: Série Democracía (ed) *Um campeão visto de perto*, Rio de Janeiro: Fundação Böll, pp 198–216.

Acosta, M.E. (2009) *Políticas de vivienda en Ecuador desde la década de los 70 – análisis, balance y aprendizajes*, Tesis de Maestría, Facultad Latinoamericana de Ciencias Sociales, Quito: FLACSO.

Argüello, N., Hernández, A. and Zúñiga, S. (1985) *Las Cooperativas de Vivienda en Quito*, Tesis de licenciatura, Quito: Facultad de Arquitectura y Urbanismo de la Universidad Central del Ecuador.

Baquero, P.L. (2011) *Ecos de revuelta: cambio social y violencia política en Quito (1931–1932)*, Quito: Flacso-Sede Ecuador.

Carrión, F. and Erazo, J. (2012) 'La forma urbana de Quito: una historia de centros y periferias', *Bulletin de l'Institut français d'études andines*, 41(3): 503–22.

COOVIAS (Cooperativa de Vivienda Alianza Solidaria) (2012a) *La Cooperativa de Vivienda Alianza Solidaria 10 años de historia: procesos y aprendizajes 1990–2010. Tomo I*, Quito: Archivo COOVIAS.

COOVIAS (2012b) *La Cooperativa de Vivienda Alianza Solidaria 10 años de historia: procesos y aprendizajes 1990–2010. Tomo 3 Planes y Propuestas Solidaridad*, Quito: Coovias Archivo COOVIAS–FEDAEPS.

Da Ros, G. (2007) 'El movimiento cooperativo en el Ecuador. Visión histórica, situación actual y perspectivas', *CIRIEC – España, Revista de Economía Pública, Social y Cooperativa*, 57: 249–84.

Ecuador (2008) *Constitución de la República del Ecuador*, Ciudad Alfaro: Asamblea Constituyente.

Fabianokueva.net (2018) 'Ciudad Modelo – Fabiano Kueva', http://fabianokueva.net/archivo/ciudad-modelo

Godard, H. (1987) 'Quito – Guayaquil: Eje Central o Bicefalía', in CEDIG (ed) *El Espacio Urbano en el Ecuador*, Quito: Instituto Geográfico Militar, pp 108–36.

Habitat III (Comité Técnico Interinstitucional para el proceso preparatorio de Habitat III) (2016) *Posición Nacional del Ecuador frente a la Nueva Agenda Urbana* (2nd edn), Quito: Imprenta Editorial Ecuador.

INEC (Instituto Ecuatoriano de Estadísticas y Censos) (2010) *VII Censo de Población y VI de Vivienda*, Quito: Administración central.

JNV-BEV (Junta Nacional de Vivienda; Banco Ecuatoriano de la Vivienda) (1984) *Ecuador 20 Años de Vivienda (ensayo)*, Quito: Ediciones CEDECO.

Larrea, A.M. (2012) *Modo de desarrollo, organización territorial y cambio constituyente en el Ecuador* (2nd edn), Quito: SENPLADES.

López, S. (2014) *El Rol de la Formación en la Construcción de Comunidad Participativas y Autogestionarias para el Buen Vivir, aplicado en el Proyecto Habitacional Alpallacta de la Cooperativa de Vivienda Alianza Solidaria*, Quito: Universidad Politécnica Salesiana Sede Quito.

López Giler, S. (2018) 'Interview with Andrés Cevallos', *OPTE*, 8 December.

Melo, F. (no date [a]) *Resumen Ejecutivo. Nuestra Propuesta Cooperativa – I Parte*, Quito: Presidencia Coovias.

Melo, F. (no date [b]) *Autogestión Comunitaria para el Buen Vivir. Una experiencia de economia solidaria para la construcción de habitat, comunidad y vivienda en entornos urbano populares*, Quito: Presidencia Coovias.

Melo, F. (no date[c]) *Construyendo Hábitat Comunitario y Autogestionario: medio ambiente, espacio público, comunidad y vivienda. Una experiencia de construcción social y cooperativa de hábitat popular en el Sur de Quito*, Quito: Presidencia Coovias.

MIDUVI (Ministerio de Desarrollo Urbano y Vivienda) (2015) *Informe Nacional del Ecuador para la Tercera Conferencia de las Naciones Unidas sobre Vivienda y Desarrollo Urbano Sostenible HABITAT III*, Quito: MIDUVI.

Miño, W. (2013) *Historia del Cooperativismo en el Ecuador* (1st edn), Quito: Ministerio de Coordinación de Política Económica.

Municipio de Quito (1991) *Plan Ciudad Quitumbe*, Quito: Editorial El Conejo.

Murillo, G. (2012) *Metodología de aplicación de una auditoría de gestión como herramienta para determinar los costos de la no calidad y elevar la productividad en el departamento de ahorros de la Mutualista Pichincha. Graduado*, Quito: Universidad Politécnica Salesiana.

Narváez, A. (2017) *Quito: Cuatro Cuentos Urbanos*, Quito: Casa de la Cultura Ecuatoriana Benjamín Carrión.

Odriozola, J. (1945) *Memoria descriptiva del proyecto del Plan Regulador para la ciudad de Quito*, Quito: Imprenta Municipal.

Paz y Miño, J. (2002) *La Revolución Juliana: Nación, Ejercito y bancocracia* (1st edn), Quito, Ecuador: Abya-Yala.

Paz y Miño, J. (2013) *La Revolución Juliana en Ecuador (1925–1931). Políticas económicas*, Serie Historia de la Política Económica del Ecuador, Quito: Ministerio Coordinador de Política Económica.

Peltre, P. (1989) 'Quebradas y riesgos naturales en Quito, período 1900–1988. Riesgos Naturales en Quito, Lahares, aluviones y derrumbes del Pichincha y del Cotopaxi', *Estudios de Geografía*, 2: 45–91.

Programa de las Naciones Unidas para los Asentamientos Humanos (2012) *Estado de las Ciudades de América Latina y el Caribe 2012: Rumbo a una nueva transición Urbana*, Nairobi: ONU-Habitat.

Ramón, G. (2004) 'Estado región y localidades en el Ecuador (1808–2000)', in S. Báez, P. Ospina and G. Valarezo (eds) *Una Breve História del Espacio Ecuatoriano*, Quito: CAMAREN – IEE.

Secretaría de Ambiente Municipal de Quito (2017) 'Distinción Ambiental Metropolitana Quito Sostenible', http://www.quitoambiente.gob.ec/ambiente/images/Secretaria_Ambiente/Buenas_Practicas_Ambientales/distincion/informacion_DAM_QS_2017.pdf.

SENPLADES (Secretaría Nacional de Planificación y Desarrollo) (2009) *Plan Nacional para el Buen Vivir 2009–2013*, Quito: Senplades.

SENPLADES (2013) *Plan Nacional del Buen Vivir 2013–2017*, Quito: Senplades.

Superintendencia de Bancos (1961) *Ley de Emergencia No. 23*, Quito: Registro Oficial del 26 de mayo de 1961.

Testori, G. (2016) 'Cooperation reconsidered: the case of Comité del Pueblo in Quito', in Seminario Internacional de Investigación en Urbanismo (ed) *VIII Seminario Internacional de Investigación en Urbanismo*, conference report, Barcelona: DUOT.

8

Residents' experiences of self-build housing

Daniël Bossuyt

Introduction

Self-build housing is driven by a variety of motivations, aspirations and dreams, and takes on different forms. This chapter is principally concerned with people's reasons for assuming the responsibility for building their own homes and how they fulfil this role in the context of an aided self-build scheme. This is a particularly interesting question in light of growing policy recognition and a proliferation of self-building initiatives throughout Europe (Mullins and Moore, 2018). Policymakers and advocates assume that self-building intrinsically leads to housing that is better attuned to the values of spatial quality, affordability and sustainability (Gemeente Almere, 2009; Parvin et al, 2011). This is the case, it is argued, because self-builders are more inclined to consider use values in development and design. Accordingly, the normative case has been made for the consolidation of citizens' 'right to build' (Parvin et al, 2011). This has aligned with a broader political discourse celebrating principles of subsidiarity, localism and civic autonomy in urban governance (Davoudi and Madanipour, 2015; Jarvis, 2015; Uitermark, 2015).

While there is growing attention to the social dynamics of self-build housing initiatives, this has often focused on motivations and values within discrete models. Meanwhile, there has been less qualitative understanding of residents' rationales and strategies in the context of facilitated self-build schemes. This is important in the light of increased government attention to enabling resident-led housing development. Research on the social dynamics of self-building has identified different drivers, such as costs and customisation (Harris, 1991; Clapham et al, 1993). There has also been attention to the different social, cultural and financial processes that are implicated in self-building practices (Brown, 2007; Cox, 2016; Benson and Hamiduddin, 2018). Still less attention has been paid to the relationship between self-building practices and the institutional and regulatory context at the level of self-builders. Institutional dimensions are central to understanding how residents fulfil their roles within facilitated self-build schemes as they set out the arrangements of enabling and constraining conditions for self-builders' rationales and strategies. The rich variety of commissioning arrangements through which self-building may take place are a central point of departure for this chapter.

This chapter aims to enrich the understanding of self-builders' rationales and strategies through a case study of the Homeruskwartier in Almere, one of the largest state-assisted self-building schemes in Europe (see Figure 8.1 and Figure 8.2). Unlike many other cases of self-build, which are often relatively small in scale, the Homeruskwartier concerns an entire neighbourhood of 6,279 residents, constructed through a broad spectrum of commissioning arrangements (Gemeente Almere, 2018). Almere is a new town, built on reclaimed land just 20 kilometres west of Amsterdam. In addition, it is a particularly interesting case as it includes self-building for different socio-economic groups, including groups that would normally be dependent on social housing. The municipality of Almere is central to understanding the scale of the project. Municipalities in the Netherlands play a strong part in land development through both public and private means. While this is slowly changing (Buitelaar, 2010), Almere's landownership enabled the provision of plots, which were coupled with sets of building guidelines. Almere had a twofold rationale for embarking on this scheme. On the one hand, the municipality posited that self-building results in a qualitative improvement in the living environment; on the other hand, it asserted that people ought to be in control of the production of their own homes (Gemeente Almere, 2009).

This chapter is concerned with three main questions: first, why do self-builders engage in building their own homes? Second, what design and development strategies do they employ? Third, how are self-builders' rationales and strategies structured by the regulatory framework? Conceptually speaking, the chapter is concerned with how self-builders narrate and argue their reasons and strategies, capturing both the subjective meanings and experiences implied in self-building practices, as well the material implications. The chapter asserts that for planning to successfully harness the potential of self-building, it must recognise the multiplicity of self-builders' rationales and strategies. First and foremost, this includes a recognition of the multifaceted nature of the self-build house as both a place to live/home and an asset/source of wealth. The pivotal role of residents in self-building potentially allows them to prioritise values related to sustainability or spatial quality.

However, self-builders also bear risk and responsibility, against which they are required to weigh their design and development decisions. This implies that financial and use value considerations should not be thought of as opposites or mutually exclusive; rather, they may overlap, clash and cross-cut in self-builders' design and development decisions and practices.

Conceptualising self-build housing

This chapter opts for a broad definition of self-build housing as the practice whereby residents produce housing for their own use. This can be done individually or collectively, drawing upon their own skills or in collaboration with other stakeholders. This broader definition relates to Duncan and Rowe's (1993) definition of self-build as cases 'where the first occupants arrange for the production of their own dwelling, and in various ways participate in its production'. It also aligns with Mullins and Moore's (2018) definition of self-organised housing as an umbrella term for all sorts of different practices pertaining to household involvement in housing production.

The chapter acknowledges the term 'collaborative housing', which has recently been used to refer to a wide variety of (collective) self-organised and self-managed forms of housing (Lang et al, 2018). However, the term 'self-build' is used here as it resonates with the terms used in public discourse, as well as the chapter's focus on practices of housing production by individual households. The advantage of this broader definition is that it directs attention towards different types and models of self-building, without excluding any one model in particular. This sits well with this chapter's objective of scrutinising different self-building practices in the context of resident-led urban development.

Understanding self-build rationales and strategies

Land and housing market dynamics are key to understanding self-building. At a structural level, self-building is associated with periods of economic downturn (Duncan and Rowe, 1993). As large market actors and public authorities fail to provide housing, self-building constitutes an alternative that is based on small-scale initiatives. Nowhere is this more apparent than in accounts of autonomous settlements in the Global South. While the contextual differences are vast, there is a similarity in terms of how the state and market are either incapable or unwilling to provide housing (Harms, 1982); in response, citizens arrange their own forms of housing (and services). Much in the same light, the recent resurgence of self-build housing initiatives in Europe has been related to the global financial crisis and austerity. On the one hand, public authorities have adopted more flexible and demand-led land development models, privileging incremental and small-scale development such as self-building (Savini, 2017). On the other hand, as institutional mechanisms have failed to provide housing, citizens have tried to find alternatives (Czischke, 2017). The proliferation of new models of self-build can be attributed to these two interrelated structural and civic dynamics.

However, we must be wary of drawing one-to-one causal linkages between observations of autonomous settlements and the recent self-building renaissance in Europe. Examples of self-building initiatives also exist in currently booming economies (Crabtree, 2018). Still, these may hint at a broader concern with affordability in the context of overheated markets. Meso-level factors pertaining to institutional norms of land development and housing are crucial in terms of understanding self-building. In countries with advanced planning systems such as the Netherlands and the UK, development control, building regulations and controlled land supply have negatively affected prospects for civic commissioning (Hardy and Ward, 1984; Bossuyt et al, 2018). In addition, we also see that welfare rescaling and retrenchment have created space for community-based housing solutions. Not only do formal institutional factors play a role, but cultural aspects, such as the North American emphasis on autonomy and self-provision (Shulist and Harris, 2002), communitarian values in Denmark (Sørvoll and Bengtsson, 2018), or anti-urbanist sentiments in Belgium (De Decker, 2008), all play their part in contributing to the ways in which actor relations in housing and land markets are structured.

At the individual level, there are two broad categories of motivations for self-building: control and costs (Clapham et al, 1993; Wallace et al, 2013). First, as residents occupy a pivotal role in procurement, they have a potentially stronger degree of control over design and development. This creates access to housing types, layouts and designs not offered by either the state or the market. Second, self-building allows for significant cost savings as there are neither profit margins nor marketing costs to consider. Moreover, residents may build more cheaply by drawing on their own skills and 'sweat equity'. The broad categories of cost and control are essential to the claimed advantages of self-building vis-a-vis regular housing, and shed light on the renewed policy attention to self-building. However, they do not fully illuminate that self-build housing ought to be understood as a social process, rather than a commodity that satisfies the need for dwelling

(Turner, 1972). This ties in to a conceptualisation of the house as a nexus for all sorts of social and economic relationships, closely tied to the affective notion of home and shaped by the socio-economic, cultural and political contexts in which it is situated (Mallett, 2004). This necessitates a multidimensional view of the self-building process, and concomitantly residents' rationales and strategies.

Policymakers and self-build advocates have posited that self-builders' strategies are characterised by a pursuit of values such as spatial quality and sustainability (Gemeente Almere, 2009; Wallace et al, 2013). Parvin et al (2011) use the concept of 'value architecture' to indicate how self-building engenders a shift from financial exchange value to use value maximisation. Residents have a strong stake in the house that they are building and are thus keen to consider the long-term effects of their design decisions. The consequence is that residents can opt for housing that suits their particular living arrangements, is more energy efficient or is of improved architectural value. Overall, this results in an improvement in the spatial quality of urban environments. Against the background of these arguments, policymakers and politicians in various European countries have called for the scaling up of self-build to address housing issues (Duivesteijn, 2014; NaCSBA, 2018; Tellinga, 2018).

Municipalities, non-profits and other intermediaries are key in terms of enabling a broader populace to engage in self-building and reap its claimed benefits. Support may be provided in terms of land, technical expertise, access to financial resources or easing development risk (Wallace et al, 2013). However, while much is known about the various models of self-building and the values underpinning them, there remains a knowledge gap pertaining to the rationales and strategies of self-builders within an aided self-build scheme. As outlined earlier, choice and affordability are key rationales for self-builders, but this remains insufficiently investigated in the example of concrete facilitated self-build schemes. This is particularly key in terms of understanding how residents' motivations and strategies are framed and how these translate into particular commissioning configurations.

This chapter hypothesises that residents' motivations may not be understood through a crude conceptualisation of costs and control as exclusive, mutually exhaustive categories. A multidimensional conceptualisation of the self-build house implies a wide range of motivations, which may compromise, clash with or cross-cut each other in residents' design and development practices. Moreover, it is expected that residents' rationales and strategies interact with economic and regulatory contexts. This is important not just in terms of the advantages offered by self-building vis-a-vis regular turnkey housing, but also for understanding how rationales and strategies are framed through institutional support. In terms of residents' relationship to the regulatory framework, we expect that this is experienced as necessary for the realisation of their practices, though self-builders may also challenge existing formal rules in their practices.

Methodology

This chapter is based on fieldwork conducted from April to October 2018 in the Homeruskwartier in Almere, a new town located on reclaimed land in the Amsterdam Metropolitan Region. The author opted for a qualitative research strategy as it was primarily concerned with how residents articulated the desire to build their own homes from their own perspectives. The author conducted 23 in-depth qualitative interviews with 30 residents of the Homeruskwartier.

As the aim was to explore rationales and strategies across a large variety of commissioning arrangements, interviewees were contacted through a combined strategy of purposeful snowball sampling and convenience sampling to ensure variety in terms of commissioning arrangements. Residents were approached through a combined strategy of Internet searches and door-to-door contact to ensure the coverage of different self-building models and plots. In addition, I asked participants for the contact information of neighbours and friends in the Homeruskwartier. Interviews lasted between 45 and 90 minutes on average and followed a semi-structured topic list covering participants' goals and motivations for self-building, how they tried to achieve these in the design and process, and their interaction with regulatory frameworks. The interviews took place in participants' homes, which facilitated relating the narratives to material dimensions of their self-build strategies. All interviews were coded, transcribed and analysed using a thematic content analysis. Interviewees were assigned a pseudonym for anonymity. In addition, the author was able to access legal documents on building regulations, deeds of conveyance and self-builders' archival materials. To complement the qualitative first-hand data, this chapter draws on secondary data on self-building in Almere. These include surveys issued by the municipality of Almere (Janssen et al, 2011; Van der Vegt et al, 2014), municipal census data (Gemeente Almere, 2014a, 2014b, 2018) and secondary material on self-builders' experiences in newspapers and books (Eckardt et al, 2013; Koole and Kämena, 2014).

The case study: the Homeruskwartier

The Homeruskwartier is a neighbourhood in the Almere Poort district, which is located on Almere's westernmost fringe, about 15 kilometres from Amsterdam. Almere has over 200,000 inhabitants and is forecasted to grow. Although it was founded as a suburb of neighbouring Amsterdam, it has more recently tried to become a city in its own right (Nio, 2016). Originally, a mix of individual, collective and co-commissioning varieties of self-build was foreseen for the neighbourhood. In the end, only individual and co-commissioning varieties of self-build were realised. This chapter deals with the motivations and strategies of individual self-builders since residents were hardly involved in the co-commissioning cases. One can distinguish between 'regular' individual self-building and 'affordable' self-building. Within each category, there exist different ways of arranging the building process.

For individual owner-builders, three models of self-building can be discerned in the Homeruskwartier. First, some residents build their own homes drawing on their own labour, including arranging design and coordinating building activities. These so-called DIY builders may employ specialised labour for particular construction activities or consult an architect. Second, residents may opt to build with a catalogue builder. In this case, residents chose a catalogue builder who builds the house, often tailored to the specific demands of the commissioner. Third, residents may contract an architect to design and build their house. The architect may work within a team of contractors and advisors from the start, or might take charge and employ contractors at a later stage. These three forms should be thought of as part of a continuum, rather than as points on a definite spectrum. A quantitative survey on self-building in Almere found that catalogue building was the most popular option (42 per cent), building with an architect or an architect team was the second most popular (39 per cent), while 19 per cent took up the DIY option.

Residents in the affordable self-building programme 'Ik bouw betaalbaar in Almere' ('I build affordably in Almere' ['Ibba']) in the Homeruskwartier were restricted to building in row housing and were recommended to select builders from a prearranged catalogue. Residents could further develop and tailor the design and layout of their house in conjunction with the building company or architect. Builders were also required to employ a construction supervisor who further assisted them in the building process. Residents could get an interest-free loan of maximally 40 per cent that was taken on top of the regular mortgage (Duivesteijn, 2014). If income growth developed

Figure 8.1: Aerial view of Homeruskwartier in the early stages of construction

Source: Top-Shot.nl

Figure 8.2: Aerial view of Homeruskwartier in the current stage of construction

Source: Top-Shot.nl

negatively, self-builders would pay interest without repaying the loan. This enabled first-time homebuyers to partake in self-building in a lowered-risk setting. The target group for the Ibba scheme are people who would normally depend on social housing, which is measured in terms of income.

Demographics and figures of self-building

Before moving on to the qualitative analysis of self-builders' rationales and strategies, it is worthwhile highlighting some secondary data on demographics, self-builders' motivations and building statistics in Almere. In terms of who builds, a municipal survey carried out among residents of Almere found a particularly strong interest in self-building among homeowners in the 18 to 45 years age bracket (Gemeente Almere, 2014a). When asked 'Why self-build?', the most popular option cited was the opportunity to determine how one's home looks (cited by 85 per cent of respondents). Costs (4 per cent) and location (5 per cent) were found to be significantly less popular options (Janssen et al, 2011). When these data are compared to census data on the Homeruskwartier, it becomes apparent that the Homeruskwartier is popular among younger residents. People aged 25 to 44 years are over-represented (at 50 per cent), as opposed to the municipal average (of 29 per cent). Meanwhile, the 45 to 64 years age category is under-represented (at 13 per cent versus 29 per cent). In terms of household make-up, there is just a slight under-representation of households with children (40 per cent), as compared to the municipal average (44 per cent). The distribution of types of housing is also different, with 21 per cent freestanding housing, 42 per cent row housing and 37 per cent apartments. This is a more even distribution compared to the municipal averages of 15 per cent, 60 per cent and 24 per cent, respectively, and can possibly be attributed to the prevalence of self-building. In addition, the Homeruskwartier has a higher proportion of owner-occupied homes (77 per cent) when compared to the average for Almere as a whole (66 per cent). Moreover, the average cadastral value in the Homeruskwartier in 2014 was €210,000, as opposed to €195,000 for Almere (Gemeente Almere, 2014b). This is potentially related to the neighbourhood being situated on Almere's western fringe, in close proximity to Amsterdam.

Moving on to motivations, Van der Vegt et al (2014) found that the primary motivation for self-builders included the possibility to 'realize the house of their dreams' (56 per cent), as well as having 'more freedom of choice in terms of housing layout' (54 per cent).

The third most chosen option was that the 'housing that is offered does not satisfy my demands' (32 per cent). Other popular options hinting at aspects of control were realising housing of higher quality (30 per cent) and having more freedom of choice in terms of architecture (29 per cent). The value aspect can be noted in obtaining 'a large house for relatively little money' (31 per cent). Less cited reasons related to intrinsic building satisfaction, combining work and living, attaining a house with a garden, and building sustainably, all of which attained around or under 10 per cent.

Looking at self-build models in Almere, catalogue builders were found to be the most popular option among individual owner-builders (42 per cent). Some 27 per cent of people employed an architect, while 12 per cent of self-builders made use of a construction team. Only 19 per cent of self-builders did everything themselves (Van der Vegt et al, 2014). This survey contrasts with the figures in the Almere housing survey, in which 54 per cent of prospective self-builders expressed the wish to build with an architect, while catalogue builders were preferred by 19 per cent (Janssen et al, 2011). Nearly two thirds of respondents in the Almere housing survey were involved in the building process in some way or another. In addition, most self-builders (74 per cent) preferred working individually or together with neighbours over hiring (sub)contractors or other professionals, which could potentially allow them to save on building costs. In terms of building satisfaction and obstacles, Van der Vegt et al (2014) found that most people expressed the wish to build again sometime in the future. Frequently cited obstacles were resources, time and lack of knowledge.

While these quantitative data hint at several frequently cited motivations and obstacles during the self-build process, they offer hardly any insight into residents' rationales as articulated from their perspectives. Notably, both surveys only allowed for a limited set of responses and thus shed no light on how motivations may conjoin or contrast. For example, the survey by Van der Vegt et al (2014) only allowed a selection of four answers out of a narrowly defined list of possible motivations. Multiple motivations may exist at the same time, either in harmony or in tension with one another. In this respect, qualitative data are more suited to showing how residents argue for self-building from their own experiences, as well as the strategies that they pursue.

Rationales and motivations

As hypothesised, there is a large heterogeneity in terms of the rationales identified by self-builders in the Homeruskwartier. However, we found two motives to be present across all self-builders: customisation and costs.

Customisation

The Homeruskwartier offered an opportunity for participants to acquire a newly built home, and with a larger degree of customisation than would otherwise have been possible. Here, self-building constituted a means realising a particular type of housing that accompanied certain changes in lifestyle or household composition, such as getting married, living alone after a divorce or buying a first house. In some cases, participants had looked into the option of buying turnkey housing but had been frustrated by the lack of customisation opportunities. The lack of self-building opportunities in this part of the Netherlands further necessitated the choice of Almere Poort. As stated by Patty and Maurice:

> 'We wanted to determine the layout ourselves, that is why we did this. And we wanted to live here [Almere Poort], but there weren't a lot of options at that time, so we had to build ourselves. And it was important to us to move closer to Amsterdam, that's 16 kilometres' difference [in the commute to work].'

Interestingly, here, the customisation motif conjoins with the proximity of Almere Poort to Amsterdam. Furthermore, the neighbourhood offered reasonable prices to self-build a house, while there was no comparable ready-made housing available.

Customisation enabled residents to build according to particular living arrangements or to meet certain aesthetic qualities. The opportunity to choose a particular design and layout according to their own ideas was frequently appreciated by self-builders. For some people, this meant creating workspaces in their domestic environment in the form of a workshop or storage space. Another example entailed a resident building two houses on the same plot, with one reserved for her and her son and the other for her daughter. A senior self-builder wanted to live in a smaller home on the ground floor, a type of housing that he could not find on the regular housing market. More mundane examples included the desire for particular room layouts or the use of particular materials, such as wood, glass or steel. Self-builders who made significant use of their own labour particularly appreciated the intrinsic satisfaction derived from building their own house.

Despite its tailored and customised nature, a self-build home is not always considered a residence that will be 'forever'. Some early residents of the Homeruskwartier were already looking to move again as their household composition or lives had changed. As explained by one resident, Bertina, a house is supposed to match where you are in your life. Now that her children had moved out, she was looking to build a new and completely different house, much smaller than her existing residence: "I am not old yet, but you're in a different phase. And I would like some more quiet and space. I don't want three flights of stairs anymore. I just want to build this last house once more and that's it." Similarly, some residents opted to downsize as they grew older. This was a key consideration mentioned by Henk, who built a 40 m² bungalow, having previously lived in an apartment in a co-commissioned project. Even though self-building permits the construction of a house that closely matches a person's particular living arrangements, people do not necessarily conceive of their home as permanent.

For most participants, the process of self-building constituted the first time in their lives that they had thoroughly had the opportunity to consider how they would like to live. For most of the Netherlands, particularly the more urbanised areas in the western part of the country, turnkey housing provided by large developers or housing associations is the norm. Hence, a lot of participants were first-time builders, who were finally able to realise long-standing dreams, thoughts or aspirations. As Piet stated: "My idea was to build a home once, all by myself, from the ground up. Here, there was an opportunity." Sometimes, this extended to a reflective attitude towards the function of housing in Dutch society, as explained by Jos: "It was always my dream to build a house – and I have done it now.... I find it important that other people start thinking – 'How would I like to live?'"

Participants posited the merits of self-building in opposition to the rigidity and uniformity of standard turnkey housing, which is strongly representative of much of the post war newly built housing in the Netherlands, and Almere in particular. The adaptability of such standardised housing is limited, as expressed by Jos: "You tear down a wall, slap on a new colour, a new tile, but still you're stuck with the concept you bought." Similar sentiments were expressed by Frank and Carola when referring to the bedrooms in their previous row house:

> 'You're stuck with it. It takes something special if you want to make something nice out of it. Often it is not suited for it in the first place. When you are in control of building

your own house, this all changes. Now you say, 'I want a big bedroom', and you'll get one.'

Self-building thus offers the opportunity to achieve more space and square meters.

Not only does self-building offer certain material benefits in terms of customised living arrangements, aesthetic qualities or more value for money; it also offers an opportunity for people to distinguish themselves and attain a sense of freedom or autonomy. Participants speak of "leaving their own mark". Individual owner-builders expressed strong sentiments of autonomy gained through the freedom to make their own choices in the development and design process. Here, again, images of regular-provided housing were invoked for contrast, as Bertina explained: "I do not want to live in a directed house that's allotted to me – because it's so conventional." The pursuit of freedom and autonomy may prevail over considerations of utilitarian customisation. As Gert explained, he was looking not for a particular living arrangement, but rather for something less conventional: "I was a bit bored with the 'standard single-family home'…. We had just split up and I did not necessarily want a home with a living room downstairs and three bedrooms upstairs."

Costs

Financial considerations were strong among all interviewed self-builders, but were expressed in different ways. Many participants emphasised the exceptional value for money that they had in self-building. As of 2018, house prices in the Homeruskwartier have increased by 6.3 per cent when compared to 2012, the date for which real estate value has first been estimated. Self-builders feel that they were able to profit from rising house prices, low mortgage interest and, more importantly, low building costs. As Willem elaborated: "At that time, we thought: 'Actually you're crazy if you don't do it!' At that time, the housing prices were already on the rise. And building costs were much lower back then. No sooner said than done, we decided to start building." Furthermore, it was felt that the cost of land in Almere Poort was particularly favourable and was often cited as the only feasible option if you wanted to self-build: "Either it's affordable self-build or you need to have a lot of money. You can forget about the last part, so this was an [excellent] opportunity" (Pascal and Marie).

In this context, residents frequently cited the increase in value of their self-build homes. The market value during the summer of 2018 was compared to 2011, when everything was at rock bottom. While individual owner-builders of the catalogue building or architect categories emphasised a strong preference that they could exercise here, things were different for self-builders of the DIY category, for whom it was the only way to attain homeownership. Drawing on their own labour and skills in the building process allowed for significant savings. Meanwhile, financial considerations were exercised differently in the development process. Many catalogue builders often explained how they had looked into building with an architect or professional designer but had finally opted for a catalogue builder as this would save them significant money. Architects were appreciated but posed a risk in terms of exceeding one's budget, as Bertina explained: "Doing it [DIY self-building] allows you to save money." Frank and Carola expressed that if they had bought a similarly sized house on the regular market, it would have cost twice the amount that they actually spent.

For participants in the affordable self-build scheme, the Homeruskwartier constituted a unique opportunity to achieve homeownership, mostly for younger adults or first-time homeowners. In this scheme, up to 40 per cent of the house was covered by an additional interest-free loan. As Bart explained, affordable self-building was an attractive and unique opportunity to finally realise his "own place", as opposed to living in a three-room apartment. Similarly, Suzan elaborated that "before, we lived in a 40 m^2 apartment.... Now we have our own home with a garden, balcony and three bedrooms for €190,000." The customisation potential was welcomed by these affordable owner-builders, but this motivation was often cited in strong conjunction with the unique avenue to homeownership that was provided through the affordable self-build scheme. For this category, owning a house was seen as a necessary step in life, as clearly expressed by Lisette: "Once we owned a real house, we could finally marry." Although, on the one hand, this scheme allowed people who had previously been tenants to access homeownership, on the other, it also limited the degree to which they could become the owner of their self-build house – depending on the amount of money that they had mortgaged or put in themselves. Still, the 150 per cent increase in value of housing in the neighbourhood was often referred to in order to justify the soundness of their decisions. At a time when lower- to middle-income households, and young people in particular, are facing increasing difficulties in attaining owner occupancy, the affordable self-build scheme offered a promising alternative, with a large degree of customisation opportunities to boot.

Strategies and qualities

In the perspective of participants, self-building presented exceptional value for money with unprecedented customisation opportunities. Moreover, the change in procurement, as opposed to conventional house building, allowed residents to fulfil roles in design and development that are normally occupied by development and construction professionals. This opens up the questions of what design and development strategies were employed, and in pursuit of what qualities did residents build.

A large variety of building strategies can be observed in the Homeruskwartier. This varies from self-builders who wished to construct a unique, state-of-the-art architectural masterpiece, to commissioners that contracted catalogue builders to attain a large amount of living space for a decent price. Dutch building law does not stipulate the use of an architect and anyone may formally request a building permit. However, in one specific neighbourhood within the Homeruskwartier, residents were required to build their homes with the help of architects. To Jos, this concept had appealed to him as "unique and innovative ... so I thought that's my spot". In contrast, we saw that many other self-builders were much more practical in their design and development considerations. In multiple cases, residents mentioned having started to work with an architect but finally deciding against it because of the costs. In light of tight budgets and other options, architects were quickly left out of the picture, as Bertina explained: "The money I would otherwise have spent on architects, I can now spend on other things." In her perspective, working with a catalogue builder was more effective and cheaper:

> 'I think, often, architects have beautiful ideas but they don't listen to you.... In my experience, architects and their creative solutions can make it really nice – but it can also deviate strongly from what you want. You go in their flow and only after you start living there do you realise it's complete rubbish. It cost too much money.'

Residents who did work with architects sometimes recollected clashes over design ideas. In one example, residents mentioned how they felt that the concerns of the architect detrimentally affected the potential exchange value of the house: "For him [the architect], it was an interesting project. But there will be a point when I will leave this place here, I would want to get rid of it, and at that point, I would like to be able to sell it – so we stopped working with him" (Frank and Carola).

Residents felt that they had to safeguard their financial interests in the face of architects solely working for aesthetic considerations:

> 'I have had a month's worth of battle with the architect to get it the way I wanted and not the way the architect wanted it. You see, architects have the tendency to look at aesthetics, rather than the practical side of things – they think in terms of 'this is nice', 'the more beautiful it is the better it is' – while I was constantly thinking 'this is my budget and I cannot exceed it.' (Henk)

As commissioners of their homes, residents carry the development risk, and the potential benefits from self-building are a direct consequence of the sum of each and every design and development decision.

Residents expressed awareness of the responsibilities and future consequences of design and development decisions. For some, this translated into a concern with the saleability of the house. Residents explained that they had built their house so that it would be easy to sell once that became necessary. This translated into building something that was not particularly wild or unique, but a house that would appeal to someone else as well. At the same time, other residents with more divergent or unique designs mentioned prioritising the uniqueness of their design, even though they knew that it would make it harder to sell their house in the future. This mostly applied to the DIY builders or people who had built with the help of architects. As Jos explained: "It has to be unique. It has to be innovative. It has to be an architectural masterpiece." Building a house for yourself may necessitate compromises in terms of the future potential ease of sale: "If I would have built it for sale, I would have built a single family home. But in that case it would not have been a house that's mine", explained Jacob, who opted for an open-plan layout.

Ecological considerations played out in different ways. Jan explained that he wanted a house that was completely recyclable, conforming to high ecological standards. This extended to a preference for a particular construction method that used prefab wooden panels. For Willem, ecological considerations related to energy, neat finishing and the potential future sale value of his home:

> 'The house should be built to match decent standards; it has to be well insulated. And if you want to make sure to do it properly, make sure all the piping runs through the

walls. Put solar panels on the roof, put a 'warm water thing' in it – that covers heating for a large part.'

The value of the self-build home was expressed in different ways, either qualitative value, related to ecology or architectural quality, or the sense of autonomy that it offered residents. Self-building could be done with reference to the particular material properties of the house, such as wood, innovative prefab panels or steel. Others spoke in quantitative terms, stressing the number of square meters that they had realised. The market value of self-builders' homes was often directly expressed through the amount of indoor space in square meters. For many self-builders, this had been a central consideration in their design strategies – in addition to the other considerations that they may have had. When asked to justify their design decisions, residents often made claims in which costs and square meters conjoined. Here, again, this appeared most strongly the case for catalogue builders and affordable self-builders. In terms of strategies and qualities, we observed how use value considerations over location, architecture and housing layout conjoined with financial considerations over budget, risk and future sale value.

Rules and finances

With the Homeruskwartier, the municipality of Almere intended to showcase different varieties of self-building, and thus it created a plan that included different building typologies and plot sizes. Although all self-builders were required to comply with national building regulations, they also faced additional plot-based rules that were included in the private legal deeds of conveyances. Such 'plot passports' included demands regarding the building line, width, materials, maximum building height and maximum built-up area per plot. Residents frequently described their experiences in relation to the plot passports in positive terms. Resident-builders felt that there were not many things that you could not do. Rather than delimit residents' creativity and imagination, plot passports created an image of what was possible and feasible.

The maximisation rationale described in the previous section created a particular dynamic in which residents would strive to cover the maximum allowed built-up area, sometimes forsaking outdoor space. As Bertina described: "OK, what are the rules? OK. I'll build as much as possible. I do not need a garden." Residents would come up with creative means to maximise indoor living space. In one particular set of plots, it was prescribed that there could only be one floor. However, there was no mention of underground construction. As a result, residents proceeded to build large multi-bedroom basements to increase their living space. One self-builder with a background in real estate, Els, felt that this was a consequence of local housing market dynamics: "In Almere, people like a lot of volume ... the quality of built objects is less important. This also complicates it for people with architectural ambition, as the value of their homes is often directly expressed through living surface." Some residents anticipated the consequences of particular plot passports in their plot choice, for instance, by opting for row housing with free views at the back and front, rather than having a free-standing house with little space in between. Since, most of the time, there were no additional requirements regarding architectural quality, some DIY builders who had spent a lot of resources and time on unique designs expressed a sense of disappointment in the overall spatial quality of the neighbourhood. Still, the sense of satisfaction with their own home remained strong.

Experiences with the regulatory framework were characterised by both feelings of freedom and restriction. Here, again, we see differences between residents who employed catalogue builders to take care of things, and people who had more direct dealings with the regulatory framework. On the one hand, self-builders felt that they had had a large degree of liberty during construction, which they had not entirely expected:

> 'The municipality didn't make themselves noticed during the construction process. Not that I disliked that, but I found it aggravating.... They never asked if I was able to [build a house]. They never asked me: 'What is your background?' All they said is 'Here is your permit and do your thing.' Now I know how to build a home, but I can imagine there are plenty of people that do not know how to do so and the result may be bad.' (Jacob)

On the other hand, self-builders described experiences with overbearing clerks and lengthy bureaucratic procedures, which slowed down their building process significantly. Henk described a situation where he had been asked about the location of the emergency exit in his small bungalow: "When they have a question [for you], the permit application is stopped for three weeks. When they have two questions, it is six weeks…. 'Free' building is not completely 'free'." Catalogue builders often did not have to deal with regulatory compliance directly and more frequently cited the advantages. The presence of formal regulations gave residents a sense of security and control.

Over time, as the neighbourhood was built up, some plots remained empty. This urged the 2012 new municipal coalition to open up the Homeruskwartier to private developers and architects, and a residency requirement was no longer necessary for certain sets of plots. For some long-standing residents, this brought about a sense of frustration as they felt that there was unequal treatment by the municipality: "When you live here as one of the first residents, they are very strict with you in terms of the plot passport. Then, at some point, you notice housing gets built which makes you think, 'Where's the plot passport?'" (Patty and Maurice). Early residents saw the neighbourhood develop over time, and witnessed changes in the land-use plan or plot passports. In these cases, residents felt that the principle of equal treatment had been violated.

Although it was hypothesised that self-builders could face difficulties in accessing finance, in practice, this often proved not to be a problem. Once a building permit had been granted by the municipality, the financing went relatively smoothly. For second- or third-time homeowners, this process was described as not being significantly different to buying a turnkey home: "You just go to the bank, get your mortgage, and done" (Paul and Emma). Collective arrangements were seldom made. In the case of affordable self-building, some people mentioned coordinating the piledriving work collectively to save up on money. In most cases, building took place on a house-by-house basis. Affordable self-builders felt that they, in particular, were able to profit from the recession in the construction industry and the consequent large supply of available building companies. Individual owner-builders often preferred to arrange things alone if they could, expressing a strong sense of self-sufficiency and individuality.

Summing up

To recapitulate, we found a wide range of rationales and strategies employed by self-builders in the Almere Homeruskwartier. Broadly speaking, rationales were related to either achieving particular living arrangements through customisation or achieving homeownership through an exceptional value-for-money deal. The latter applied to residents in the affordable self-build scheme, who would otherwise not have been able to own a house. However, it also applied to other individual self-builders, who mentioned having been able to get a lot of value for money. The value of the self-build home was expressed through qualitative goals such as sustainability or architectural quality, as well as in material or financial terms, which related directly to the market value of their homes. These multiple values were taken into consideration in residents' design decisions in self-build practices.

Conclusion

This chapter offered an in-depth, qualitative analysis of the rationales and strategies of self-builders in a comprehensive, aided self-building scheme in the Netherlands. The case of the Homeruskwartier is particularly interesting not only because of its scale and geographic context on reclaimed land, but also because it catered to a large variety of people in terms of social backgrounds. This was enabled by variation in terms of plot size, plot passports and the creation of an affordable self-build scheme.

A large variation in terms of rationales and strategies exists among self-builders in the Homeruskwartier. While some self-builders articulated their motivations as the result of a long-standing wish or demand, others were motivated to engage in self-building by more pragmatic reasons related to achieving a particular housing layout or homeownership at reduced costs. For all self-builders, the customisation potential offered them access to unique living arrangements. This is exceptional in the Netherlands, where people are often dependent on turnkey housing provided by large developers or housing associations. In this context, participants were able to consider for the first time how they would like to live. Design and development decisions were frequently framed in opposition to the material properties of regular Dutch housing, perceived as inflexible and uniform. The material properties and qualities of self-build homes in the Homeruskwartier are indicative of what regular turnkey housing in the Netherlands fails to offer. As self-builders assumed a central responsibility for development and design, they were required to weigh decisions in terms of use value, costs and potential future saleability. In some cases, this led to a preference for catalogue builders over architects. Foreclosing on expensive materials and finishing and maximising floor living space were also strategies pursued to increase potential resale value. The regulatory framework had a double-edged role: on the one hand, it provided security and fostered creative freedom by showing what was feasible; yet, on the other hand, at times, residents had to deal with administrative procedures that slowed down the building process. Financially speaking, there were people who drew on previous housing assets to build their homes, as well as first-time homeowners who appreciated the project as an affordable opportunity to acquire homeownership. Self-builders felt that they had profited from rising housing values. In addition, the absence of intermediaries and a surplus of contractors (as a result of the economic crisis) further enabled them to cut down on building costs.

Although a strong degree of resident involvement was central to procurement in each example, the configuration and extent of involvement varied on a case-by-case basis. This accentuates the importance of defining self-building as a practice, rather than a discrete model, where residents take on a commissioning role in the production of housing for their own use. The centrality of residents in procurement allows for the pursuit of different values. While this may entail certain qualitative use values pertaining to architectural concerns or sustainability, it may also involve the pursuit of maximal financial exchange value. This should be taken into consideration when arguing in favour of governmental support for self-build schemes.

Two lessons can be drawn with respect to understanding self-builders' agency. First, institutional and economic structures are essential to understanding why people do what they do. Studies of self-build housing should pay attention not just to the case-study level, but also to the contextualisation of the practice in relation to structuring institutional and economic logics. Second, rationales and strategies are multifaceted. This chapter has highlighted multiple rationales to do with customisation, freedom, finances and thrift. While each of these addresses singular concerns, we observed that, depending on their situation, self-builders are sometimes able to combine multiple concerns, while, at other times, these concerns clash, conflict or are fused into a compromise.

References

Benson, M. and Hamiduddin, I. (2018) *Self-Build Homes: Social Discourse, Experiences and Directions*, London: UCL Press.

Bossuyt, D., Salet, W. and Majoor, S. (2018) 'Commissioning as the cornerstone of self-build. Assessing the constraints and opportunities of self build housing in the Netherlands', *Land Use Policy*, 77: 524–33.

Brown, R. (2007) 'Identity and narrativity in homes made by amateurs', *Home Cult*, 4: 261–85, https://doi.org/10.2752/174063107X247305

Buitelaar, E. (2010) 'Window on the Netherlands: cracks in the myth: challenges to land policy in the Netherlands', *Tijdschrift Voor Economische en Sociale Geografie*, 101: 349–56, https://doi.org/10.1111/j.1467-9663.2010.00604.x

Clapham, D., Kintrea, K. and McAdam, G. (1993) 'Individual self-provision and the Scottish housing system', *Urban Studies*, 30: 1355–69, https://doi.org/10.1080/00420989320081301

Cox, R. (2016) 'What are homes made of? Building materials, DIY and the homeyness of homes', *Home Cult*, 13: 63–82, https://doi.org/10.1080/17406315.2016.1122966

Crabtree, L. (2018) 'Self-organised housing in Australia: housing diversity in an age of market heat', *International Journal of Housing Policy*, 18(1): 15–34.

Czischke, D. (2017) 'Collaborative housing and housing providers: towards an analytical framework of multi-stakeholder collaboration in housing co-production', *International Journal of Housing Policy*, 1247, https://doi.org/10.1080/19491247.2017.1331593

Davoudi, S. and Madanipour, A. (2015) *Reconsidering Localism*, London and New York, NY: Routledge.

De Decker, P. (2008) 'Facets of housing and housing policies in Belgium', *Journal of Housing and the Built Environment*, 23: 155–71, https://doi.org/10.1007/s10901-008-9110-4

Duivesteijn, A. (2014) 'De Wooncoöperatie: op weg naar een zichzelf organiserende samenleving', www.adriduivesteijn.nl/wp-content/uploads/De-Woonco%C3%B6peratie.pdf

Duncan, S.S.. and Rowe, A. (1993) 'Self-provided housing: the First World's hidden housing', *Urban Studies* 30(8): 1331–54.

Eckardt, F., Heijne, K., Hinterleitner, J., Roos, C. and Tellinga, J. (eds) (2013) *Hoe bouwt de particuliere opdrachtgever?*, Rotterdam: Nai010.

Gemeente Almere (2009) *Meerjarenprogramma IkbouwmijnhuisinAlmere 2010–2014*, Almere: Gemeente Almere.

Gemeente Almere (2014a) 'De Staat van de Stad', www.almere.nl/fileadmin/files/almere/overalmere/TOTAAL_DE_STAAT_VAN_DE_STAD.pdf

Gemeente Almere (2014b) *De Sociale Atlas van Almere. Wijkprofielen*, Almere: Gemeente Almere.

Gemeente Almere (2018) 'Website Wijkmonitor Almere', https://wijkmonitoralmere.nl/nl/almere-poort/homeruskwartier%2bhogekant%2bpampus%2bmiddenkant.html

Hardy, D. and Ward, C. (1984) *Arcadia for All: The Legacy of the Makeshift Landscape*, London: Mansell Publishing.

Harms, H. (1982) 'Historical perspectives on the practice and purpose of self-help housing', in P.M. Ward (ed) *Self-Help Housing: A Critique*, London: Mansell, pp 15–55.

Harris, R. (1991) 'The impact of building controls on residential development in Toronto, 1900–40', *Planning Perspectives*, 6: 269–96, https://doi.org/10.1080/02665439108725731

Janssen, T., Huisman, M. and Gorter, H. (2011) *Woononderzoek Almere 2011*, Almere: Gemeente Almere/SBZ/Onderzoek & Statistiek.

Jarvis, H. (2015) 'Community-led housing and "slow" opposition to corporate development: citizen participation as common ground?', *Geography Compass*, 9(4): 202–13.

Koole, C. and Kämena, R. (2014) *De democratie van het zand*, Amsterdam: Prometheus/Bert Bakker.

Lang, R., Carriou, C. and Czischke, D. (2018) 'Collaborative housing research (1990–2017): a systematic review and thematic analysis of the field', *Housing, Theory and Society*, 1-29 DOI: 10.1080/14036096.2018.1536077

Mallet, S. (2004) 'Understanding home: a critical review of the literature', *Sociological Review*, 52(1): 63–89.

Mullins, D. and Moore, T. (2018) 'Self-organised and civil society participation in housing provision', *International Journal of Housing and Policy*, 18: 1–14, https://doi.org/10.1080/19491247.2018.1422320

NaCSBA (National Custom & Self-Build Association) (2018) 'The campaign for custom and self build in the UK', Right to Build Portal, www.righttobuildportal.org/

Nio, I. (2016) 'Moderniteit en suburbaniteit in de nieuwe stad: Almere, Cergy-Pontoise, Milton Keynes', dissertation, University of Amsterdam, the Netherlands.

Parvin, A., Saxby, D., Cerulli, C. and Schneider, T. (2011) 'A right to build', *Architecture 00*: University of Sheffield School of Architecture, Sheffield; London.

Savini, F. (2017) 'Planning, uncertainty and risk: the neoliberal logics of Amsterdam urbanism', *Environment and Planning A*, https://doi.org/10.1177/0308518X16684520

Shulist, T. and Harris, R. (2002) 'Build your own home': state-assisted self-help housing in Canada, 1942–75', *Planning Perspectives*, 17: 345–72, https://doi.org/10.1080/02665430210154759

Sørvoll, J. and Bengtsson, B. (2018) 'Mechanisms of solidarity in collaborative housing – the case of co-operative housing in Denmark 1980–2017', *Housing Theory and Society*,: 1–17, https://doi.org/10.1080/14036096.2018.1467341

Tellinga, J. (2018) 'Zelfbouw is remedie tegen groeiende economische ongelijkheid', *Het Financieel Dagblad*, 27 July.

Turner, J. (1972) *Freedom to Build*, Basingstoke: Macmillan.

Uitermark, J. (2015) 'Longing for Wikitopia: the study and politics of self-organisation', *Urban Studies*, 52: 2301–12, https://doi.org/10.1177/0042098015577334

Van der Vegt, J., Adriaanse, C. and Jansen, S. (2014) *Proces, kosten en tevredenheid bij zelfbouw in Almere*, Delft: TU Delft.

Wallace, A., Ford, J. and Quilgars, D. (2013) *Build-It-Yourself? Understanding the Changing Landscape of the UK Self-Build Market*, York: University of York and Lloyds Banking Group.

9

Residential experiences in times of shifting housing regimes in Istanbul

Zeynep Enlil and İclal Dinçer

Introduction

Turkey has been a rapidly urbanising country since the 1950s. Its major cities experienced massive migratory flows.[1] The share of population living in cities was only 25 per cent in 1950; this increased to 70 per cent by 2012 and it is expected to reach 85 per cent by 2050 (Balaban, 2012). As the economic engine of the country, Istanbul has always been an attraction point for both investments and people, and has been under constant growth pressures. The population of the city increased from 1.1 million in 1950 to 4.7 million by 1980, and with a population of 15 million by 2017, Istanbul became the largest city in Europe. Housing the mounting population has been one of the major challenges facing cities in Turkey, including Istanbul. The rapid pace of urbanisation resulted in the emergence of improvised solutions to the housing problem, leading to different forms of self-regulation and the formation of a dual structure where formal and informal settlements coexisted.

Rapid urbanisation was paralleled by skyrocketing land values and a highly speculative land market in Istanbul. However, as Öncü (1988) points out, the enormous growth of urban land rents cannot be explained by the scarcity of land alone vis-a-vis the rapidly increasing population. Urban land in the Turkish context has a much wider role. It has not only been a major source of securing funds in a highly inflationary economy, but also been a major source of accumulation for all sectors of society − rich and poor alike. Tapping the lucrative land market meant wide-ranging alliances between various actors that changed over time in line with shifting housing regimes, making Istanbul a contested terrain of urban governance reflecting the 'tensions between societal self-regulation initiatives, market forces and governmental regulation' (Salet et al, 2020:2).

The state took different stances in the different phases of Turkish urbanisation from the 1950s. Three periods can be identified regarding the production of space in line with the socio-economic policies adopted by the state, which also connoted shifting housing regimes. The first is the period from 1950 to 1980. It is marked by massive urbanisation with minimal state intervention in housing production and witnessed the emergence of two forms of self-build housing forms: *gecekondu* and *yap-sat*. The second period encompasses the two decades from 1980 to 2000, characterised by changing economic policies embracing a neoliberal outlook. Although the state's role diminished in the economic sphere, it began to interfere in the housing market through new mechanisms. From the 2000s onwards is the third period, which marks the second phase of neoliberalism in Turkey. This period involved sweeping institutional changes, with the state assuming an increasingly entrepreneurial role, pursuing growth strategies focused on the urban land market and becoming more aggressive and hegemonic. The organisation of housing production radically transformed with these changes and the introduction of new financial instruments. This chapter critically analyses the shifting housing regimes and their repercussions on place making and the quality of Istanbul's neighbourhoods, which aroused considerable dissent and resistance among residents.

Shifting housing regimes in Istanbul

Emergent forms of self-building in housing production: 1950–80

The 1950s mark a significant era of transformation in Turkey. The transition to a multi-party system in government, rapid industrialisation paralleled by an equally rapid urbanisation, fuelled by the mechanisation and commercialisation of agriculture that triggered massive migratory flows from rural areas to the major cities, are the major markers of the 30 years from 1950 to 1980. In Turkey, as in most developing countries during the post-war period, there was a shift in national development policy towards import-substituting industrialisation aimed at developing an industry oriented to manufacturing consumer goods for the internal market (Öncü, 1988). In this context, Istanbul became the locus of large-scale industrial developments established by government subsidies.

Industrial production promoted by the market-oriented governmental incentives, coupled with modernisation in agriculture, stimulated a high rate of urbanisation and created significant housing need. However, due to limited financial resources and institutional shortcomings, there has never been a comprehensive social housing policy in Turkey. Instead, socio-economic policies during this period placed greater importance on industrial development and economic growth, leaving urbanisation to spontaneous processes, with minimum regulation and intervention by the state. In the absence of state policies oriented towards sheltering the mounting urban population, people improvised their own solutions. Two forms of self-building emerged in response to pressing housing need and became predominant modes of housing production: *'gecekondu'* ('squatter houses') and *'yap-sat'* ('build-and-sell'). *Gecekondu* entails the occupation of publically owned vacant land and building an unauthorised house on it. It literally means, 'build overnight' in reference to the rapid and makeshift way in which the first generation of *gecekondus* were mostly constructed, often with the help of relatives. *Yap-sat* ('build-and-sell') for the middle classes, on the other hand, was a peculiar form of commissioning between plot owners and small contractors in the planned sections of the city.

As Istanbul became the core of industrial development, tens of thousands of migrants who provided the main workforce for the expanding industry built themselves squatter houses or *gecekondus*, mainly on public land around the industrial establishments and in the periphery. They not only provided the cheap unskilled labour pool that the expanding industry needed, but also contributed to its growth as consumers (Şenyapılı, 1998, cited in Özdemir, 2011). The increasing need for the unskilled cheap labour force, on the other hand, provided for the *gecekondu* communities an advantageous position, justifying and guaranteeing their presence in big cities (Enlil et al, 2015). Thus, the vast extent of these self-build *gecekondu* neighbourhoods constituted a major component of urbanisation as well as an important issue on the political agenda for many years to come (Enlil, 2011). An important feature of these informal settlements was that they were built for use value determined by the immediate needs of their users and reflected the mobility and flexibility of the positions of the newcomers in the labour market (Şenyapılı, 2004). Although there were several attempts to regulate and prevent the *gecekondu* settlements, they were rather weak and none of them were sufficiently enforced. The lack of governmental policies and the reluctance to take action resulted in a tremendous increase in the number of *gecekondus*, from 8,239 in 1950 to 61,400 in 1959 (Erman, 2001; Kılınçaslan et al, 2009); by 1963, 35 per cent of Istanbul's population were living in *gecekondus* (Kılınçaslan et al, 2009).

The substantial spread of the informal housing areas eventually obliged the government to take action and the first comprehensive initiative to address the mounting problem in major cities came in 1966 with the enactment of the Squatter Housing Law (Act #775). This law defined three types of intervention zones in *gecekondu* areas: improvement zones, stipulating the improvement of those *gecekondu* areas that were in relatively good condition by providing infrastructure and services; demolition zones, stipulating the demolition of those that were dilapidated; and prevention zones, stipulating the prevention of further *gecekondu* formation by holding the municipalities responsible for the provision of housing for people living in these areas.

The state thus laid the institutional foundations by providing a legal framework and the infrastructure and services that improved the living conditions in some *gecekondu* areas. However, it did not strongly enforce demolitions since housing provision in prevention zones remained rather limited and, in line with the principle based on the welfarist approach adopted in the 1960s, no *gecekondus* were to be demolished before the people living in them were properly rehoused in prevention zones.[2] Although public lands were transferred to municipalities for the provision of housing, that alone was not enough to solve the housing problem of the *gecekondu* population since neither the institutional capacity nor resources of municipalities were sufficient to undertake this task, especially given the fact that the sheer number of *gecekondu* dwellers steadily swelled. On the other hand, as urbanisation continued apace, most of the public lands allocated for prevention purposes were soon occupied by *gecekondus* as well. Thus, the Squatter Housing Law far from solved the *gecekondu* problem; the issue of legal title largely remained unresolved and the chances for providing urban land necessary for building affordable housing was wasted. The law only legitimised unauthorised housing and eventually led to its commodification. What the government could not provide was undertaken by the private sector (Yönder, 1987). Land profiteers appeared, subdividing and selling private lands on the urban fringe to new newcomers. This form of producing land for residential development is known as *hisseli tapu*, meaning 'shared title deeds' or 'split deeds'. They were un-plotted large tracks of land that carried restrictions on housing construction. Squatter houses built on these plots acquired semi-secure status because the ownership of the land was legal, though its subdivision and the construction of buildings on it were unauthorised. Soon, a market dominated by 'squatter lords' began to emerge. From the mid-1970s onwards, as the possibilities of seizing publicly owned vacant land on the outskirts of the city was exhausted, newcomers had to pay large lump sums to buy a 'split-deed' plots further out on the periphery. By the 1980s, more than half of Istanbul's population was living in unauthorised self-built informal housing, whether in *gecekondu* areas occupying public lands or in the 'split-deed' settlements (Öncü, 1988; Enlil et al, 2015).

In the formal sections of the city, there was also a steadily increasing housing need yet a scarcity of urban land. As the population of the city rapidly increased, land values skyrocketed. Although the state was not directly involved in the provision of housing, it provided long-term housing credits with low-interest rates to individuals and cooperatives, as well as land below market rates. Furthermore, national development plans gradually reduced the government investment in housing and defined the 'role of the state as a regulator rather than an investor', leaving the solution of the housing problem to the market mechanism and encouraging cooperatives and providing support to entrepreneurs (Sey, 1984; Keleş, 1990). Despite these incentives, housing production by cooperatives remained rather limited.[3]

The period witnessed the emergence of another form of improvised housing production by new market actors, frequently referred as *yap-sat* or 'build and sell', which was yet another 'way of organizing the self-building practices' (Salet et al, 2020:2). It involved a peculiar alliance between the owners of urban land and small capital owners or contractors (*yapsatçı*). This system reflected the scarcity of resources of all the parties involved: the landowner lacked the means to undertake the production of a larger building; and the entrepreneur did not have enough capital to buy urban land and construct a building upon it. Therefore, an agreement was made between the landowner and the entrepreneur to put their limited resources together in order to capitalise on rising urban land values. Depending upon the deal, the landowner got a certain share of the flats in the apartment building to be built in exchange for the land and the entrepreneur got the rest (Öncü, 1988; Enlil, 2011). Usually, the units were sold during the process and helped to finance the construction.[4] This mode of building involved relatively small lots in the city where there were modest single-family houses, as well as large plots of 19th-century mansions. In the latter cases, it usually involved the subdivision of the large plots into smaller pieces on which apartment buildings were constructed (Enlil, 2011).

The 'build and sell' method was an almost-miraculous solution, which provided easy profits for those who either had the means or the capabilities to organise the construction process. It provided housing for large segments of society, ranging from the lower-middle to the upper-middle classes. Moreover, it took the burden off the shoulders of governments who had a constitutional responsibility to provide a decent shelter for every citizen. Meanwhile, the Condominium Law, first enacted in 1958 and amended in 1965, made flat ownership legally possible, which gave momentum to the construction of new apartment buildings. Within less than two decades, the urban structure of Istanbul was significantly changed. The traditional urban fabric, with many wooden houses and mansions, was largely torn down and replaced by much denser neighbourhoods composed of apartment buildings, which were deemed to be 'modern' and more convenient to live in (Dinçer and Enlil, 1996; Enlil, 2011).

In sum, during the 1950–80 period, socio-economic policies placed greater importance on restoring economic growth, leaving spatial development to spontaneous processes. *Gecekondu* was seen as a bottom-up buffer mechanism, which provided housing for the cheap labour force indispensable for the growing industries. Unable to compensate for the economic gap created between different social groups, the state pursued lax land policies concerning the informal housing market and low-income migrants (Enlil et al, 2015). Given the clientelist nature of urban politics in Turkey too, turning a blind eye to the occupation of public lands was a key component of the 'silent alliance' between the state and the newcomers (Işık and Pınarcıoğlu, 2001: 116). The immense stretch of self-build *gecekondus* served as a redistribution strategy to underprivileged groups of the surplus value created through the use of urban land, compensating for the lack of welfare state provisions, including housing with economic advantages (Enlil et al, 2015). In fact, rapid urbanisation was financed by the redistribution of lucrative rents created by rapid urban growth. All sectors of society rushed to build and gained something out of rising land values. A major part of this city building took place through self-organised processes under a broad consensus and wide-ranging alliances, which were to change as a result of shifting housing regimes after the 1980s.

From consensus to tension in the era of emergent neoliberalism: 1980–2000

The 1980s was yet another significant turning point in Turkey. In a similar vein as the global restructuring, there was a major shift towards a neoliberal economic model, which involved the replacement of the import-substituting industrialisation policies implemented since the 1960s with export-oriented growth based on privatisation and the deregulation of the economy geared towards opening up the market to foreign investment. Correspondingly, Istanbul was conceived as the primary driver of change connecting the Turkish economy with world markets and attracting footloose global capital. At the same time, the state withdrew its resources from industry and privatised production facilities while directing its investments to infrastructure projects, including energy and communication sectors. As industry was drawn into the background, tourism, finance and investment in urban land became the prime areas for private sector interest (Öktem, 2005). In order to attract multinational companies, finance organisations and global capital to Istanbul, large-scale projects became a priority on the political agenda. Accordingly, just like the economy, the urbanisation process was deregulated and remodelled through a series of adjustments.

The planning laws during this period were reshaped and certain central government bodies were bestowed with the power to use privileged development rights that bypassed existing local plans, which made piecemeal interventions in line with the needs of investors possible. Yet, paradoxically enough, local authorities were granted more decision-making powers and were positioned as the facilitators of the new phase of the capitalist system functioning via accumulation through the built environment and urban land. With this new process, local authorities were restructured towards an 'urban entrepreneurialism' in which new coalitions with capital groups started governing urban development (Harvey, 1989; Brenner, 2004).

The transition to a neoliberal regime under the ANAP (Motherland Party) government during the 1980s witnessed a novel combination of uncompromising pro-market ideology and a new form of urban populism (Keyder and Öncü, 1993).[5] This first phase of neoliberalism had important repercussions on the production of housing and the redistributive mechanisms previously employed. Two major developments marked the changes in the housing regime and opened up a new era for housing production. The first was a set of amnesty laws passed during the 1980s. With these amnesties, not only were the *gecekondus* that illegally occupied public lands authorised and granted title deeds, but illegal constructions in areas of 'split-deed ownership' were also pardoned. Hence, all unplanned and uncontrolled developments were legitimised. Moreover, the Amnesty Law of 1984 (Act #2981) introduced the concept of 'rehabilitation plans', through which environmental quality was to be improved in these self-built housing areas. However, a right to build up to four storeys in height was permitted in the areas for which 'rehabilitation plans' were to be made. This was yet another bonus offered to the unauthorised settlements, which triggered a fast and massive verticalisation, as well as an unplanned, low-quality urban fabric. The 1984 Amnesty Law not only allowed increased densities, but also stated that in making 'rehabilitation plans', the existing built-up conditions should be taken into account and it was not obligatory to attain the standards for facilities such as parks, schools and other community areas (Enlil et al, 1998). Thus, no significant improvement in environmental quality was achieved. On the contrary, conditions were made even worse by the increased densities (see Figure 9.1).

The amnesty laws of the 1980s did not intend to resolve the informal housing problem like the previous Squatter Housing Law (Act #775), which stipulated physical improvements as well as social housing provision. Instead, they only aimed at settling the property issues through the legalisation of informal areas and initiated a significant spatial transformation (Şenyapılı, 2004). Having secured property rights through these amnesties, many *gecekondu* dwellers turned their one- to two-storey houses into multi-storey apartment buildings (Balaban, 2011), usually through the *yap-sat* method of commissioning the construction process to a contractor in exchange for a number of flats, which provided new sources of income through flats and rent from the land they formerly occupied. Hence, *gecekondu* housing that was seen as an owner-built and owner-occupied low-income solution to housing commercialised and became the subject of land speculation (Enlil, 2011). For low-income migrants, it was no longer a means of gaining a foothold in the city, but a means of substantial accumulation and a way out of poverty (Öncü, 1988; Işık and Pınarcıoğlu, 2001).

The second major development was the foundation of the Mass Housing Administration (TOKI)[6] in 1984 with the purposes of meeting the housing needs of especially low-income groups, to provide low-cost credits to housing cooperatives and mass housing developers, and to give a new boost to the construction sector. However, TOKI mainly served middle- and upper-middle-income groups as it was designed to function within the framework of a free-market economy, becoming a handy tool for the government, which sought to encourage private initiative in housing construction (Keyder and Öncü, 1993). Through TOKI, the state not only provided resources to finance the housing sector, but also got involved in the sector as a developer.

The funds generated by TOKI were used as policy tools for producing patches of mass housing areas in big cities, primarily in Istanbul, which also triggered the emergence of cooperatives as an important actor shaping the periphery. Consequently, the share of housing cooperatives in total housing supply increased from 8.7 per cent in 1980 to 25.2 per cent in 1990 (Berkman and Osmay, 1996, cited in

Figure 9.1: Former *gecekondu* densified by low-quality apartment buildings following the amnesties (in between, it is possible to detect one- to two-storey *gecekondus*)

Source: Evrim Yilmaz

Özdemir, 2011). However, since eligibility for these credits were not strictly controlled, the beneficiaries were mostly middle- and upper-middle-income groups (Özdemir, 2011). On the other hand, housing production by small builders through *yap-sat* was steadily decreasing due to the depletion of available plots and skyrocketing land values in central areas, making housing construction for the middle classes a less profitable endeavour. While small-scale entrepreneurs were struggling to develop strategies to stay in the market, housing for the middle-income groups was made available by the cooperatives that rushed to build on the relatively cheaper lands in the periphery. Using clientelist relationships, some of these cooperatives even managed to get a hold of the public lands that were allocated as *gecekondu* prevention areas.

At the same time, the incapacity of the industries to create enough surplus value directed the investment to the built environment and secondary circuit of capital accumulation (Harvey, 1978). This coincided with the new conception of the city as a finance and business centre, which involved a wide span of strategies, including large-scale urban transformation projects and the emergence of a new CBD (Central Business District). In line with this new vision of Istanbul, the policies implemented during the period oriented capitalists to invest in urban land by easing regulatory frameworks and preparing favourable conditions for surplus gain from urbanisation. The capital, which thrived upon the support provided by the import-substituting economic policies of the state during the previous period, now began to invest not only in major urban transformation projects such as office towers and luxury hotels, but also in housing for the upper and upper-middle classes. Hence, the structure of capital in housing production began to change as large-scale companies emerged as important actors in the construction sector. As Tekeli (1991) puts it, this signalled the transition from city building with small-scale capital towards large-scale capital, a process that became predominant after the 2000s, leading to new configurations of redistributive relations.

The political consensus generated through the redistributive mechanisms of the previous period was the cornerstone of what Işık and Pınarcıoğlu (2001) refer as 'soft and inclusionary urbanisation'. However, as urban land became the major means of accumulation and as actors who competed for easy profits gained through the highly speculative diversification of the urban land market, this consensus eroded, leading to a 'tension-ridden, exclusionary urbanisation'.

The rise of supply-led housing provision and the role of the state in the new phase of aggressive neoliberalism: the 2000s

Although stimulated by governments for some decades, both of these self-build housing environments almost disappeared under the new regime of capital accumulation based on aggressive real-estate development adopted from the 2000s onwards. As the increasing importance of globalisation, international competition between leading cities and the neoliberal market logic took a toll on the urban agenda, global capital's choice of location started steering the spatial development of cities. Subsequently, the aspiration to make Istanbul a global city, the engine of socio-economic change and a centre of finance and business services was accelerated with the coming to power of the Justice and Development Party (AKP) in 2002. Furthermore, the urban land speculation and construction that emerged in the 1980s fully developed as the tools of capitalistic accumulation through urbanisation.

The city increasingly became a space of contestation as the control of space was largely left to market forces, with the state taking a different stance in this phase of the Turkish neoliberal experience (Bayırbağ, 2013). During the previous period between 1980 and 1990, the deregulation of the economy and refraining from economic interventionism was the dominant stance that governments adopted, and in order to gain support from diverse segments of society, a property regime that offered opportunities to various classes was followed. However, during the 2000s, the neoliberal policies pursued by the AKP government became increasingly aggressive and hegemonic. The government built its economic growth strategies on the urban land market and the construction sector, and increasingly became interventionist and authoritarian in order to ensure the continued growth of these sectors. This shift primarily manifested itself in frequently made revisions of planning legislation, which vested a number of central state departments with rights and responsibilities in planning (Eraydın and Tasan-Kok, 2013), and gave discretionary authority to the government (Enlil et al, 2015). The new policies, which involved substantial institutional restructuring, hastened the integration of the housing sector and finance by preparing the legal conditions and ad hoc decisions that facilitated certain lucrative projects for big investors to shape the urbanisation process.

There were several reasons behind these institutional changes. First, due to the rapid expansion of the city, urban land became a rather scarce commodity in both the centre and the periphery. This gave rise to the need for the production of developable land since it had become the major means of capital accumulation. Second, as the project of linking Turkey to global markets was gaining precedence and Istanbul was being restructured towards becoming a 'global city', dilapidated historical areas as well as self-build *gecekondu* and '*yap-sat*' neighbourhoods that occupied valuable land were seen as major obstacles to further lucrative development and as also obscuring this new image of the city. Thus, they became major targets of urban transformation projects in order to create urban land that was no longer available in the central locations of the city (Çelik et al, 2015). On the other hand, the 1999 earthquake that devastated large areas in the Marmara region and also threatened Istanbul marked a turning point in policy circles, which prioritised earthquake-resilient building and legitimised the 'property-led redevelopment' strategy adopted by the central government.

Furthermore, the government took on an entrepreneurial approach (Lovering and Evren, 2011), enacting a variety of laws that reregulated the urban land market, commodified publicly owned lands and devised new financial instruments in order to stimulate the construction sector, which was, at the same time, seen as a way out of the crises that the Turkish economy had experienced in 2001. With the sweeping regulatory changes and the introduction of new financial instruments, the organisation of housing production began to be radically transformed.

As the AKP consolidated its administrative authority, regulatory changes involving a series of laws that 'reshuffled' the legal framework to centralise planning powers, such as the planning authority given to TOKI and the foundation of the Ministry of Environment and Urbanism in 2011, nearly monopolised all kinds of plan making, revision and approval authorities in its hands. The adjustments restraining some of the authority given to local municipalities demonstrated that they were being reorganised almost as the executive organs of the central authorities for making urban development plans. In 2005, the Renewal Law (#5366) and later, in 2012, the Law on the 'Transformation of Areas Under Disaster Risk' (#6306), known as the infamous 'Disaster Law', were enacted. While the Renewal Law gave local municipalities the power to declare 'renewal areas' in protected zones, paving the way for the implementation of renewal projects in historical or natural protection areas in their jurisdiction, the Disaster Law not only gave the Ministry of Environment and Urbanism an all-encompassing authority to designate 'risky areas' anywhere in the country, but also made the Ministry the ultimate planning authority in these areas.[7] As a result, highly contested state-led urban transformation projects began in a number of neighbourhoods in the historical core as well as in squatter areas. These projects not only commodified these areas, but also led to the displacement of the poor from their neighbourhoods (Dinçer, 2011; Kuyucu, 2014). The Disaster Law also annulled the former Amnesty Law of 1984 and placed the *gecekondu* areas under risk by eliminating the possibility of legalisation and the acquisition of land titles for these settlements (Enlil et al, 2015).

On the other hand, the new financial instruments comprised new forms of consumer finance, including for housing, which culminated in a new mortgage law enacted in 2007, the emergence of Real Estate Investment Trusts (REITs) and the restructuring of TOKI in congruence with the changing role of the state (Akçay, 2018). The AKP government started a 'Housing Campaign' and enacted various laws and by-laws, which granted TOKI unprecedented powers (Balaban, 2012; Altınok, 2016), making it the most crucial institution and source of development finance through which the neoliberal urban agenda was put into action. With the new arrangements, the scope and impact of TOKI's power far surpassed the previous period.[8] TOKI began undertaking profit-oriented projects in partnership with private companies on state-owned lands, mostly based on the revenue-sharing model. In addition, all the assets and duties of the former Land Office were transferred to TOKI, expanding its land stock from 16,500,000 m^2 to 194,000,000 m^2 (Çelik et al, 2015), thereby transforming TOKI into 'a real estate giant and the primary producer of market-rate housing in Turkey' (Karaman, 2013: 87). Thus, TOKI's share of the housing market increased from a mere 1.1 per cent in 2003 to 18.6 per cent in 2007 (Törüner, 2008 in Karaman, 2013). From 2003 to 2010, TOKI built 445,000 housing units, half of which targeted middle- and high-income groups (Balaban, 2012), and by 2015, this number had reached 640,726 housing units (Çelik et al, 2015). At the same time, TOKI was given the authority to make plans at all scales, including urban transformation projects in *gecekondu* areas, in the historic centre or in other dilapidated inner-city neighbourhoods, as well as on all the state-owned lands under its responsibility (see Figure 9.2). Moreover, the Disaster Law of 2012 vested TOKI, along with the Ministry of the Environment and Urbanism, with planning powers in the areas declared as 'risky'.

The changing role and approach of the state to housing and urban land also meant a significant shift in how housing production was organised. The organisation of housing production and the profile of investors also changed, shifting from small-scale construction by petty builders on a lot basis to large-scale mass production by large-scale construction companies. In other words, small-scale *yap-sat* builders were gradually driven out of the market and the 'build-and-sell' model of small-scale contractors – in which they secured access to land through an agreement promising a share to the landowner and sold the flats during the construction process to help finance the building – was replaced by a 'sell-and-build' system, where large firms undertaking the construction sell the flats before actually erecting the buildings.

Figure 9.2: In the foreground is an apartment building from the pre-1980s built through *yap-sat*, while in the background are high rises of the urban transformation era

Source: Evrim Yilmaz

The shortage of buildable/renewable plots within central areas of the city was one of the reasons why this kind of small-scale, self-organised housing production faded away,[9] paving the way for a supply-led, large-scale housing provision by larger construction companies and developers, mostly supported by state institutions like TOKI with the transfer of public land – mostly below market rate – to the companies in exchange for a share from real estate development (Enlil et al, 2017). Clientelist and hegemonic relationships led to the emergence of a circle of developers and construction firms who have been repeatedly awarded these lucrative contracts. The concentration of power in institutions like TOKI, Emlak Konut REIT and the Ministry of Environment and Urbanisation created an unfair competitive environment for firms who were not able or willing to enter the close circles of the government (Enlil et al, 2017).

The implementations of new tools like REITs[10] and mortgages have also given a boost to real estate development. Emlak Konut REIT is the major REIT in Turkey. It is a state-owned company as its largest shareholder is TOKI. Its connection to this powerful institution with an extensive land portfolio makes Emlak Konut the leading REIT monopolising the market.[11] Given the scarcity of large plots suitable for development, large-scale projects are predominantly enabled by bids put out by TOKI and Emlak Konut REIT on publicly owned lands. Emlak Konut REIT works largely with a 'revenue-sharing model', with land being provided either by Emlak Konut REIT or

TOKI through an open tender where contractors are invited to offer an estimate of 'minimum sales revenue' and a 'company share ratio'[12] in return for providing the most scarcely found resource, the land. The revenue offered to Emlak Konut REIT should be equivalent to or higher than the appraised value of the land provided. This works as a hidden subsidy since TOKI values the land below its actual market price (Karaman, 2013), providing a competitive edge to the contractor.

TOKI uses some of the revenue generated through the 'revenue-sharing model' to construct low- and middle-income housing as well as for *gecekondu* redevelopment projects since the strategy of legalising *gecekondus* has been abandoned and a more stringent policy is pursued towards these settlements. TOKI also started numerous transformation projects targeting the informal settlement areas of Istanbul, mainly using the Disaster Law as a pretext for clearing up public lands occupied by self-build *gecekondus* for further investment, including large-scale projects. These projects either displaced the residents to buildings constructed by TOKI with inadequate services and inconvenient living conditions outside the city, or proposed housing in the newly built estates that are far from being affordable for the population of these informal settlements.[13]

Although gecekondu production came almost to a halt, new versions of self-building and commissioning practices arose, which led to new forms of tension between the state, market actors and civil society. In some neighbourhoods declared as 'risky areas', TOKI is not involved in the redevelopment process either as a developer or as an arbiter, leaving the organisation of the transformation process to market forces. In such areas, property-owners and developers enter into a negotiation process, setting the terms of agreement for the redevelopment of the land in exchange for the flats to be built. Although akin to the *build-and-sell* or *yap-sat* method, this process diverges from the previous modes of self-organisation and commissioning in some fundamental ways. First, it involves area-based transformation as opposed to the lot-based small-scale operations of the *yap-sat*. Second, instead of a single landowner, it involves many owners, not only because the 'risky areas' are composed of many individual lots, but also because each lot usually has multiple ownership, with a number of flat-owners. Hence, it is a much more complicated process and takes a longer period of negotiation, involving higher risks for both the residents and the developers.[14] Third, property-owners usually end up having a single smaller flat as compensation for the increased value of a brand new home in a renewed area, as opposed to the single landowner who got at least half of the flats that were built through the *yap-sat* process, which

Figure 9.3: Different generations of housing

Source: Evrim Yilmaz

was a major means of accumulation. Finally, the transformation process involves large construction firms or a consortium of firms depending upon the scale of the area to be redeveloped, as opposed to the small-scale *yap-sat* contractor (see Figure 9.3).

Another version of this process involves a lot-based renewal of the apartment buildings built earlier, where the flat-owners agree with a contractor commissioning the renewal of the building and apply to the ministry to get their building declared as a 'risky building', which allows substantial tax deductions, lowering the cost of renewal and making the residents eligible to receive a monthly rent subsidy from the government until the construction is completed.[15] The period starting from the 2000s onwards witnessed the consolidation of the link between urban space and capital accumulation, deepening the commodification of urban space and its exposure to the expropriation processes enabling capital's intervention in cities and urban land.

Transformation of the quality of place in the context of shifting housing regimes: from use value to exchange value

The rapid urbanisation experience in Turkey since the 1950s entailed different forms of self-building, namely, the *gecekondu* and *yap-sat*, which were both encouraged by populist policies and clientelist relations that varied according to the ideological positions and political agendas of different periods. Although these improvised solutions helped to ease the problems of rapid urbanisation not only by providing shelter, but

Figure 9.4: Different generations of housing with new CBD in the background

Source: Evrim Yilmaz

also by offering opportunities for capital accumulation and as a way out of poverty, their social and environmental costs have been rather high. The impact of the populist legal arrangements to facilitate surplus gain for the lower and middle classes was a self-organised urban morphology boosted in density due to the legalisation of the previously unregulated and unplanned developments, on the one hand, and increased building rights, on the other. Hence, not only were the inner-city neighbourhoods renewed at the expense of the historic urban fabric, becoming much denser, but the peripheral areas also sprawled at the expense of forests, water basins and farmlands, eroding the natural values for generations to come. The result was a low-quality living environment where self-organising, bottom-up initiatives were transformed into an instrumental tool for redistributing urban rents, resulting in a switch from use value to exchange value in the production of housing and urban space (see Figure 9.4).

The increasingly market-oriented housing provision model adopted by the state, especially over the last two decades, and the frenzy for urban transformation led to the further commodification of housing, making it a major means of investment and capital accumulation rather than a place to live in dignity, where the place qualities of urban space and the quality of life contained in it were of secondary importance. The institutional and legal rearrangements, including the financialisation of housing, exacerbate inequalities and social exclusion, increasing the threats of gentrification and the displacement of disadvantaged groups and the urban poor from their communities.

In a Lefebvreian sense, the contradiction between use value and exchange value was spatialised, reflecting capitalist social relations in which inhabitants who 'use' the city are marginalised and subordinated to those who seek to benefit from the 'exchange' value of urban space (Kuymulu, 2013). In this process, TOKI has been one of the major public institutions supporting the financialisation of housing and the commodification of urban space, undermining the right to decent and affordable housing and quality urban space for every citizen. These urban practices and interventions of the state in urban space aroused considerable dissent and led to the emergence of new urban movements. Those who bore the brunt of eviction and displacement because of urban transformation projects targeting *gecekondu* areas and dilapidated historic neighbourhoods formed fronts of resistance. They founded neighbourhood associations in order to organise collective opposition against these projects. Through meetings, press statements and lawsuits, they have been struggling to gain the right to housing, property ownership and participation in decision-making (Çelik et al, 2015). However, the basis of the struggles and the demands differed according to ownership patterns, the nature of the projects and the historical and political background of the neighbourhood in question. In some cases, opposition movements were quickly depoliticised and turned merely into a vehicle of negotiation with the government in order to improve property rights or raise the expropriation value since the residents were obliged to settle an agreement with the government and had no chance of rejecting the project.[16] Nevertheless, these movements were a leap forward in the defence of housing rights, as well as the 'right to the city' backed up by activists.

Discontent with government policies was not limited to the residents of low-income, disadvantaged neighbourhoods. As urban space became increasingly commodified, public lands were privatised, and as cultural and natural values were damaged or lost due to the urban transformation projects, another strand of opposition grew from professional chambers, academics, non-governmental organisations (NGOs) and 'neighbourhood beautification associations' of middle-income groups who stood against these projects (Eraydın and Tasan-Kok, 2013; Çelik et al, 2015). These groups also allied with the neighbourhood movements. Taken together, all these experiences culminated in the Taksim Gezi Park resistance of June 2013, which started with the cutting down of trees in an inner-city park to make way for a shopping mall. The Gezi protest was not 'just about a few trees'; rather, it was an opposition mobilised by a much larger discontent with state-led neoliberal urbanisation: 'a refusal of a new kind of spatial neoliberalism nourished by authoritarian and religious governmental practices, which have become dominant in Turkey over the last decade' (Erdi-Lelandis, 2016: 288).

Notes

[1] The research for this article was supported by the Scientific and Technological Research Council of Turkey (TÜBİTAK), project no. 113K028.
[2] State Planning Organization, '1st Five Year National Development Plan', DPT Yayını, 1962, p 120, cited in Arslan (1989)
[3] The 2nd Five Year National Development Plan (1968–72) reduced state investment in housing to 17 per cent of total investments, whereas the share of housing was 20 per cent in the previous plan. The 3rd Five Year National Development Plan further reduced it to 15 per cent (Keleş, 1990).
[4] *Yap-sat* is usually thought as a mode of building that takes place in the formal domain whereas *gecekondu* belongs to the informal. However, when examined more closely, it is apparent that the *yap-sat* also involves a similarly informal, self-organised production of housing.
[5] According to Keyder and Öncü (1993: 20), due to electoral concerns, the ideological preference of governments during the previous period was for rural populism. However, this ideological focus shifted with the ANAP government towards urban populism.
[6] TOKİ became one of the prime actors in the transformation of *gecekondu* areas after the amendments made to the law granting the administration extensive authority after the 2000s.
[7] In addition, this law provided in areas declared as 'risky' not only an exemption from the provisions of a variety of other laws such as the City Planning Law or the Conservation Law, but also freedom from the restrictions of existing plans, once more consolidating the planning power of the central authority and the supremacy of its decisions over existing planning laws and regulations.
[8] TOKİ was also given the power of establishing its own companies, making partnership agreements with private companies in and outside the country, providing credit and land, and/or directly undertaking urban transformation projects.
[9] However, over the last couple of years, there has been a feverish process of renewal on a lot basis, especially in the Kadıköy district, which was again modelled after build-and-sell and stimulated by the Disaster Law. It is a process involving many owners and medium-scale firms.
[10] In December 2008, there were 14 REITs with a total portfolio of US$2,652 million, whereas by March 2016, the number of REITs had increased to 31 with a total portfolio of US$8,315 million (see:www.spk.gov.tr/SiteApps/Yayin/AylikIstatistikBultenleri)).
[11] Emlak Konut REIT describes its business activities as 'purchasing land in Turkey and developing real estate projects for middle and upper-middle income groups'www.emlakkonut.com.tr/_Assets/Upload/Images/file/YatirimciSunumu/Turkce-Y-13.11.15.pdf (reached 20.11.2015) Due to the fact that TOKİ holds 49.34 per

cent of the shares of Emlak Konut REIT, it is also free from audit and many other regulations that TOKI is immune to as a semi-governmental institution.

[12] In the projects carried out through a revenue-sharing model so far, the company share ratio has varied from 16 per cent to 40 per cent (see: www.emlakkonut.com.tr/_Assets/Upload/Images/file/YatirimciSunumu/Turkce-Y-13.11.15.pdf accessed 20.11.2015)

[13] In this context, between 2003 and 2011, TOKI had 169 projects transforming 233,055 *gecekondus* in Turkey (Kara, 2011).

[14] According to the Disaster Law, although the acceptance of two thirds of the residents suffices to reach an agreement about the transformation of the property declared as risky, the property-owners who do not agree with the terms of the contract have the right to take it to court. Then the process takes time, which involves losses for all parties. Second, the developer may not be able to complete the redevelopment, leaving the residents homeless.

[15] Government subsidy is given for a maximum of 18 months. The contractor also pays an agreed-upon amount of monthly rent to the flat-owners who have to reside elsewhere until the construction of the new building is completed.

[16] The owners in the project areas were offered only limited choices: sell their property at the designated price to the public body in question (usually TOKI or the municipality); pay an additional amount in lieu of the increased value of their property after reconstruction by using long-term credits; or move into one of the housing complexes, again by using credit, built by TOKI, usually on the fringes away from the centre where their jobs are located.

References

Akçay, Ü. (2018) *Neoliberal Populism in Turkey and Its Crisis*, Working Paper No. 100/2018, Berlin: Institute for International Political Economy Berlin.

Altınok, E. (2016) 'Neoliberalleşme sürecinde TOKİ ve toplu konut biçiminde kentleşmenin ekonomi politiği' ['The role of TOKI in the neoliberalisation process and political economy of urbanisation through mass housing'], *Arredamento Mimarlık*, 4(300): 65–72.

Arslan, R. (1989) 'Gecekondulaşmanın evrimi' ['The evolution of *Gecekondu* development], *Mimarlık*, 6: 34–7.

Balaban, O. (2012) 'The negative effects of construction boom on urban planning and environment in Turkey: unraveling the role of the public sector', *Habitat International*, 36(1): 26–35.

Balaban, U. (2011) 'The enclosure of urban space and consolidation of capitalist land regime in Turkish cities', *Urban Studies*, 48(10): 2162–79.

Bayırbağ, M.K. (2013) 'Continuity and change in public policy: redistribution, exclusion and state rescaling in Turkey', *IJJUR*, 37(4): 123–46.

Berkman, G. and Osmay, S. (1996) *1984 Sonrası konut kooperatifçiliği* [*The Housing Cooperative System After 1984*], Konut Araştırmaları Dizisi [Housing Studies Series], Ankara: TOKI, 16.

Brenner, N. (2004) 'Urban governance and the production of new state spaces in Western Europe, 1960–2000', *Review of International Political Economy*, 11(3): 447–8.

Çelik, Ö., Topal, A. and Yalman, G. (2015) 'Finance and system of provision of housing, the case of Istanbul, Turkey', FESSUD – Financialisation, Economy, Society and Sustainable Development, EU, FP7, Grant # 266800, Working Paper No. 152, http://fessud.eu/wp-content/uploads/2015/03/Housing_Istanbul_WP152-FESSUD.pdf

Dinçer, İ. (2011) 'Impact of neoliberal policies on historic urban space: areas of urban renewal in Istanbul', *International Planning Studies*, 16(1): 43–60.

Dinçer, İ. and Enlil, Z. (1996) 'New owners of old quarters: migrants and the reproduction of historic urban spaces', in E.M. Komut (ed) *Housing Question of the Others, Habitat II Pre-Conference*, Ankara: Chamber of Architects, pp 267–80.

Enlil, Z.M. (2011) 'The neoliberal agenda and the changing urban form of Istanbul', *International Planning Studies*, 16(1): 6–25.

Enlil, Z.M., Görgülü, Z. and Dinçer, İ. (1998) 'Management and mismanagement of change in the "grand water allée": the case of the Bosphorus', paper presented at the Land and Water: Integrated Planning for a Sustainable Future, 34th International Planning Congress – ISOCARP, Azores, Portugal, 26 September–2 October, pp 257–62.

Enlil, Z., Dinçer, İ., Akyos, C. and Can Çetin, B. (2015) 'Changing spatialities of Istanbul: from a bottom-up informal development towards a state-led flexible urban transformation', in A. Gospodini (2015). *2nd International Conference on Changing Cities, Spatial Design Landscape and Socio-economic Dimensions*, 22–26 June, Greece: Portoheli Peleponnese, pp 30–9.

Enlil, Z., Dinçer, İ., Can Çetin, B. and Yılmaz E. (2017) 'Chapter III: Kartal, İstanbul planning between flexibility and control: contradictions, uncertainties and power relations in urban transformation', in F. Savini and W. Salet (eds) *Planning Projects in Transition Interventions, Regulations and Investments*, Berlin: JOVIS Verlag GmbH, pp 46–71.

Eraydın, A. and Tasan-Kok, T. (2013) 'State response to contemporary urban movements in Turkey: a critical overview of state entrepreneurialism and authoritarian interventions', *Antipode*, 46(1): 110–29.

Erdi Lelandis, G. (2016) 'Gezi protests and beyond urban resistance', in M. Mayer, C. Thorn and H. Thorn (eds) *Urban Uprisings: Challenging Neoliberal Urbanism in Europe*, London: Palgrave Macmillan, pp 283–308.

Erman, T. (2001) 'The politics of squatter *(gecekondu)* studies in Turkey: the changing representations of rural migrants in the academic discourse', *Urban Studies*, 38(7): 983–1002.

Harvey, D. (1978) 'The urban process under capitalism: a framework for analysis', *International Journal of Urban and Regional Research*, 2(1–4): 101–31.

Harvey, D. (1989) 'From managerialism to entrepreneurialism: the transformation in urban governance, late capitalism', *Geografiska Annaler, Series B, Human Geography, The Roots of Geographical Change: 1973 to the Present*, 71(1): 3–17.

Işık, O. and Pınarcıoğlu, M. (2001) *Nöbetleşe yoksulluk: gecekondulaşma ve kent yoksulları, Sultanbeyli örneği* [*Poverty in Turns: Squatter Development and Urban Poverty, the Case of Sultanbeyli*] (1st edn), İstanbul: İletişim.

Kara, M. (2011) 'Türkiye'de gecekondu dönüşüm projelerinin konut sorununun çözümündeki rolü' ['The role of *gecekondu* transformation projects in solving the housing problem in Turkey'], *Girişimcilik ve Kalkınma Dergisi*, 6(2): 171–94.

Karaman, O. (2013) 'Urban renewal in Istanbul: reconfigured spaces, robotic lives', *IJJUR*, 37(2): 715–33.

Keleş, R. (1990) *Kentleşme Politikası* [*Urban Policies*], Ankara: İmge Kitapevi.

Keyder, Ç. and Öncü, A. (1993) *İstanbul and the Concept of World Cities*, İstanbul: Friedrich Ebert Vakfı.

Kılınçaslan, İ., Erkut, G., Gülersoy, N.Z., Özsoy, A., Dinçer, İ., Gezici, F. and Kerimoğlu, E. (2009) 'An evaluation on squatter housing and ownership patterns in two neighbourhoods of İstanbul', in N.Z. Gülersoy F. Gezici, A.B. Önem and K.Y. Arslanlı. (eds) *New Approaches in Urban and Regional Planning*, İstanbul: ITU Urban and Environmental Planning and Research Centre, pp 114–33.

Kuymulu, M.B. (2013) 'The vortex of rights: "right to the city" at a crossroads', *International Journal of Urban and Regional Research*, 37(3): 923–40.

Kuyucu, T. (2014) 'Law, property and ambiguity: the uses and abuses of legal ambiguity in remaking Istanbul's informal settlements', *International Journal of Urban and Regional Research*, 38(2): 609–27.

Lovering, J. and Evren, Y. (2011) 'Urban development and planning in Istanbul', *International Planning Studies*, 16(1): 1–4.

Öktem, B. (2005) 'Küresel kent söyleminin kentsel mekanı dönüştürmedeki rolü: Büyükdere-Maslak Aksı' ['The impact of global city discourse on the transformation of urban space'], in H. Kurtuluş (ed) *İstanbul'da Kentsel Ayrışma* [*Urban Segregation in Istanbul*], İstanbul: Bağlam Press, pp 25–76.

Öncü, A. (1988) 'The politics of urban land market in Turkey: 1950–1980', *IJURR*, 12(1): 38–63.

Özdemir, D. (2011) 'The role of the public sector in the provision of housing supply in Turkey 1950–2009', *IJURR*, 6(35): 1099–117.

Salet, W., D'Ottaviano, C., Majoor, S. and Bossuyt, D. (2020) Selfbuilding as a right to the city', in W. Salet, C. D'Ottaviano, S. Majoor and D. Bossuyt (eds) *The Self-Build Experience: Institutionalisation, Place-Making and City Building*, Bristol: Policy Press, 1–19.

Şenyapılı, T. (1998) '"Cumhuriyet" in 75. yılı gecekondunun 50. yılı' ['The 75th year of the republic; the 50th year of *gecekondu* housing'], in *75 Yılda degisen kent ve mimarlik* [*The Changing City and Architecture After 75 Years*], Istanbul: Türk Tarih Vakfı Yayınları.

Şenyapılı, T. (2004) 'Charting the voyage of squatter housing in urban spatial quadruped', *European Journal of Turkish Studies*, 1: 1–19.

Sey, Y. (1984) 'To house the new citizens: housing policies and mass housing', in R. Holod and A. Evin (eds) *Modern Turkish Architecture*, Philadelphia, PA: University of Pennsylvania Press, pp 153–77.

Tekeli, İ. (1991) *Kent Planlaması Konuşmaları* [*Urban Planning Talks*], Ankara: TMMOB, Mimarlar Odası.

Törüner, Y. (2008), Insaat sektörü krizden nasıl etkilenir? [How will the construction sector be affected by the crisis?] *Milliyet* 29 January www.milliyet.com.tr/2008/01/29/yazar/toruner.htm

Yönder, A. (1987) 'Informal land and housing markets: the case of Istanbul, Turkey', *Journal of the American Planning Association*, 53(2): 213–19.

10

The experience of an African city: urban areas in Ouagadougou, Burkina Faso

Adama Belemviré

Introduction

In Burkina Faso, the rate of urbanisation has increased successively from 6.4 per cent in 1975 to 15.5 per cent in 1996. In 2006, this rate is estimated at 20.3 per cent and it could reach 35 per cent by 2026. These urbanisation rates are among the lowest in the sub-region. Urban growth or urbanisation is often synonymous with improving the physical living environment of the population (the construction of superstructure equipment, infrastructure, the servicing of living spaces, basic urban services and so on). However, the population explosion in Burkina Faso is accompanied by disjointed urbanisation, posing a crucial problem in the near future: access to decent housing, especially for the poor. The paradox in underdeveloped African countries in general, and in Burkina Faso in particular, is that the process of urbanisation is generating enormous social deficits and a high social demand that is almost unfulfilled when we consider the resources available for development. In Burkina Faso, urban growth is fundamentally characterised by a simple increase of the population living in cities (Ministère de l'Habitat et de l'Urbanisme, 2008; Cities Alliance, 2012), which has as immediate corollaries: (1) a lack of basic infrastructure and difficult access to basic urban services (health, education, sanitation, transport, environment and so on); (2) a growing housing deficit; (3) endemic unemployment and underemployment; and (4) urban insecurity development.

The spontaneous and uncontrolled growth of urban centres will invariably produce social inequities that are detrimental to the harmonious development of the whole country. This chapter looks at self-construction experiences in Ouagadougou and their implications for urban development. It also explores how self-construction or changing relationships in housing production are related to major urbanisation issues, such as those outlined in Chapter 1 on 'contested urban governance'. The chapter is built around the following points: (1) the historical stages of urban development in Burkina Faso; (2) inconsistencies in public housing measures; (3) actors in real estate promotion; and (4) the emergence of a civil society in the planning of housing and town planning.

The historical stages of urban development in Burkina

The development of cities on Burkinabe territory is the consequence of a historical evolution. There are four main periods in the establishment of the urban network in Burkina Faso (Ministère de l'Habitat et de l'Urbanisme, 2008): the pre-colonial and colonial periods; the period of independence to 1983; the period from 1983 to 1995; and the period from 1995 to the present day.

Pre-colonial and colonial periods

Before colonisation, on the territory of the future Upper Volta and the current Burkina Faso, cities appeared when the conquering peoples set themselves up before the first contacts with Europe in 1895. This resulted in the subdivision of the territory into political and economic entities administered by capitals with city functions. The level of equipment in administrative, socio-economic or health infrastructures, and also the political and administrative, commercial and sociocultural functions that these cities embodied for their populations, explain their existence and their importance. Thus, on the central plateau, corresponding to the moaga country (Moogho or Empire of the Moose), the function was political and administrative, while in the west and north of the territory, it was more commercial and sociocultural. There were cities in pre-colonial Burkina Faso and colonisers relied on them to establish their domination. In accordance with the objectives of the coloniser, the urban configuration of these cities was somewhat modified. The territory was subdivided into ten circles with that of Ouagadougou in the centre, from which control of the whole territory was assured. The circles were structured into subdivisions and these, in turn, into cantons. Most of the pre-colonial cities became centres of circles where colonial domination was exercised.

In terms of land policy, French colonisers criticised traditional agrarian and land tenure structures for maintaining obscure rights, dangerous for credit and incompatible with development. To encourage the development of land and induce economic development, decrees of 24 July 1906 and 26 July 1932 introduced in French West Africa (AOF) a land registration system based on the individualisation of land rights by private property. However, Africans showed little interest in registration, which led the French to make changes to the text. Thus, the legislator had to intervene by a new decree to institute the system of the administrative certificate or the native land title. It was a transitional regime between the customary tenure system and the registration system that recognised customary tenure rights for the first time. This system also failed. From the point of view of urban practices, it should be noted that spatial segregation has greatly influenced all actions in terms of urban management: on the one hand, there was the European city with all the urban facilities; on the other, the unhealthy native city with deprived equipment; and between the two, the shops. In terms of housing production, the interventions of the colonial administration were limited to the production of the official homes of the main officials.

Period from independence to 1983

Burkina Faso gained independence on 5 August 1960, when the most important cities were Ouagadougou (60,000 inhabitants) and Bobo-Dioulasso (55,000 inhabitants). In 1975, according to the criteria used to define a city, there were five city centres: Ouagadougou (centre), Bobo-Dioulasso (west), Koudougou (centre-west), Ouahigouya (north) and Banfora (West). In terms of land policy, sharing a desire to develop the maximum land in its territory and respect for customary law, the new independent state regulated land by Law No. 77-60/AN of 12 July 1960, while Law No. 29–63 of 24 July 1963 authorised the government to reserve for the state a portion of land subject to spatial development or land with few or no settlements. Regarding urban development, several projects have been initiated on external financing, most of which were tested in Ouagadougou. The period from 1960 to 1983 was marked by the start of real estate development, with the construction of about 200 medium and high-class houses by real estate companies.

Period from 1983 to 1995

In 1983, with the advent of the revolutionary political regime, there was a radical change in the policy of land-use planning, urban planning and housing promotion in Burkina Faso. A law on agrarian and land reorganisation was developed and implemented, with the aim to establish state sovereignty over land. With the slogan 'a household, a plot', the authorities of the era of the revolution adopted a policy of massive subdivisions via the production of plots, socio-economic housing, community amenities and also sanitation. Rental housing prices were rigorously controlled to relieve non-homeowners. Ouagadougou, the capital, until then rather a big village, underwent an urban renewal. A special account entitled 'Urban and rural centres subdivision operations account' was created to support the financing of urban development operations. A housing fund was also created to support the efforts of the services of real estate development companies and certain categories of state agents for the financing of housing.

Period from 1996 to the present

The year 1996 is marked by a resumption of the process of decentralisation in Burkina Faso, which had been interrupted since 1966. This process took place in a context of democracy and economic liberalism in which the state gradually disengaged from the sector of housing production, to the benefit of the private real estate development companies. With decentralisation, local authorities become major actors in production and land management. However, the state has not abandoned its role as developer, despite the absence of a comprehensive strategy in the housing and urban development sector and the inadequacy of the legal framework (Ministère de l'Habitat et de l'Urbanisme, 2010). This is how major projects were started at the Ouagadougou level in an unclear context where the minister in charge of the housing sector failed to assert his policy in an elaborate strategy. In 2006, the creation of a Ministry of Habitat (set up an urban database) and Bank of the Habitat, and the adoption of the code of town planning and construction, allowed a renewal of the habitat sector and of urbanism, and was the beginning of urban development.

The inconsistencies in public housing measures

Inconsistencies in public housing measures and legal aspects point to the absence of a unique frame of reference that takes into account the entire housing and urban development sector. This is why the laws regulating the sector have been subject to limited objectives until now. In this section, we discuss the housing situation in Burkina Faso, the structure of housing costs and the inconsistency of public measures in housing.

The housing situation

The housing situation in Burkina Faso is characterised by a gap between the faster growth of the population living in the city and the supply of housing; hence, a housing deficit grew (Ministère de l'Habitat et de l'Urbanisme, 2008). The appearance of spontaneous and precarious settlements in slums is one example of this. Demand for housing consists of households that are displaced (outside their place of residence) or urged to move (to leave the parental home), from different socio-professional categories: workers, shopkeepers, the unemployed, students, migrants from the rural exodus and so on. For its part, the housing offer is made up of all standards and essentially individual owners and real estate companies (Daniel and Florence, 2017). It is therefore an 'imperfect market' so that the supply of and demand for, or free trade in, housing also works imperfectly. This housing market, insufficiently regulated by the state if not by taxation, is also handled by more or less informally structured real estate agents (intermediaries or marketers).

In non-lot areas

In 2003, 37 per cent of households were unable to meet basic needs (Ministère de l'Habitat et de l'Urbanisme, 2008). This especially rural poverty also concerns cities as they are centres of attraction for young people of all regions of Burkina Faso, where many find themselves unemployed and consequently in precarious conditions. In Ouagadougou, these migrants converge on the outskirts, which are now neighbourhoods under construction with hopes of land appropriation, professional integration and family success. They are therefore confronted with the problems of training, employment, housing, health and social integration, the management of which requires, among other things, considerable financial resources that the municipality alone cannot provide. In these so-called spontaneous neighbourhoods, households often live in deplorable hygienic conditions, without basic equipment and infrastructures (schools, primary care centres, drinking water, electricity), but especially in land insecurity due to not having an official title guaranteeing occupation. The increase in the population in these non-settled areas in recent years has forced the authorities to provide them with some basic social services, such as school education, health services and drinking water supply networks.

In these unplanned areas, houses built in a disordered way are usually made of unsustainable materials (*banco*) because they can be destroyed during subdivisions, which discourages people from investing in *solid structures*, even if they would have the means to do so. As soon as there is a subdivision project for a neighbourhood, newcomers will be installed who build unplanned precarious homes. The land becomes an object of speculation, with very profitable economic potential. In principle, the management of land is the responsibility of the state alone, but in practice, actors such as landowners or customary leaders, as well as speculators (traders and so on) in search of monetary gains from the sale or resale of plots of land to applicants, need to be taken into account. The number of plots available is always lower than the number of applicants, and after the awards, the unlucky ones are forced to leave and settle elsewhere, which contributes to the spread of the city.

Owning one's home is a major aspiration for any Burkinabe household, as illustrated by this well-known maxim in Burkina: 'sleeping under the roof or on the mat of others is sleeping outside or on the ground'. In fact, most households own their homes: 81.2 per cent for the whole country, 93.4 per cent for rural households and 59.7 per cent for urban households. In the central region, where the capital is Ouagadougou, 11.5 per cent of households own property, 36.9 per cent rent-to-own and 39.5 per cent rented (Ministère de l'Habitat et de l'Urbanisme, 2008). In the Hauts Bassins region, with Bobo-Dioulasso as the county seat, 9.2% of households own property, 25.6% rent-to-own and 22% rented.

In plot areas

In plots of land, the inhabitants of plots make efforts to build sustainable housing with adequate materials. However, the vast majority of households do not have sufficient income, cannot resort to private actors and build their own housing. Thus, they face the very high cost of building materials (cement, iron, aggregate sheets and so on), some of which are subject to taxes. The main mode of housing production is therefore self-construction (90 per cent). Currently, a review is being carried out at the level of the Ministry of Housing and Town Planning to help low-income households to self-build so that they have a decent habitat. In Burkina Faso, according to the 2006 Recensement General de la Population et de l'Habitat (RGPH, 2006), the majority of dwellings are of low standing (42.1 per cent) and at least 15 per cent is indecent. Depending on the area of residence, high-class housing is located in urban areas. In non-parcelled areas, those of average standing are represented more in rural areas (45.9 per cent) than in urban areas (31.7 per cent).

The structure of housing cost

In the past, the promotion of housing was organised by the state through the establishment of housing finance mechanisms such as the Habitat Fund, created in 1986, to support the efforts of the services and companies. Economic operators, state-owned companies, banks and insurance companies were also called upon to finance housing. Thus, plots have been cleared and housing has been built and made available to the population in the form of renting or hire-purchase. Unfortunately, their very high costs make them accessible only to the haves, who are in the minority. Currently, state companies in this area are: the National Urban Land Development Company (SONATUR) and the City Management Centre (CEGECI), which is the structure responsible for the implementation of government policy in terms of access to decent housing, with a mission to manage the cities built by the state and also to build housing.

However, the state is in the process of withdrawing from real estate production to the benefit of private developers such as Aziz Immobilier (AZIMMO), the Real Estate and Mobiliar Company of Burkina Faso (SIMOB), the agency CAP Immobilier, GELPAZ-IMMO, Abdul Service International and so on, which do not have social concerns. Confronting the increasing demand for housing by young executives, the state is currently engaged in the production of social housing in some cities across the country, some of which are made of local materials. The project Promotion of Local Building Materials (LOCOMAT), which researches the production and use of local building materials, has allowed the creation of know-how and various skills for their exploitation. Regarding the rental phenomenon, it contributes to the reduction of housing insufficiency and is currently increasing in large cities such as Ouagadougou and Bobo-Dioulasso. However, due to the non-application of legislation regulating and controlling rent prices, we are witnessing speculation that is causing housing costs to rise excessively. Thus, many tenants live in indecent conditions and are subject to the whims of landlords who increase rental fees at any time, without thinking of offering them any increase in comfort (which the National Coalition for Housing denounces). Aware that the sustainable human development of a country also requires the equitable and transparent management of land and the decent housing of its population, the Ministry of Housing and Urban Planning has developed a national policy of housing and urban development with a 2009–18 action plan, which is being implemented, including the construction and allocation of social housing to some applicants.

The high cost of housing is unanimously recognised by all and singularly by the Ouagalais. The high price of a good results either from its rarity (the shortage or insufficiency of the offer) or from its real cost. In the case of housing in Burkina Faso, the second thesis is more plausible and also explains the first. In fact, the structure of the cost of housing is made up of equally prohibitive elements. First, for the acquisition of land for residential use in Ouagadougou, for example, the average discounted price is at least 10,000 CFA francs per square meter, or 3 million CFA francs per plot of 300 m^2 (Kaboré, 2012). This outbidding is explained, on the one hand, by the inadequacy of urban development and especially its capture by the plutocrats of the present times, and, on the other hand, by the land speculation that follows. Then, for the transfer of ownership, the purchaser finds himself facing the state administration, with all its heaviness, red tape and ruthless taxation in a context of the active bribery of certain public officials and money-hungry touts, who harass and squeeze people, pulling them to the bottom.

The cost of obtaining building permits far exceeds the reach of the Burkinabè, exceeding 2 million CFA francs to obtain a soil analysis at the National Laboratory of Building and Public Works (LNBTP), develop all plans, pay the Centre for Facilitation of Acts of Building (CEFAC) for the boundary plan, pay the costs of filing, pay for procedures with fire-fighters and so on (Kaboré, 2012). Beyond these fees, it is uncertain how long it will take to get a building permit; CEFAC will take three weeks alone to issue the permit. To have a complete file, the architect will take at least six months for the different plans, and the building engineer will take an average of one month to establish the quantity and quality of materials to be used for construction. Worse, the LNBTP, the only accredited laboratory, will take a minimum of ten months to conduct the soil survey and one month to transmit its results. In Burkina Faso, the main mode of housing production remains constrained self-construction in the context of poverty and low wages (Kaboré, 2012). The domestic market for (final) building materials is dominated by a few large importers. In such a situation, it is the latter who dictate their prices to buyers, which is why the world prices of some materials (for example, iron) are not enough to justify their sometimes very prohibitive prices on the local market.

Regarding cement, the national cement plant is unable to meet domestic demand despite its de facto monopoly. To this incapacity is added speculation in the distribution circuit of this cement. In addition, the high cost of aggregates and the cost of certain services such as SONABEL are not negligible in the development of the land.

Finally, for the exploitation of buildings, informal intermediaries (sellers) between owners and tenants are found. Indeed, many large real estate owners in the country are not openly exposed for a variety of reasons, including appearance or ownership. As a result, these shady landlords use touts (or nominees) to find tenants and collect their rents. In doing so, there is generally a different (lower) price for the owner compared with the price for the intermediary. Those who are no longer satisfied with the remuneration for their services become true sub-donors. According to some estimates, the surplus earnings of this chain of intermediaries sometimes reach 30 per cent of the rent fixed by the owner. This bidding explains why many houses remain unoccupied for a long time due to a lack of takers (see Figure 10.1 and Figure 10.2).

The inconsistency of public measures in housing

Faced with these recurring housing issues, the public authorities have taken measures, among which we can include: the Single Window Land (GUF), the CEFAC, the Housing Bank, the construction of social housing (including those of 11 December) and so on (Kaboré, 2012). What about the effectiveness of these measures in meeting people's expectations for housing? The primary objective of the creation of the GUF is the simplification (facilitation) of the formalities of real estate

Figure 10.1: Traditional habitat

Source: Théophile Mone, (2016). *La crise et l'accès au logement au Faso: quellessolutions durables?* Lesechosdufaso.net (2016).

Figure 10.2: Modern habitat

Source: Théophile Mone (2016). *La Crise et l'accès au logement au Faso: quelles solutions durables?,* Lesechosdufaso.net (2016).

deeds. After a few years of existence and in the light of the current functioning of this GUF, this objective seems very elusive as it is unlikely that it will be reached in the long run. Indeed, the GUF's formalities are neither facilitated nor simplified. Administrative burdens persist, with the consequent failure to meet deadlines, favouritism and corruption, as affirmed by the large presence in these places of solicitors. Even if the GUF was perfect in design, its operation leaves the precepts that prevailed at its creation intact. As such, an organisational audit of the GUF is more than necessary in order to reorganise it in the hope of achieving the much-desired speed.

After the GUF, the self-builder must also traverse the same obstacle course at CEFAC, which shares the same defects as its counterpart as a one-stop shop. Indeed, the various service providers of documents constituting CEFAC files (architects, national soil laboratory, fire brigade, town halls and so on) are dispersed, with some having monopolies. As a result, despite the reduction measures taken by the state, the cost of a file from CEFAC remains still very high in the cost of housing, and the deadlines announced by this centre are never respected. One of the important housing issues remains, without question, funding. Indeed, most financial institutions do not have any financial products that are attractive and adapted to Burkinabe housing issues. Indeed, many of these institutions do not offer a loan 'to individuals' of even five years duration, which is unsuitable for real estate investment in the context of low wages in Burkina. Added to this are prohibitive interest rates on loans. In addition, there is a conflict of interest between financial institutions and real estate companies because they are the same people as the shareholders or the owners.

Social housing is another state solution to the housing issue in Burkina Faso. For decades, the construction of social housing has mostly been done by state programmes, with the revolutionary period being more productive. The applicants for these types of housing are characterised by the modesty of their income and the urgency of housing need, with a more or less numerous family. Unfortunately, the conditions and methods of access to these dwellings are inaccessible to many potential applicants today. In order to benefit from it, one needs a sufficient period of service before retirement in order to have an initial personal contribution and a certain transferable quota. By way of comparison, during the revolutionary period, the flexibility of the grant conditions allowed many low-income workers to benefit from social housing (the cities of the Revolution 4-Aout, An-2, An-3, An-4, 1200-logements).

As for housing and infrastructure built as part of the celebrations of 11 December, many of these investments are economically irrational and ostentatious (aerodromes). For example, while the average official has problems finding a home in Fada (and certainly also Ouahigouya, Bobo, Koudougou, Dori and Kaya), the majestic city of 11 December (or citées des forces vives) seeks in vain for occupants. Let us not forget that it is development (emergence) that gives rise to beautiful buildings and not the other way around.

The actors of real estate promotion

Real estate developers

The housing issue is at the heart of concerns for Burkinabe. For its resolution, the activity of real estate development has emerged. A real estate developer is any natural or legal person who carries out the activities defined in Article 2 of the Law No. 057-2008/AN of 20 November 2008 relating to property development in Burkina Faso. This concerns urban planning and development operations, in particular, the construction, improvement, rehabilitation or extension of buildings on developed land. One may only exercise the activity of real estate and/or land development if they have been approved by the Ministry of Urban Planning and Construction. This definition comes from law 057-2008/AN of 20 November 2008 on real estate development in Burkina Faso. Thanks to this law, the sector once monopolised by some operators with large financial means will be opened to others.

Real estate development as a commercial activity of the formal sector has experienced a particular boom since 2008 thanks to the adoption of a number of laws and their implementing decrees. From this period, there has been a real 'boom' in property development activity, with the creation of many companies that now ensure performance. To date, there are about 50 real estate developers. As the demographic boom has led to overcrowding in major urban centres, the Burkinabè, anxious to have a home, has convinced many to invest in real estate, claiming that it remains a good deal. Housing supply is becoming increasingly insufficient in the face of ever-increasing demand in the respective political and economic capital cities of Ouagadougou and Bobo-Dioulasso. This imbalance has led to an explosion in plot prices. The recent sale of land in Ouaga in 2000 by the SONATUR is a good example. SONATUR sold land for a house on the edge of an unpaved roadway for the square meter price of 14,000 FCFA (25 USD). For an area of 324 square meters, that is 4,536,000 CFA francs (7,893 USD). For a house with a paved road, the square meter price was 25,000 FCFA (44 USD) or 7,400,000 CFA francs (12,876 USD) for an area of 296 square meters. The highest cost was CFAF 95,550,000 (166,257 USD) for a plot of 1,470 square meters for commercial use and a tarred service at the corner. For this transaction, the company sold 421 parcels to 37,367 subscribers. Like SONATUR, natural or legal persons will start selling parcels or housing. While some do well in the markets granted by the state for the construction of social housing for the benefit of citizens, others have shown by their inability to do the same. One of the reasons is probably related to the financial issue. A common practice prevailing in this environment is that it is enough to raise 100 million FCFA (174,000 USD) with some documents to obtain approval as a real estate developer. Once this document is in the bag, these economic operators bid on markets that are beyond their financial means. In the end, the work is either suspended or poorly executed.

The main actors of housing promotion in Burkina

The main actors of housing promotion are public promoters, private developers and financial institutions. Public promoters are state-owned companies and government-sponsored project programmes. They undertake, among other activities, the development of land and the production of real estate for the benefit of national and foreign investors. This is the case of SONATUR. To these are added private real estate developers. As indicated by the aforementioned law, these are natural or legal persons whose tasks consist in carrying out or having carried out urban planning and development operations. Most of them are 'men or women of business'. In other words, in addition to real estate, they carry out other activities. Financial institutions are also stakeholders in real estate development. As traditional partners, they play an active role in the financing of real estate. To better defend their interests, promoters are grouped into associations or unions. Among them is the National Union of Real Estate Developers of Burkina (SYNAPIB), created in 2013. This union aims to defend the collective and individual protection of members' interests. Members are involved in the construction of housing, including those of the city of Bassinko. The real estate developer may decide to support the state by building housing. In this case, they submit a project for validation to the competent authorities of the ministry in charge of the habitat. The developer may also purchase land with the intention of selling it on or erecting dwellings intended for sale.

In addition to SYNAPIB, there is another framework for the exchange of promoters. This is the National Union of Real Estate Developers, created on 12 November 2016. These promoters have expressed a need to be gathered around a reference structure that could act as an interlocutor for all partners. The aim of SYNAPIB is to bring about a change in the organisation and to reflect on how to better organise the sector in order to improve the activities of promoters. This union proposes the immediate organisation of real estate forums and days. It must also reflect on its contribution to the implementation of different projects. A relevant question is why so many structures exist for the same activity. More questions may be raised. The real estate development sector seems to be the preserve of men, though there are still women involved. Another big difficulty mentioned by promoters remains the mobilisation of funds. Many promoters contribute to the establishment of the city of Bassinko.

A sector to reorganise

Like other sectors, real estate development is struggling. There is a need for good organisation on all sides: promoters, administration and financial partners. There is a need to take strong measures to find suitable financing. Promoters deplore delays in administration, and the issue of tax exemption is acute. For developers, if dwellings were duty-free, the costs would not be as high. According to them, the high price of building materials, insufficient financing and low purchasing power hinder the development of real estate activity in Burkina Faso. Another impediment to real estate development is that the mortgage market remains unreachable, especially for the poorest segments of the population who are most in need. In other words, the conditions under which banks grant mortgages are limiting demand. Loan opportunities do not reach the neediest. Those who are eligible find that interest rates remain high. In spite of all these difficulties, property developers must know how to succeed. They are the ones able to mobilise resources to carry out real estate projects, adapted to the needs of the population. Developers, not to be confused with construction companies, must have the ability to innovate in order to offer products that fit the needs of customers.

An activity often badly perceived

Real estate developers do not necessarily enjoy a good reputation among citizens (due to land grabbing, dubious housing quality, the unrestrained search for profits and so on). There are doubts about the quality of social housing. Also, it misses mechanisms of correction by the state. For communities, these promoters are getting rich on the backs of citizens. They sell expensive plots, and the social housing that they build as part of partnerships with the state are very often not of good quality. Even worse, there is often corruption. Indeed, officially, only the state has the right to sell land through SONATUR and town halls. However, the state removed the subdivisions from the hands of mayors after all the diversions that took place in their management of subdivisions. The Burkinabè citizen had thought that removing the subdivisions from the mayors was in order to better organise the process in favour of the population.

Unfortunately, what we see is worse. Abdoul Service, for example, is a company that has a licence for real estate development, like SOCOGIB CEGECI and SONATUR, who built villas and rented them out. With a building project for sale, Abdoul Service received authorisation from the state to acquire land, and therefore came into contact with the landowners. Once the agreement is got with the latter, a bulldozer arrives to scrape the land and subdivide it into parcels. In place of serviced parcels, there are boundaries that are placed to delimit the parcels. While serviced parcels must be served by an access road and connections to drinking water, electricity, telephone, and sanitation.

The approval of the real estate developer is for the purpose of building priority houses with all amenities. The approval of the real estate developer allows it to build priority houses with all amenities. This is not the case at most real estate development agencies. Worse, the property development agency "Abdoul Service" makes subdivisions and grants simple parcels to landowners. In Saaba, a neighbouring commune, east of the capital Ouagadougou, this agency was awarded an area through false deliberations signed by a High Commissioner. By substituting for SONATUR to sell simple parcels instead of built houses, this agency is making land grabbing. Landowners who do not measure the scope of their actions are thus selling off their land for subsidies. That is why the state should be more concerned about the activities of real estate developers and not leave citizens at their mercy. They set prices for plots and dwellings as they see fit, suggesting that real estate development is a profitable business that helps to sharpen speculation over plots. However, for real estate developers, the high price of parcels can be justified by the fact that many parameters must be taken into account. They buy land from landowners and then have to pay taxes to the municipality and the state. These are all expenses that must be borne for the same plot and, according to developers, explains why the price of the plot is high. Services (electricity, water, roads, gutters and so on) also have a cost. However, proponents believe that if the government could reduce some of the costs, housing will be cheaper. They compare the situation with social housing, where, according to the real estate developers, the government promised duty-free exemptions.

For the state, the main difficulty facing real estate development is financial. The delay in site development is often a hindrance and there is a lack of substantial budget allocations to support the servicing works (drinking water supply, electrification and road development). The real estate sector is an important part of a country's economy, with the world's strong economies based on real estate. In this stage, it is important to build a guiding policy vision for the future while taking into account the concerns of the present.

The emergence of a civil society in housing planning

It should be noted that decentralisation and subdivision operations across the country have fostered the emergence of grass-roots communities and a civil society in the field of housing and urbanism, acting against forced evictions and for the more transparent management of urban land. Thus, in unplanned areas, newly built or old neighbourhoods whose inhabitants have to leave, we are witnessing the birth of 'associations of residents' and 'crisis committees', which are sometimes supported by non-governmental organisations (NGOs), such as the Burkinabè Movement of Rights Human Rights and Peoples (MBDHP), who denounce the operation of evictions and especially argue for the transparent management of land. Several associations working in the field of housing and urban planning are active in Burkina (Worldmap,

2017), among which we can mention the National Coalition for Housing (CNHa), the Solidarity Association for the Right to Housing (ASP/DROL) and the Information and Communication Network for Hygiene and Drinking Water and Sanitation. These associations also mobilise inhabitants to improve the daily life of their neighbourhood, in particular, relating to questions of improving the living environment (safety, building standpipes and so on) and development projects (mobilisation and awareness of residents in the case of an immunisation campaign, street children, and so on).

Conclusion

The relevance of the role played by public authorities in housing is hardly perceptible in a country where the main mode of production of housing is self-construction. At a time when 'old' capitalism is oscillating on its own, informal economies must not and cannot do without state interventionism. Indeed, according to economists, to lower the price of a good on the market in a liberal context, it is enough to pull the levers of the demand for and supply of this good. To do this, the state has a powerful instrument: taxation. In the case of housing, if it is not acceptable for the state to fix the prices of materials and rents, it is necessary that it intervenes to regulate them (for example, import competition in the cement market). In addition, the presence of the state on the real estate market as a tenant of buildings on its behalf (many administrative services are in rented buildings) necessarily creates a perverse effect: the effect of eviction. The state must instead give itself the means to build for its own needs, and to continue the subdivisions and other urban developments.

A housing policy cannot ignore taxation in this area. It must also take into account a simplification of transfer procedures, which are a real problem nowadays. In fact, a parcel buyer who does not have a Burkinabè national identity card (CIB) in their current transfer file is blocked. Moreover, if for whatever reason your seller cannot find his CIB, you may run into a big problem. It is important that the state diligently addresses these many particular cases and generally reduces the red tape surrounding these transactions. With political will, another more simplified procedure for transactions and acts of construction is possible. Perhaps the effectiveness of GUF and CEFAC may be improved. The state could also be the promoter of collective housing (apartments), which are more economical and should prevail in urban habitats. In addition, there are still no structured public instruments for housing finance.

Many questions require new policy guidelines. What about the LOCOMAT project that raised so many hopes? What about the creation of the housing promotion agency, the tax exemption for real estate loans and so on? In short, the question of housing in Burkina concerns several factors, including the cost of materials, the thresholds of appropriate financing, red tape, fairness in the real estate market and so on. We summarise the problems around three main constraints: (1) the scarcity of appropriate and accessible funding for all segments of the population; (2) the weakness of the purchasing power of the population, which cannot support the terms of mortgages and their interest rates; and (3) the costs of construction that continue to rise following input prices. Faced with this situation, some measures taken so far by the public authorities have shown their limits. The lack of political will due to conflicts of interest with wealthy real estate developers is the main factor limiting the formulation and, above all, the effective implementation of a real social housing policy in this country. The role of the state is not to take ownership of housing construction; however, it does have an obligation to facilitate access to decent housing for all. The magnitude of this challenge requires all parties (the state and communities, financial institutions, landlords and real estate companies, tenants, agencies, and real estate marketers) to contribute their share to the answer.

References

Cities Alliance (Cities without Slum) (2012) 'Etat des lieux sur l'urbain et positionnement du Programme-Pays Urbain du Burkina Faso (PPUB)', August, Burkina Faso, http://habitat-worldmap.org/pays/afrique/burkina-faso

Daniel, D. and Florence, B. (2017) *Habiter Ouagadougou. Ouagadougou, Burkina Faso, Afrique subsaharienne*, Paris: IEDES Université Paris 1 Panthéon-Sorbonne, www.researchgate.net/publication/316845380_Habiter_Ouagadougou

Kaboré, N. (2012) *Question de l'habitat au Burkina*, Ouagadougou: Le fasonet.bf, http://lefaso.net/spip.php?article46983

Ministère de l'Habitat et de l'Urbanisme (2008) 'Politique Nationale de l'Habitat et du Développement Urbain', http://urbanlex.unhabitat.org/sites/default/files/bu_nup_politique_nationale_de_lhabitat_et_du_developpement_urbain_2008.pdf

Ministère de l'Habitat et de l'Urbanisme (2010) *Etude pour un dispositif d'assistance à l'auto- construction au Burkina Faso*, Ouagadougou: Ministère de l'Habitat et de l'Urbanisme.

RGPH (Recensement Général de la Population et de l'Habitat) (2006) Ouagadoougou, Burkina Faso.

Worldmap (2017) Burkina Faso Maps http://habitat-worldmap.org/en/pais/africa/burkina-faso-3/

11

The implications of self-build for the social and spatial shape of city-regions: exemplifying the cases of São Paulo and Amsterdam

Camila D'Ottaviano, Stan Majoor, Suzana Pasternak and Willem Salet

Introduction

Self-building, and the partly informal city that is created by this practice, is a common characteristic in Brazilian city-regions. The urban fabric is a complex cohabitation of more formal and informal – affordable – city quarters, realised in a situation of extensive urban growth over the last decades. In Europe, the impact of low- and middle-income housing on the social and spatial shape of city-regions differs highly among states and regions with different forms of welfare capitalism (Esping-Andersen, 1990; Kemeny, 1995). Such as outlined in Chapter 3, there are huge differences between the economically advanced city-regions of North-Western Europe, characterised by historic trajectories of professional and affluent social housing, and Southern Europe, where there has often been no extensive social housing sector established and low- and middle-income residents largely depend on access to densely occupied, private sector family homes. In Eastern Europe, the transition of state estates to individual homeownership has created new needs to develop some sort of social housing. Generally speaking, the self-build constructions that are so pivotal for housing production in Latin America are not common in Europe. Almost everywhere historic traces of self-build and cooperative processes exist, and on a modest scale, some new initiatives in European cities appear, but there is no evidence of similarity with the current experiences in Latin American.

Yet, it makes sense to compare the underlying conditions of contested urban regimes in both cases. Characteristic for an urban regime perspective is that it shows how local government occupies two often contrasting positions. It has to generate income from economic growth and the prosperity of its residents (the institutional condition of financial accountability), and it has to be responsive to the political electorate (the institutional condition of electoral accountability). Urban regime theory investigates how these conditions are interrelated in urban practices (Elkin, 1987). In empirical practices, this tender relationship is almost never in balance. In the US, cities tend to be one-sidedly dependent on economic growth within their territory, which may explain their straight market orientation and their competitive attitude to other municipalities. In Europe, on the other hand, central states often intervened so intensely that many cities felt relieved to give in to the social preferences of the electorate. In Brazil, there has been a strong switch in political rationales over the last decades between more interventionist and more liberal policies. It is crucial to investigate these relationships in detail, including the structure of intergovernmental relationships. These relationships differ between city-regions and they differ over periods of time, in each case conditioning the prices and uses of land.

The economic pressure of capitalising markets on the lower segments of housing is visible in both systems. One of the most important laws of urban economy (going back to Pareto) demonstrates that the price of land does not depend on the land as such, but more particularly on the activities that take place on the land. When economic activities in cities grow, the price of urban land tends to increase. The mechanism of capitalising on the economic growth of urban land underlies the political-economic explanation of social dispossession and spatial disposition (Harvey, 1989). When urban economies grow, the lower returning uses of urban land tend to be rejected. The importance of this economic law cannot be denied – it permanently pushes the material pressure cooker on the uses of urban land – however, it does not fully explain the actual values and uses of urban land. At the same time mechanisms of social and political (electoral) power are visible (Lefebvre, 1996). The urban laboratory is conditioned by the contestation and negotiation of these institutional parameters. The material outcomes differ everywhere – over time and space – but it makes sense to focus this comparative analysis on the ways in which these institutional conditions operate and influence the actual housing situation in different local contexts.

The chapter compares city-building practices in the Brazilian city of São Paulo and the Dutch capital city of Amsterdam in more detail. The extraordinary large share of social housing in Amsterdam makes this an 'extreme' case in international comparison. With 34 per cent social housing and 6 per cent private rent nationwide in the Netherlands, and an even larger share of 44 per cent social housing in Amsterdam, this 'egalitarian city' (Fainstein, 1997) represents about the largest possible contrast with the empirical figures of São Paulo. Focusing the comparison on regime conditions is intended not to stow away the enormous material differences, but to enable us to unpack the contesting grammar of socio-political and economic institutions. This analysis focuses on the different roles and interrelationships between the residents, the municipality and higher echelons of government, the market, and the established providing agencies (founded in the public or private sector). The spatial impact on city building will be presented in interaction with these regime conditions.

The spatial impact of regime conditions in São Paulo and Brazil

In Brazil, self-construction, as broadly defined in this book, has been one of the main forms of access to housing. It is important to notice that, historically, there are fundamental differences in the way in which high-, middle- and low-income groups produce their homes through self-construction. In the Brazilian case, self-construction as 'the practice by which people commission the production of housing and neighbourhood facilities for their own use' applies only to the lower-income groups. The 'on demand' construction of isolated single-family houses on individual plots has been the predominant practice of housing provision for the highest-income population throughout the 20th century in Brazilian cities. It is a practice linked to groups that choose the project and hire, within the specialists in the market, the managers and constructors of the civil works.

What differentiates it from the practices of self-construction for the lower-income groups is that all urban infrastructure and neighbourhood facilities are implemented by the public authority and not by the residents; in addition, the entire process is permitted and complies with urban norms and building codes. Both the project and the civil works conform to the directives of public norms. Taxes are paid and construction workers are hired within the parameters of labour laws. These practices are therefore a component of the so-called *legal city*. The co-presence of the development of the legal city with alternative practices of housing development and urbanisation are seen as quintessential of Brazilian urban development over the last century (Ferreto, 2018). We distinguish four episodes.

Urban development: pre-1940

In 1940, the São Paulo municipality had 1,326,261 inhabitants according to the official statistics. Until then, it was a dense and compact city, where layers of distinct incomes shared the same urban space. The dominant pattern of housing alternatives – for all classes – was rent, and tenements represented the only alternative housing for the very poor population (Rolnik et al, 1990).

Urban sprawl and the centre–periphery pattern: 1940–70

In 1950, the municipality of São Paulo had 2,198,096 inhabitants, reaching 5,929,206 inhabitants by 1970, with rates of population growth of more than 4 per cent per year in all decades (5.18 per cent per year between 1940 and 1950, 5.58 per cent between 1950 and 1960, and 4.79 per cent in the 1960s). This was a period of transition from an agro-export economy to early industrialisation during the Getúlio Vargas government (1930–45), which opened space for emerging industrial elites and the formation of an urban middle class, supported by labour laws. São Paulo, as well as many Brazilian cities, showed an expressive growth of its urban area, evidencing the formation of the first popular neighbourhoods and establishing a clear distinction between the centre – a place for the better-equipped elites – and the nascent popular periphery. Dwellings of the popular strata were accessed through what was commonly called the tripod: 'irregular subdivision–homeownership–self-construction'. Data from the São Paulo Plano Urbanístico Básico (Basic Urban Plan) of 1968 show that only 47.6 per cent of municipal dwellings had public water, 84.1 per cent had garbage collection and only 65.7 per cent were located on paved streets. It was on this sprawling dispersed and deprived urban fabric that mostly migrants built their low-income houses, typically by self-construction.

Suburbanisation and the centre–periphery model consolidation: 1970–90

This is a period characterised by the industrialisation of the economy and intensive urbanisation. The population of the municipality in 1980 was 8,493,226 inhabitants, reaching 9,610,659 inhabitants in 1991, according to official numbers. Although the volume is enormous, there was a decrease in growth rates: between 1970 and 1980, the annual growth rate reduced to 3.66 per cent, and between 1980 and

1990, it was 1.13 per cent. Between 1980 and 1991, all of São Paulo's population growth of 1.12 million people was in the outskirts of the city. The spreading of the urban area followed the previous logic – private irregular land subdivisions – but also the actions of the state, which built popular housing complexes in the periphery under the aegis of the National Housing Bank (BNH). The state production of housing started in the 1970s and showed its results in 1991: 4.77 per cent of households in São Paulo were in these complexes, mainly in the peripheral ring, where 9.52 per cent of housing units belonged to this category (Bogus and Pasternak, 2004). The total of irregular real estate in 1989 was estimated at 347,614 units (Rolnik et al, 1990), approximately 13 per cent of the total of 2.63 million households in the municipality. It is extremely difficult to estimate the amount of irregular real estate produced by self-construction. After a certain time, the property and the neighbourhoods were legalised. Its final form usually mimics that of legally built real estate. A possible estimation was made by Menna Barreto and Pozzi de Castro (1997). The authors found that between 1980 and 1991, less than 200,000 housing units were licensed by City Hall and about 80,000 housing units were marketed by public agencies.

According to the demographic censuses of 1980 and 1991, the number of households in the period was 645,205 units. The 1991 census showed the existence of about 270,000 vacant dwellings. However, it can be estimated that the number of units actually produced in the 1980–91 period is between 500,000 and 750,000. These include:

1. apartments and houses built by real estate companies;
2. approved construction on private plots (production 'on demand');
3. public housing complexes;
4. irregular subdivision of existing buildings or the construction of rooms at the bottom of a plot, generally for rent (including tenements);
5. construction without approval in regular or irregular settlements[1]; and
6. construction on irregularly occupied land (*favelas*[2]).

A quick estimate would be that 42 per cent of the city's households were produced with some kind of illegality between 1980 and 1991. These households fall under the last three listed alternatives. Thus, it is a larger estimate than that of self-construction. The exhaustion of the alternative of irregular land subdivision with self-constructed houses in the late 1970s through the enactment of Law 6.766 in 1979, which defines urban planning requirements for the approval of land division and regulates the responsibility of landowners, typifying illegal settlements as a crime against the public administration, placed a limitation on this form of subdivision at the federal level. Since then, the *favelas*, with their self-built dwellings, became the main housing option for the poor population. São Paulo's *favelas* housed 71,000 households in 1980. In 1991, there were already 147,000, reaching 7.46 per cent of the municipal population. The increase of *favela* units in the period represented 12 per cent of the total increase and about 16 per cent of the occupied homes.

Intra-urban restructure and new patterns of segregation: 1990–2018

The beginning of the 21st century saw the intensification of globalisation and productive restructuring. In Brazil, the resumption of a democratic regime began in 1985. During the 1970s and 1980s, the real estate market was responsible for the provision of a new model of housing for the middle and upper classes: apartments in vertical condominiums. In the 1990s, a second model of housing offered by the market became increasingly important: houses in horizontal gated condominiums (D'Ottaviano, 2008). However, even in those cases, the public authorities continued to be in charge of urban infrastructure and neighbourhood facilities. At the intra-urban scale, there is an overlapping of processes: public investments in housing via the My House, My Life Program (Programa Minha Casa Minha Vida [PMCMV]); the resumption of the construction of large complexes in the periphery; and upper-class gated condominiums that reframed the Brazilian urban periphery.

In the city of São Paulo, some public services reached the periphery in this era: in 2000, almost all households were connected to the electricity grid and to the public water system, while 88 per cent was connected to sewage and practically all households were served by garbage collection. However, the periphery remained a space devoid of social facilities and urban mobility. The lower-income population continues to access housing through self-construction on irregular peripheral subdivisions, self-construction in occupied areas (*favelas*) or large peripheral public housing complexes built from the 1970s by BNH and now by the PMCMV. The *favelas* continue to grow, reaching 9.95 per cent of the total population of São Paulo in 2010. Within the total increase of housing units between 2000 and 2010 (589,871), the increase in households in *favelas* (132,640) represents 22.5 per cent of the total.

Due to this precarious housing production based on self-help without any governmental support, from 1950 on, the urban fabric of Brazilian cities has been characterised by two different types of city: the *'legal city'*, with designed land divisions approved by the municipal public authority and paved roads, neighbourhood facilities, green areas and other facilities; and the *'illegal city'*, produced in a spontaneous way, with practically no type of neighbourhood facilities, where precariousness is present both in the housing units and in the urban space.

Self-build: towards recognition and legalisation

The gradual institutionalisation of self-build must be explained a bit in more detail. In 1973, a study directed by Marta Godinho (1974) indicated that half of the migrants arriving in São Paulo accessed housing through family ties and 16 per cent through friends. These data show the importance of mutual aid in access to housing. Sampaio and Lemos (1993), in a survey begun in the 1960s, pointed out that 45 per cent of self-built houses in São Paulo used contracted labour, 43.8 per cent were executed by the family itself and 11 per cent were constructed by a group of people unknown to the family. They argue that as early as 1965, most of the simplistic (architectural) solutions found in their research derived from the precariousness of resources. Sérgio Ferro (1975) points out that 'the precision imposed by the economy of means rises with the precision in the production, bitter precision, not the result of the programmed and chosen ingenuity, but the result of infinite scarcities'. São Paulo's periphery is grey and dispersed. The construction materials used by the self-builders are a consequence of the materials and techniques provided by the building materials industry. The industry is an important component of the peripheral landscape and the process of self-construction.

Only in the 1970s did public authorities recognise the *'illegal city'*, either through the first research on *favelas* or through the first intervention and housing improvement programmes. The first federal programmes were then launched to intervene in precarious areas or assist self-help construction, such as the Urbanised Lands Financing Programme (PROFILURB) in 1975, Construction Financing, Conclusion, Expansion or Improvement of Social Interest Housing (FICAM) in 1977 and the Programme for the Eradication of Sub-habitation (PROMORAR) in 1979. The federal government's self-construction or self-management programmes sought to serve very low-income families not served by the programmes of the BNH (1964–85) and Housing Finance System (SFH). However, within

Table 11.1: Housing programmes SFH/BNH, 1964–85

Year	Programme	Number of loans and units	
		#	%
1964	BNH	4,356,963	100.0
1964	COHAB (Conventional Programmes)	1,206,879	27.7
1975	PROFILURB	73,742	0.02
1977	FICAM	81,872	0.07
1979	PROMORAR	206,607	2.80
1984	PROJETO JOAO DE BARRO (Self-help National Programme)	7,000	0.09

Source: Sachs (1999) and Arretche da Silva (1990)

the national housing provision policy, investments in these so-called 'alternative' programmes were less representative, accounting for less than 3 per cent of the total invested by BNH (see Table 11.1).

During the 1970s, the city of São Paulo implemented an experimental programme of assisted self-construction for the low-income population, based in part on research and surveys that were being carried out both by City Hall and by universities. At that moment, Maricato (1979) affirms that the housing production of the low-income population by self-construction represented the 'possible architecture'. Since the 1980s, this possible architecture (or city) has been the subject of public projects at the municipal, state and federal levels. Pasternak (2008), analysing data from the 2000 census in her paper 'The *favela* that became city', showed that after two decades of public intervention in *favelas*, its dwellings and population were being incorporated in an effective way into the formal city.

Brazilian urban fabric today

Census data for 2010 indicate that there are 11.4 million people living in *favelas*, which is 7 per cent of the Brazilian population. These data do not include people living in irregular or clandestine settlements, which are very difficult to measure at a national level. Even so, some municipalities and state capitals have a significant number of people concentrated in slums: 54 per cent of the population of Belém do Pará lived in households located in *favelas in* 2010; 33 per cent in Salvador; 22 per cent in Recife and Rio de Janeiro; and 11 per cent in São Paulo. A total of 60 per cent of the households living in *favelas* are located

Table 11.2: Total households and *favela* households, and annual growth, per region

Region/ year	Total households			Favela households		
	2000	2010	Annual growth 2000–10	2000	2010	Annual growth 2000–10
North	3,353,764	3,988,832	1.75%	178,326	463,444	10.02%
North-East	13,911,413	14,957,608	0.73%	306,395	926,370	11.70%
South-East	24,699,909	25,227,877	0.21%	1,038,608	1,607,375	4.46%
South	85,092,284	8,904,120	0.45%	110,411	170,054	4.41%
Midwest	3,791,248	4,349,562	1.38%	16,808	57,286	3.05%
Brazil	54,267,618	57,427,999	0.57%	1,650,548	3,224,520	6.93%

Source: D'Ottaviano and Pasternak (2015)

in 15 Brazilian municipalities with more than 1 million inhabitants.[3] (see Table 11.2).

Analysis of census data shows that the reality in Brazilian *favelas* has changed a lot over the last 20 years. In addition to programmes for urban improvements and neighbourhood facilities, with major works of sanitation, redevelopment or the construction of new housing units, land regularisation programmes, especially after the 2001 City Statute, changed the way of accessing housing in the *favelas*. The City Statute implemented normative issues to guarantee the permanence of the *favela* population in their homes. Instruments such as the Concession of Special Use for Housing Purposes (CUEM) and urban or collective misappropriation represented important advances for the population living in irregular settlements. The creation of the Ministry of Cities in 2003, with its secretariats of Housing, Transport and Mobility, Sanitation and Urban Programmes, was an important indicator of the weight that the urban issue had for the then President Lula (2003–10).

However, with regard to urban infrastructure and the upgrading of *favelas*, the recent event with the greatest impact was the Growth Acceleration Program (PAC). PAC 1 was responsible for 621 operations that benefited 1.24 million families. Some of the interventions financed by PAC are works such as: the integrated urbanisation of *favelas* in the Billings and Guarapiranga Dams (São Paulo), which included the environmental recovery of the springs; the urban planning of Complexo do Alemão (Rio de Janeiro), which includes works for mobility and the construction of new housing; and the integrated urbanisation of the Beberibe River Basin (Recife), with the removal of stilts and the construction of 5,070 housing units (D'Ottaviano and Pasternak, 2015).

To conclude on the Brazilian case: in Brazil, after decades of public policies for low-income housing and large investments in precarious settlements, self-construction, the densification of precarious areas such as *favelas* and peripheral irregular settlements are still the reality for large parts of the population. In addition, the high-income population continues to occupy consolidated neighbourhoods in more central areas and has also built new houses in subdivisions and gated communities on the outskirts of Brazilian cities, both in large cities and medium-sized cities. Even with improvements in the indicators of Brazilian households' access to basic infrastructure, Brazilian cities therefore remain characterised by a fairly dual urban configuration, with parts of the cities respecting all urban and construction standards, and parts with quite precarious conditions and a very irregular urban fabric.

The spatial impact of regime conditions in Amsterdam and the Netherlands

Amsterdam is an internationally acclaimed example in which the process of capitalising on the increasing commercial value of urban land was heavily mitigated by the organisation of social and political power. Considering the preferences of the electorate, Amsterdam has developed as a 'red city', not just in short intervals of political articulation, but more structurally, throughout about the entire 20th century. The municipality of Amsterdam has become the largest landowner of the city (almost acting as a monopoly), social housing associations have grown into the largest landlords of the city and land use is conditioned by urban zoning and other spatial policy instruments of the politically committed local government. The spatial impact of these 'local negotiation' regime conditions is even visible in the uses of the exclusive and historic inner-city spaces. The prestigious residences along the canals may be habituated by the international elite but the side streets show a more mixed picture and some parts are even exploited by social housing associations. The early 20th-century neighbourhoods around the core and the post-war extensions beyond the urban ring tend to be mixed, albeit with different proportions.

Since nationwide liberalisation processes in the social housing sector started at the end of 1980s and the beginning of 1990s, the established social, political and economic relations in real estate development and planning have changed considerably but social housing is still prominent in Amsterdam even today (Savini et al, 2016). Hereafter, we investigate the development of the most important regimes in the last five decades in more detail.

Mixed urban spaces in the post-war regime of the state, non-profit suppliers and cities: 1960–90

The blending of social and economic relationships had already been settled in the pre-war circumstances of Dutch cities, resulting in active urban planning, municipal housing, municipal hospitals and municipal organisations for public transportation. However, the level of social and economic prosperity was low before the Second World War (1940–45), local public facilities used to be of a very modest quality and public facilities were overused in all cases (for instance, densely packed social and private rent housing). This situation became even worse in the first decades after the Second World War when priority was given to the recovery of the economy and young families were urged to live in their parental homes. The new economic welfare of the 1960s saw a professional upgrading of public facilities, a huge expansion of the volumes of facilities and a widening of accessibility to low- and middle-income groups. To enhance this threefold mission of the *quality, quantity and social access of public facilities*, a supply-side welfare policy regime was established, consisting of the central government and the nationally organised non-governmental, privately based providers of facilities (such as social housing associations, educational and health organisations, and so on).

Municipal and non-governmental organisations at the local level were strongly involved in the implementation of centrally arranged policies. Public facilities were provided by non-governmental agencies, financed and conditioned by the national government. A crucial condition of this large welfare package was that it was not exclusively directed to the poor. It was the explicit mission of the dominant Christian Democratic politics at the national level to provide mixed facilities, accessible by both low- and middle-income groups, in order to prevent the social and political residualisation of the poor in local concentrations of dependency. Also in the cities with their historic signature of the political left, the socially mixed access to public facilities became the general line of public policy.

The regime of the government, the nationally organised non-profit providers and the implementing public and private agencies in the cities was extremely effective. In the field of housing, the volume of dwellings (mostly social rent) grew drastically: the social housing stock tripled in 30 years between 1960 and 1990. Social housing for low- and middle-income groups peaked in the mid-1970s with more than 75 per cent of all new housing in the major cities of Amsterdam and Rotterdam in this sector. The spatial emphasis in this period in Amsterdam, as in other larger cities in the Netherlands, was on: (1) urban expansion within the cities and in the surrounding fringe in green fields with large modernist housing schemes; and (2), from the 1970s onwards, a process of inner-city regeneration focused on housing in neighbourhoods built at the turn of the 20th century. Both practices were heavily egalitarian with a dominance of lower- and middle-income housing.

Cities did attract many low-educated migrants but had affluent social policies in the 1970s (for housing, education, health, social benefits). Yet, local income generation was meagre because of troubling urban economies in the 1970s. The secret of the egalitarian city was that public expenditures were mostly covered by the national state. Dutch municipalities only generated about 5 per cent of their income from municipal taxes and levies in that period, the rest arrived via general and specific grants from central government. The social dimension of urban policies was strongly backed by the massive urban electorate but it was only partly produced by them. The inhabitants (and the other users of social facilities, such as patients, students and so on) were not very directly involved in the provision and exploitation of these facilities. The production was enabled and in its local implementation highly conditioned by the coalition of the government, non-profit organisations and local government. Both the local organisations (municipalities and housing associations) and the residents had become recipients in the supply-side coalitions of paternalist welfare provision at the central level (Bossuyt et al, 2018).

Liberalisation of the regime: 1990–2005

These regime conditions shifted in the 1990s and 2000s. A structural reform of national housing policies in 1989 radically changed the financial and subsidy conditions for the social housing sector. Financial investment in social housing was transferred from the government to the capital market, and subsidies to housing associations were abolished. Financial guarantees for investment in housing were decentralised (making private local agencies accountable in the first instance and municipalities in the second). Under favourable market conditions in the 1990s (large availability of capital, low rents) and national policy to keep rents for dwellings above cyclical fluctuations, housing associations successfully managed to make this shift. Housing associations achieved more financial autonomy but were still beholden to the established normative conditions of supplying housing for low- and middle-income groups (in particular, for residents in a vulnerable position), and they were also urged to reinvest profits in social housing provision. Profits were allowed (most of these 'non-profits' made profits) but the commercial use of profits (financial speculation) was not allowed. This liberalisation called for a 'social entrepreneurship' of housing associations. In order to empower this social entrepreneurship, the government incited two funds: the first was a 'guarantee fund' that enabled the attraction of cumulated loans (joining all individual housing associations) on the capital market, in this way providing lower rent on commercial loans; the second was a mutual 'solidarity fund' fed by all housing associations in order to financially assist those housing associations that had run into financial trouble. Thus, the central government had liberalised its productive roles in housing but had also settled framework conditions to keep this liberalised sector within the social margins.

In the course of the 1990s, however, the government lost its disciplinary grip on the normative conditions. Many housing associations explored the margins of their action space, in particular, the financial margins. Capital could easily be invested on the capital market in the 1990s. Some started to speculate with social capital, beyond the control of the government and the stakeholders. In the early 2000s, the liberal shift in regimes had not yet crystallised into a new solid regime. Central government had retreated, housing associations were in search of new responsibilities in a hesitating *'nolens volens'* coalition with the municipality (the municipality without the financial backing of the state but with a number of political claims versus the unchained housing associations, which were fixed first of all on their autonomous potential), and residents remained waiting in a position of dependency. Political conditions became increasingly uncertain in the 2000s. At the national level, the proverbial 'politics of the mid' (with a traditional role of Christian Democrat politics in the centre of political power) gave way to new liberal coalitions, and also at the level of the city of Amsterdam, political configurations had become more dynamic. National politics was driven by ideals of marginalising social housing to low-income groups and opening up liberal markets for middle-income groups.

New transitional stage: 2005–18

The international financial crisis in the middle of the 2000s led to a severe stagnation of the housing market. The private sector crashed and the social sector was paralysed by political constraints. Due to regulations from the European Union from 2010 onwards, social housing was limited to households earning a maximum of €33,000 and 'fat' housing associations were sanctioned with national levies, which were also meant to increase pressure on them to sell the better parts of their housing stock. At level of urban politics in Amsterdam, concerns had also grown about the prominent role of housing associations (owning 44 per cent of the housing stock). Local politics shifted its priority from the 'worker' to the new prominent reality of the middle-class 'knowledge worker'.

With a slight delay, the 2008–09 global financial crisis hit the Netherlands hard. The municipality of Amsterdam ended more than 50 per cent of ongoing plans and absorbed the financial losses of land rent itself. The stagnation of the established agencies on the housing market enabled a spectacular emergence of grass-roots self-building initiatives. Empty office buildings, empty spaces (even in the urban core), neglected spots and the lack of finances for investment in housing enabled the penny-saving self-builders to open new horizons for new construction or refitting and refurbishing the built environment, which had been impossible in times of urban growth. This led to more dynamics on the local housing market. In the period of crisis, supply-side agencies and policy actors began to realise the significance of effective demand on the market. A diversity of financing agencies, developers, housing associations and policy agencies started to innovate in order to service the multiple demands in the city (Savini and Salet, 2016). Residents raised their voices, also within the lethargic housing associations, leading to a number of resident-led initiatives of housing block refurbishment for instance.

In the aftermath of the financial crisis, the economic conditions of the housing market changed radically again. The internationally connected economy of Amsterdam fiercely revived, and within a few years, increased explosively. The housing market overheated after years of stagnated construction. The demand for housing by middle-class knowledge workers grew but could not immediately be accommodated. The demand-oriented market shifted again to a supply-driven market. The combination of scarcity of supply and growing needs propelled the prices of land, leading to an increasing selectivity of housing production and distribution, in particular, in the core city of Amsterdam (excluding lower-income groups). Land became too scarce and expensive for self-building initiatives, though an interesting social experiment should be mentioned here. The municipality decided to develop ten spots throughout the city for lodging young political refugees and students in integrated housing, amounting to temporary housing for a total of 5,000 persons, provided by the municipality and housing associations but opening ways for autonomous management (Czischke, 2017). More particular initiatives – usually temporary and substandard – were taken to accommodate the most urgent needs of incoming refugees, who will eventually require regular housing provision.

Under the pressing economic figures, the overall tendency was an increasingly explicit residualisation. The need for housing grew explosively, in particular, among the low- and middle-income groups. However, the higher echelons of this group could not adequately be accommodated by new market players in the private rent and private home sector. This urged the municipality to again actively negotiate with the housing associations. It is difficult to draw a structural balance of this transitional period. The central government retreated from social housing but it still sanctions this sector (accounting for 2 billion per year in additional taxes), narrows the action space through maximum income limits (which have recently been a somewhat increased in Amsterdam) and urges housing associations to sell their housing stock to make way for private rent and homeownership. The municipality initially shared at least a part of this mission and also started to sell its land to homeowners. However, recognising the explosive needs for housing of low- and middle-income groups, it recently initiated a very ambitious plan of housing construction of 52,000 new homes over the next seven years (to 2025): housing associations are assumed to take a leading role (24,000 units); social/private rent will contribute 10,000 homes for middle-income groups; commercial rent will contribute 8,000 homes for higher-income groups; and 20,000 private home will be built (Marijnissen, 2018). Obviously, drawing up plans is easier than their implementation but these are signs of emerging new coalitions at the local level. At this stage, it is too early to talk about a new urban regime.

Tendencies of city design

The spatial implications of the aforementioned dynamics of market conditions, regimes and housing policies for the development and design of cities are evident. Home construction is not simply a particular act of production by individuals or individual production agencies. The production of activities at particular places is conditioned and enabled by a dynamic set of conditions in a field of tension between the market, the public sector agencies, the organised providers of homes and the residents. It is a highly dynamic socially, economically and politically indicated field of tension. A particular aspect of spatial organisation at the city-level scale is the enlargement and decentralisation of the idea of the city. Until 1990, the expansion of cities like Amsterdam had been overwhelmingly compact and centred around their cores and closely surrounding areas. Between 1970 and 1990, this development was strongly supported by national and local politics, as well as importantly by economic investment (as long as enough building land was indicated) and by the agricultural and recreational lobbies that aimed to curb further urban expansion. However, this discipline increased in the explosive social and economic prosperity of the 1990s. Governmental plans for urbanisation kept their compact focus but markets organised the spatial periphery of the city in their own fragmentary ways. The cocktail of market-led, fragmented urban outskirts and increasing spatial displacement in the urban core fed concerns of emerging social polarisation in urban peripheries (separating all sorts of social and economic specialisations, including new concentrations of the poor and the rich), which is already characterising urban development in a number of European city-regions. This calls for upgrading the transient urban regime to the level of the city-region.

Conclusion

This chapter investigated the underlying conditions of contested urban regimes in the Brazilian and Dutch contexts, with a focus on city building and affordable housing production in particular. The cities of Sao Paulo and Amsterdam can easily be contrasted in numerous social, political, economic and demographic parameters. A regime perspective helps to focus on the comparative processes behind these obvious differences. In both cities, the local government has to navigate between pressures of financial accountability and responsiveness to the political electorate.

The Brazilian case shows a development over time in which there has always been enormous demand for low-income housing but only slowly emerging political recognition and support to realise it in a somewhat more organised way. There was never a strong Brazilian welfare state. Pressures for financial accountability topped political pleas for government intervention. This created the conditions for the radical self-organisation of groups that built large parts of the city in an informal way. The Amsterdam case shows the long-time dominance of an almost opposite regime. Here, there was abundant political clout for the local government to support low- and middle-income housing, even in the most prestigious parts of the city. The numerous housing corporations became dominant players in Amsterdam's urban landscape.

However, under changing political and economic parameters, both in the city-region and at the level of national and European politics, the regime started to shift more towards an entrepreneurial and financial perspective on urban matters. Social housing became less of a political priority. This movement slowly energised a search for alternative, self-build initiatives in the city in order to cater for the still substantial need for affordable housing. After the global financial crisis, the urban regime in Amsterdam is again searching for a new balance to cater for economic prosperity and affordable housing.

In Brazil, the regimes towards affordable housing have been slowly changing over the last three decades. From an institutional point of view, the 1988 Federal Constitution defined housing as one of the fundamental social citizen rights (Article 6). The 2001 City Statute recognised the right to housing of the population living in irregular settlements, and determined the need to fulfil the social function of property. It is with these steps that dwellers of informal settlements, slums, irregular settlements and even occupied buildings could fight for affordable housing policies, and against forced evictions and foreclosures.

Under political pressure from the electorate, some public housing programmes were created. Although the housing shortage is still large, over the last three decades, we have seen an overall development of the illegal city being definitively incorporated into public policies, and the rights of its dwellers starting to become better recognised (Fundação João Pinheiro, 2016).[4]

Regime conditions are always moving in both cases. However, underlying the enormous differences between Sao Paulo and Amsterdam, we observe a slowly emerging consensus in their regimes that economic growth and creating responsive policies for affordable housing are not two mutually exclusive pathways. An emerging political consensus is visible in both cases that forms of well-organised affordable housing are a key aspect of any well-functioning city.

Notes

1. Plots are obtained through purchase. Families generally only have an informal document that attests to the purchase from a third party while the houses are built without any control or oversight by the public authority.
2. Usually, *favelas* are constructed on occupied public areas. The houses are built without any control or inspection by the public authority.
3. According to the 2010 census, these are Belém, Belo Horizonte, Brasília, Campinas, Curitiba, Fortaleza, Goiânia, Guarulhos, Manaus, Porto Alegre, Recife, Rio de Janeiro, Salvador, São Luis and São Paulo.
4. Currently, there is enormous uncertainty regarding the continuity of Brazilian housing and urban policies. The new federal government (2019–22) has an ultra-liberal and Extreme Right bias, and is proposing a new model of 'minimal state' with great reductions in public investments, especially in social areas.

References

Arretche da Silva, M.T. (1990) *Estado e mercado na provisão habitacional: três modelos de politica* [*State and Market in Housing Provision: Three Policy Models*], master's thesis, Campinas: Unicamp.

Bogus, L. and Pasternak, S. (eds.) (2004) 'Como anda São Paulo?' ['How is São Paulo?'], *Cadernos Metrópole*, São Paulo: Éditions Educ, pp 1–90.

Bossuyt, D., Salet, W. and Majoor, S. (2018) 'Commissioning as the cornerstone of self-build. Assessing the constraints and opportunities of self-build housing in the Netherlands', *Land Use Policy*, 77: 524–33.

Czischke, D. (2017) 'Collaborative housing and housing providers: towards an analytical framework of multi-stakeholder collaboration in housing co-production', *International Journal of Housing Policy*, 1247, https://doi.org/10.1080/19491247.2017.1331593

D'Ottaviano, C. (2008) *Condomínios fechados na Região Metropolitana de São Paulo: fim do modelo centro rico versus periferia pobre?* [*Gated Communities in São Paulo Metropolitan Region: The End of the Rich Centre Versus Poor Periphery Model?*], PhD dissertation, São Paulo: FAUUSP.

D'Ottaviano, C. and Pasternak, S. (2015) 'Políticas recentes de melhorias urbanas: municípios pequenos e médios e favelas' ['Recent urban improvement policies: small and medium-sized municipalities and *favelas*'], *RBEUR*, 17(1): 75–88.

Elkin, S.L. (1987) *City and Regime in the American Republic*, Chicago, IL: Chicago University Press.

Esping-Andersen, G. (1990) *The Three Worlds of Welfare Capitalism*, Cambridge: Polity Press.

Fainstein, S.S. (1997) 'The egalitarian city: the restructuring of Amsterdam', *International Planning Studies*, 2(3): 295–314.

Ferreto, D. (2018) *Segregação socioespacial em cidades medias* [*Socio-Spatial Segregation in Medium-Sized Cities*], PhD dissertation, São Paulo: FAUUSP.

Ferro, S. (1975) *A casa popular* [*The Popular House*], São Paulo: GFAU.
Fundação João Pinheiro, (2016). Déficit Habitacional no Brasil | 2013-2014 [Housing Deficit in Brazil. 2013-2014]. Belo Horizonte: Fundação João Pinheiro.
Godinho, M.T. (1974) *Metropolização e planejamento social* [*Metropolisation and social planning*], São Paulo: PUC, 2 v.
Harvey, D. (1989) *The Urban Experience*, Oxford: Blackwell.
Kemeny, J. (1995) *From Public Housing to Social Market*, London: Routledge.
Lefebvre, H. (1996) *Writings on Cities*, Oxford: Blackwell.
Maricato, E. (1979) 'Autoconstrução, a arquitetura possível' ['Self-construction, the architecture of the possible'], in E. Maricato (ed) *A produção capitalista da casa (e da cidade) no Brasil Industrial* [*The Capitalist Production of the House (and the City) in Industrial Brazil*], São Paulo: Alfa-Ômega, pp 71–94.
Marijnissen, H. (2018) 'Amsterdam kondigt derde bouwrevolutie aan', *Trouw*, 22 November.
Menna Barreto, H. and Pozzi de Castro, C. (1997) 'A Legislação, o mercado e o acesso à habitação em São Paulo' ['Legislation, the market and access to housing in São Paulo'], *Proceedings Workshop Habitação: como ampliar o Mercado?* [*Housing: How to Enlarge the Market?*], São Paulo: Lincoln Institute of Land Policy/LabHab FAUUSP.
Pasternak, S. (2008) 'A favela que virou cidade' ['The *favela* that became a city'], in M. De Moraes Valença (ed) *Cidade (i)Legal* [*(Il)Legal City*], Rio de Janeiro: Maud, pp 109–34.
Rolnik, R., Kowarick, L. and Somekh, N. (1990) *São Paulo: crise e mudança* [*São Paulo: Crisis and Change*], São Paulo: Prefeitura de São Paulo/Brasiliense.
Sachs, C. (1999) *São Paulo: Políticas Públicas e Habitação Popular* [*Public Policies and Popular Housing*], São Paulo: EDUSP.
Sampaio, M.R. and Lemos, C. (1993) *Casas Proletárias em São Paulo* [*Proletarian Houses in São Paulo*], São Paulo: FAUUSP.
Savini, F. and Salet, W. (eds) (2016) *Planning Projects in Transition: Interventions, Regulations and Investments*, Berlin: Jovis.
Savini, F., Boterman, W.R., Van Gent, W.P.C. and Majoor, S.J.H. (2016) 'Amsterdam in the 21st century: geography, housing, spatial development and politics', *Cities*, 52: 103–13.

12

From neighbourhood self-organisation to city building: the case of Bathore, Kamëz (Albania)

Ledio Allkja

Introduction

In 1991, after 45 years of dictatorship, Albania agreed to implement a new democratic political system. Differently from other similar contexts in the Eastern Bloc (with a few exceptions), Albania applied shock therapy at the beginning of the transition period (Aliaj et al, 2009). The results of the transition, which are evident in Albania's abolition of previous institutional structures, can also be seen in the urban development field. The basis for the rise of the informal urban sector included primarily low institutional and governance capacities to respond to the new changing context and citizens' need, people's freedom of movement, and the failure of the socialist economic model (Aliaj, 2008).

Prior to 1991, Albania was a highly centralised country where every aspect of life was controlled by the central government and the leadership of the Socialist Party; the local authorities were mainly an executive branch. Strong emphasis was put on the country's industrialisation and urbanisation, with many new towns and cities being created to foster industrial development (Aliaj, 2003). The movement of individuals and their locations of work, and even the creation of new urban settlements and decisions about their populations, were decided at the central level of government. The fall of the existing regime in the early 1990s meant that many 'new cities', which had been created for industrial development purposes, could no longer offer employment and services due to the failure of the economic structure. Many people decided to emigrate from Albania to the neighbouring countries of Italy and Greece, while others moved to the capital city of Tirana (Janku et al, 2014). At this time, both the state and the real estate market were unprepared to respond to the high demand for housing in Tirana (Aliaj et al, 2009), and migrating low-income families could not afford the market prices for housing. Thus, many families, taking advantage of the breakdown of the former state, opted for informal development. Most of the peripheries of the city of Tirana were state-owned agricultural or natural lands. Hence, the new inhabitants were able to (illegally) appropriate these lands (Aliaj, 2008).

The small settlement of Kamëz is situated in the northern part of the city of Tirana. Before the 1990s, it had a population of 6,000 inhabitants, most of whom worked in agriculture, at the Agricultural University of Tirana or at state enterprises in the industrial sector. Over the last three decades, Kamëz has seen a rapid and intense population increase, which is also reflected in the expansion of urban territory. In the first decade of democracy, all agricultural lands in the area were converted into low-rise housing, while the population grew exponentially. This process was also fuelled by remittances coming from abroad as each family had at least one person outside of Albania (Janku et al, 2014). Most families decided to invest all of their savings in real estate. Due to the availability of finance, the houses that they built were of relatively good quality compared to typical informal settlements, which are associated with poor-quality construction; however, these newly created neighbourhoods lacked public infrastructure, social and public services, and other amenities necessary for a good quality of life.

The quick growth of informal settlements initially attracted the attention of few international actors, which supported initiatives aimed at promoting cooperation with communities in neighbourhood upgrading. During the first decade, the government was either apathetic or unresponsive towards this new urban development phenomenon being shaped in Tirana's suburb. A local non-governmental organisation (NGO), Co-PLAN (Institute for Habitat Development), was the first to try working with the community to improve these settlements (Aliaj et al, 2009). What was initially refused by the inhabitants soon became one of the most successful models for the improvement of these neighbourhoods throughout the country. Co-PLAN's strategy attracted further interest from donors and the government, which invested in the improvement of the settlements' infrastructure. Following this practice, the community grew stronger and individuals started to work together to improve the neighbourhood (Co-PLAN, 2018). This commitment to improvement soon spread from local neighbourhoods to the entire city.

This chapter focuses on the case of Bathore (Kamëz), describing the evolution of a practice from a small, informal neighbourhood to a city-wide scale. The chapter tries to answer the questions as to what the main drivers of self-building in Albania were, as well as what the main institutional frameworks allowing for collective action and community improvements were. The chapter is divided into three key time frames that shaped the evolution of Kamëz from the perspective of self-building. Initially, experiences with self-building during communism are analysed. During the second time frame, when there was little or no state intervention, the evolution of the neighbourhood is analysed purely from a self-regulation perspective. Lastly, during the period 1997–2004, a more complex situation is analysed where different actors work together for the improvement of the city.

The state-led housing supply before the 1990s

During the period 1945–91, the central government controlled most aspects of a citizen's life, and private property, economic activity and private initiatives were all banned (Danemark, 1993). The dictatorial regime installed in Albania applied a strong policy of abolishing private land and property. Agricultural and rural development was organised in cooperative entities owned by the state. Another aim of the Albanian government was to industrialise the country, a process that was initiated with support from international Eastern Bloc partners (Aliaj et al, 2009). Many new settlements were created with the aim of supporting industrial production and bringing the workforce closer to its location of work (Aliaj, 2003). People moved from peripheral rural areas to new cities, as well as Tirana. The urbanisation process at the time required new housing estates for the workforce. Considering Kamëz's highly productive land, a large cooperative focused on the production of fruits, and different crops were installed. This cooperative aimed to supply the capital city of Tirana. The Institute of Agriculture was opened in 1951 near Kamëz in order to better utilise the fertile land (Universiteti Bujqesor i Tiranes, 2018). Notably, this institute was later turned into the first university in the country. Many individuals came from other areas of Albania to work in the cooperative, at the university and at other state-owned enterprises operating in the area. In addition, the opening of the Tirana Rinas Airport, the Valiasi Mine and a brick factory brought new people to the community. The economic activity of the surrounding area also started to shape Kamëz's social structure and urban layout.

As a response to the employment needs of the aforementioned activities, the small town of Kamëz was created. The town was planned through a quadratic system, with apartment blocks of four to five storeys. There were two neighbourhoods: one in 'Kamëz Hill' (Kodër Kamëz), housing people working in the university; and the other in 'Central Kamëz', housing people working in agriculture and industry. During this time, the government supplied housing through direct construction by state enterprises or through a combination of inhabitants' voluntary work and the supply of materials and expertise from the state (Aliaj, 2003). Those working in state enterprises or cooperatives (in different sectors) would join forces with their enterprise or cooperative and voluntarily build their new homes. It needs to be understood that this was not a 'free' choice as voluntarism was conditioned among citizens by the regime. Kamëz was one of the areas where this practice was applied. As reported in interviews with one of the community representatives who lived in Kamëz during that time, people working at cooperatives – and, later on, those working in the mining sector in Valias – were involved in the co-production of their own homes and neighbourhoods.

At the onset of this process, an enterprise or cooperative would make a request for new housing to the head offices of the executive government or the Socialist Party, or, alternately, the party would 'propose' the construction of new housing. Once a proposal was approved at the central level, the design phase would begin. This phase was usually implemented by different architects working in the government in Tirana. These architects would provide designs for the new urban quarter, not only for buildings, but also for different social services and infrastructural needs (Aliaj, 2003). The entire design process was conducted under the strong control and censorship of the Socialist Party. High compliance with socialist urban development standards (Aliaj et al, 2009) was imperative for any kind of new development. In addition, formal discussions and consultations were conducted by the government with the inhabitants regarding their new quarters (see Figure 12.1).

Once the design phase was finished, the construction process would start. The state would provide the machinery and the construction materials. For each construction site, a team of engineers was appointed by the state to direct the work. Meanwhile, all the construction work was conducted through the 'voluntary' engagement of the end users: the citizens. It should be emphasised that the newly built houses were owned by the state, while citizens received usage rights through the payment of a small and symbolic monthly rent.

This experience during the dictatorial regime does not fall under the definition of 'self-built' used in this book, for various reasons. Most of the process was dictated by the authorities, and local citizens had limited input into the process. Nonetheless, this experience is important as it reveals two aspects of the communities in Albania:

Figure 12.1: State-led development and voluntary housing

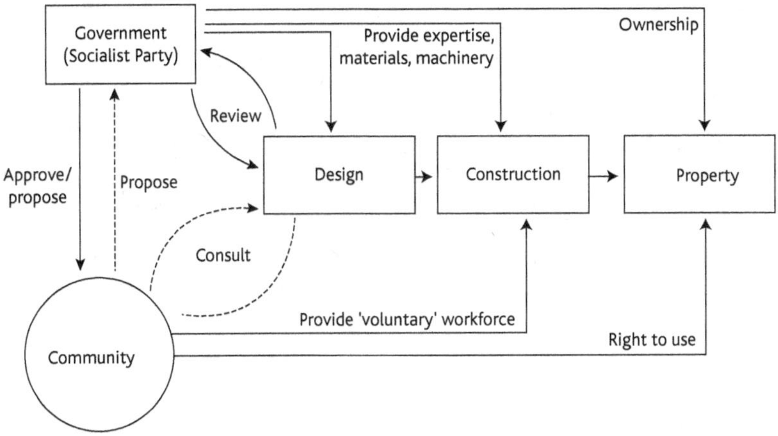

1. the experience of people working together to provide better housing; and
2. the strengthening of the community through working together to improve people's quality of life.

Nevertheless, the second point also has another interpretation that is nowadays manifested in community development to a certain extent. People were obliged to work together in order to ensure housing and maintain public spaces at the neighbourhood level. The fact that they were obliged meant that they would not value the process as collective action necessary to provide common goods, but as a form of working closely together for individual needs. Collective action was also diminished by the fact that people would not always get the apartment that they worked for; in some cases, they might not even get an apartment at all, despite the fact that they had contributed to the process. The distribution of apartments to the community was highly dependent on the Socialist Party and not based on fairness and contribution. The fact that this collaboration in terms of city making was to a certain extent fake was proven after 1990, when in the absence of a strong government, people protesting against the regime destroyed many collective resources.

Informal urban development in Albania: 1991–97

This stage of development marks another important aspect of the Albanian experience, especially for those in Kamëz. Post-dictatorship

Figure 12.2: Urban expansion of Tirana

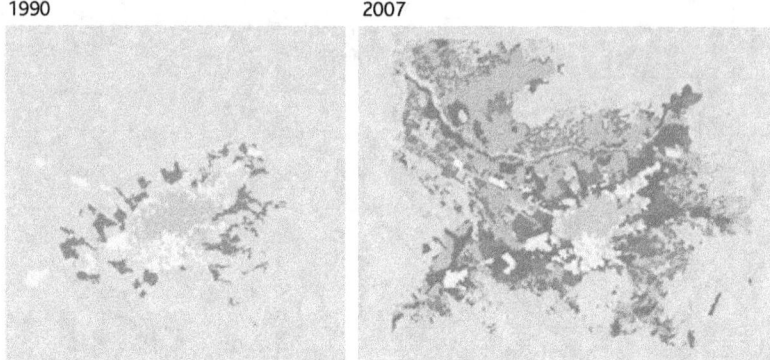

Source: Aliaj et al (2009: 100–1)

Albania was faced with great challenges in terms of urban development (Janku et al, 2014). The population in Tirana was growing very rapidly (see Figure 12.2) and could not be accommodated either by the slow-moving, confused government or by the newly formed housing market at that time (Aliaj, 2008).

The absence of appropriate legislation and planning practices that could deal with new forms of private development made the situation even more difficult. The rigidity of the planning system (Toto, 201a2– combined with the *nation's* legislative vacuum, the inability of the state to control territorial development and a series of peculiar land reforms initiated in the early 1990s (Pojani, 2011) – provided an opportunity for the rise of an informal housing market. However, before delving deeper into this informal housing development, four of the main aspects that led to informality should be highlighted: the planning system; the process of migration; the landownership reforms made during the early stages of democracy; and the social crises in 1997. The planning system and practices that existed in Albania during communism reflected a typical socialist ideology (Allkja and Marjanovic, 2017). As most economic and social issues were centrally decided, planning was developed as a discipline that mainly focused on urban regulations and standards (Ministry of Urban Development, 2014). The main instruments were urban regulatory plans, and architects were central in designing and engineering the new settlements (Aliaj et al, 1997). Consultations and participation were only formally applied as most issues were dealt with by the central government.

In 1993, Law 7693 on urban planning was approved. This was the first legislation that attempted to deal with urban development in the new framework of the democratic system (Toto, 2012a). However, considering the evolution of the planning discipline over 50 years of communism (and isolation from Western influences), one could not expect a reinvention of urban planning (Çobo and Toto, 2010). This law was mainly an adaptation of previous legislation from the limited experience of the democratic system (between 1991 and 1993). The legislation treated planning from a strong technical viewpoint but did not capture the socio-economic changes occurring in the country (Toto, 2012a]). The system was rigid and difficult to implement due to issues with property ownership. Therefore, the process of gaining building permission during this time was difficult, time consuming and highly bureaucratic.

In 1991, Law 7501 on agricultural land was approved. One of the main proposals of this law was to grant landownership rights to workers at agricultural cooperatives. As such, most people working in the agricultural cooperatives of Kamëz became entitled to landownership. In 1995, Law 8053 on the ownership of agricultural land entitled users of agricultural lands to claim ownership over those lands (Kelm et al, 2000). Lastly, in 1998, Law 8398 proposed that all former landowners before the communist regime should be compensated for their lands. Compensation could occur through the direct reclamation of their land, or claimants could be given land in another similar area. Alternatively, claimants could be awarded the monetary value of the land they lost. These three laws created confusion regarding the way in which land could be owned; therefore, in certain cases, there were multiple individuals claiming the land (Pojani, 2011). The inability to move these reforms forward created a peculiar situation (Kelm et al, 2000), where the rule of the strongest individual predominated in land claims (Pojani, 2011). This served as an enabling situation for informal urban development, especially in the area of Bathore and Kamëz, where most of the land was state-owned.

Migration to Tirana began soon after the communist system fell. The failure of state-owned industrial enterprises and the cooperative system in agriculture left many individuals unemployed. In addition, the whole architecture of the public services designed during communism fell apart because the new democratic government had neither the power nor the financial capacity to support it (Aliaj, 2008; Janku et al, 2014). Poor infrastructure and limited access to the new market, as well as a lack of working opportunities, aggravated the situation. Therefore, many people from peripheral regions all over the country had no other option but to migrate to other countries or towards the capital and other main cities in the country.

The north of Albania was one of the most persecuted and least developed regions during communism. Thus, the first people to move towards the capital were from this region (Pojani, 2011) . Another important aspect of migration at the time was the sociocultural background of the people moving to Tirana. Living in an isolated region and being persecuted by the state, strong hierarchical families were the norm for most people, with the elderly making the decisions on most matters. Therefore, they decided who would migrate outside of Albania and who would migrate towards the centre (Pojani, 2011). In an interview with one of these community elders, the interviewee explained that the typical family from Northern Albania was relatively large. Thus, families would send one or two of their members (usually younger men in their 20s) to European countries in order to work and send money back to the rest of the family, while elder sons would go to Tirana and start building their new home, which would be developed through remittances from abroad. Very soon, these remittances from migration would become the grounds for financing informal development.

In addition, buying a home was more expensive in the formal market than in the informal one, with prices at least double or triple in the former. An apartment in Tirana would cost at least three times as much as building a private informal villa on the city's outskirts. According to Slootweg (1998), a finished one-floor villa in Bathore would have cost between US$5,000 and US$10,000 in 1997, whereas buying an apartment in the formal market in Tirana (on the outskirts of the city) would cost around US$40,000. The architecture of the houses that were built expressed the current and future needs of the family. Coming from a strong patriarchal background, the idea was that the whole family should stay under the same roof or within the same garden. Thus, it became quite common to find large three- to four-storey villas where each floor had its own staircase offering private access. Since the banking system in Albania was weak at this time, gaining financing for housing was impossible for low-income families (Aliaj et al, 2009). The only solution was to build a home step by step as savings accrued or as family members living abroad sent money home. Therefore, these informally built houses were under continuous construction, which could not be accommodated within a building permit framework.

These contextual factors served as the basis for the flourishing of informal urban development. The process of building a villa started with the occupation of land. Individuals, usually coming from a different part of the country, would go to agricultural areas that were formerly state-owned and occupy a small plot of land (Aliaj et al,

2009). They would initially put a fence around the land to make their claim. Many who had claimed large amounts of land started to subdivide it; they would donate areas of land to family members, build other houses or sell individual plots in the informal land market (Co-PLAN, 2018). The exchange of properties was not done on a contractual basis; there were no deeds or any kind of property title, just verbal agreements.

Lastly, in 1994/95, a series of financial schemes started to emerge in Albania that offered high returns. Known as pyramid or Ponzi schemes, these financial arrangements were short lived and were closed in 1996, but the results were devastating for the country and its citizens (Janku et al, 2014). Many people put all of their money into these schemes with the hope of achieving quick financial gains. Most of the money was from savings and income sent home by family members living abroad, but in some cases, people even sold their properties to be a part of these schemes. In the end, enormous amounts of capital were lost, leading the country into massive turmoil. The closure of these Ponzi schemes was followed by massive social unrest and an internal 'civil war' (Janku et al, 2014). People broke into army depots to make use of the guns stored there, and most civilians had access to guns of different calibres. Following these events, *informal building practices were* accelerated even more as inhabitants, who lacked confidence in the governance and banking systems, started to invest more in housing and construction (Aliaj et al, 2009). In addition, this upheaval increased social insecurity and unrest, as well as the power available to civilians to claim and defend land.

In rapid succession, an individual who had claimed or informally purchased agricultural land would build the foundation of their house and raise the main structure of the building. In most cases, this project was self-built or done through support from *others who lived in the informal settlement*. In some cases, people from the same family or from the same area would occupy adjacent land and support each other in the construction process.

Once the structure was erected, the process of finishing one of the floors, typically the first floor, would start. This was also done very quickly so that the family could move into their new home. The ground floor was typically left undeveloped due to security reasons and to maintain the prospect of starting a small business venture there in the future (see Figure 12.3). In this process, everything was regulated by the new inhabitants, and there was no government intervention. Importantly, this process did not always go through negotiation channels; in some cases, (armed) conflicts between citizens were also

Figure 12.3: Process of informal development

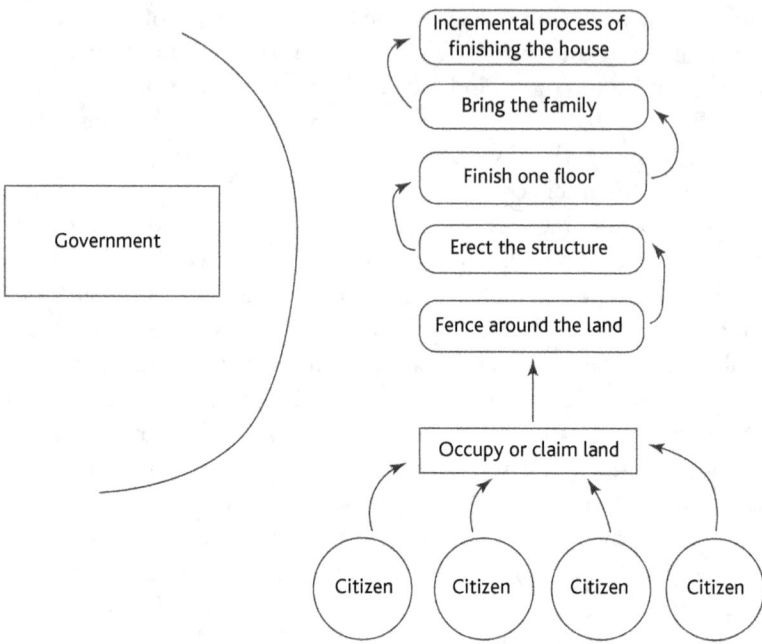

part of the practice (Pojani, 2011). Neither the government nor any other non-state actor had a say in this process. Aside from such conflicts, this process of informal construction did help to establish community leaders, usually individuals with strong credibility and integrity who could help in the development process. These community leaders would resolve conflicts and try to establish some regulations for informal developments. At this time, great amounts of energy and money were invested in property development (Aliaj, 2008).

The role of non-state actors

According to Misja (1998), by 1995, almost 70 per cent of new housing in the Tirana district (including Kamëz) was informally constructed. With informal development growing so quickly in the Kamëz area, the state had tried to intervene. Nevertheless, since then, no state authority has tried to enter the area. Although housing was developed quickly, the area lacked infrastructure and social services (Shutina and Slootweg, 1998). The municipal government of Kamëz was unable to support the community in this regard. Even though there was political will to improve the situation among local authorities, the local government's low financial capacity, combined with its lack of experience in urban planning, could not offer the community the required support (Shutina and Slootweg, 1998).

Following the social unrest in 1997, a newly created NGO called Co-PLAN emerged on the informal urban development scene, trying to fill a gap left by the government. One of their first projects concentrated on the Bathore area, with the aim of upgrading the informal settlement. At first, the community did not want to negotiate or cooperate. After the persistence of the NGO, people's attitudes slowly started to change (Aliaj et al, 2009). Creating trust and new models of cooperation was one of the key factors in this respect. A partnership with the municipality of Kamëz was also set up in order to improve community infrastructure.

The first aim of the NGO was to identify community leaders and enable them to start improving and developing their communities (Shutina and Slootweg, 1998). The whole process was based on strong consultations, collaborations and negotiations with community leaders, as well as with individual families (Aliaj et al, 2009). Once the project started to show positive results, international donors and the Albanian government became involved in the upgrading of the community. The logic was that through the work of Co-PLAN, the municipality of Kamëz and the community leaders – via intensive consultations with community groups and citizens – would evidence the needs of the community and provide a way to move forward with infrastructural projects (Shutina and Slootweg, 1998). Citizens would relinquish part of their land to facilitate the creation of roads or any other infrastructural needs. The Albanian government and international donors (mainly the World Bank) would finance infrastructural improvements. In addition, the inhabitants of the area had to contribute to the projects through co-financing, which, in this case, was done not on a direct monetary basis, but through directly working for and contributing to the provision of infrastructure (Shutina and Slootweg, 1998). The main principle was as follows: 'The Albanian government will borrow from the World Bank 10 million USD and the total project will be about 16 million of which over 4 million will come from project beneficiaries' (Shutina and Slootweg, 1998: 120) (see Figure 12.4).

After the successful experience with Bathore, Co-PLAN and the municipality created a partnership to take participatory planning to another level and the municipality of Kamëz became one of the few Albanian municipalities to undergo the strategic urban development of its territory (Aliaj et al, 2009). It was agreed that community leaders would join the periodical meetings of the municipal council and that

Figure 12.4: Multi-actor community improvement

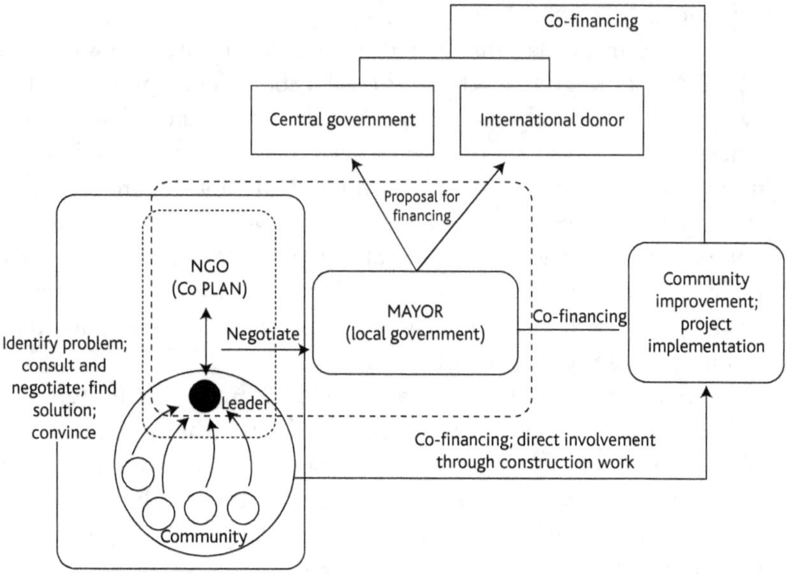

they would have the right to vote on community issues (Aliaj et al, 2009). Bathore served as a pilot case for the municipality of Kamëz, creating a practice that could be continued. The finalisation of the project did not succeed in stopping informal development in the municipality of Kamëz, nor did it stop self-building. However, it created a new practice of collective action and community planning.

This experience shows the important mediation role of non-state actors in improvements for these types of communities. In this case, the local NGO was the mediator between the government and the community. Through this process, rules of self-regulation were established within the community as well, which helped in shaping its future and facilitating infrastructural improvements.

Conclusion

The aim of this chapter was to analyse the case study of Bathore, Kamëz, through three stages of its development from a self-built perspective. In the early stages of the development of Kamëz during the dictatorial communist regime, the process was state-led and the community had little say in the process aside from 'voluntarily' contributing construction work for their apartment. During this phase, the main driver for self-building was the need to increasing the housing stock in order to bring people closer to their workplaces and foster economic development. Although there was a certain degree of voluntarism, with people directly contributing to the building of their homes, the process was highly dictated by the state. Nevertheless, it was seen as a quick and cheap solution in the provision of housing.

The second stage between 1991 and 1997 was the complete opposite. The town was developed under self-regulation and in the total absence of government actors. The result was a large neighbourhood composed of different individual villas with a complete absence of infrastructure, social and public services, and community amenities. Although the quality of the individual buildings was often of a high standard, the overall quality of the town had serious drawbacks; more work was needed in terms of making the area liveable. Self-building was driven by financial challenges and the inability of the real estate market to respond to people's needs. The difficulties of accessing the market and the high availability of public land in the surroundings of Tirana drove people to informal urban development and self-building as the quickest and cheapest solution in housing.

The dominant characteristic of Bathore's evolution was the appropriation of land. This land, taken by citizens in various different ways, had an unclear status due to the different legal reforms of landownership that had been passed. Therefore, for one plot of land, there could be more than just one claim. Another unifying characteristic is continuity between the buildings, such as the column extensions on the terrace of each building. Due to the way in which land was appropriated and claimed, as well as the social unrest in 1997, the area was unsafe. Most of the dwellings were surrounded by high walls and fences. The absence of collective action and the complete absence of regulations and rules showed that individual interests prevailed, leaving the community with little or no amenities.

The third stage between 1997 and 2004 offers a different picture and form of collective action. What started from a small pilot project in the area of Bathore afterwards became a relatively successful case that spread to the city. Citizens, community leaders, local and central government, NGOs, and international donors all cooperated in the improvement of the city. This approach, which became common practice, showed how low- to medium-level community groups could be involved in the co-production of space. Nevertheless, the role of a trustworthy actor, such as a local NGO that serves as a mediator between the state and citizens, is highly important in the successful upgrading and provision of services. The role of the mediator helped in building trust among the different parties and in increasing the exchange of knowledge on the costs and benefits of the various scenarios.

This helped in articulating the difference between keeping the status quo or engaging in collective action for neighbourhood upgrading, and in creating related community ownership and leadership. Lastly, considering the capacities of local government, it also helped the municipality in building the capacity to deal with the context. Although the project focused mainly on providing basic infrastructure, in the end, the creation of a successful practice resulted in even greater improvements. The creation of schools, health centres, public spaces and other community amenities was achieved through the power of negotiation.

This chapter shows that self-building in Albania has been a common practice under different governmental forms. In all three time frames, self-building was driven by economic conditions and the pressure of housing needs. The self-built experience shows that it is a cheaper and quicker way of providing housing, as well as of fulfilling people's needs and desires. Nevertheless, what this experience shows is the need for certain prerequisites to be developed before such ideas of self-building can be achieved, such as trust, leadership (political and community), negotiation and an understanding of the local circumstances and context-specific approaches.

Acknowledgements

I would like to thank Co-PLAN (Institute for Habitat Development) for their support and for allowing me to use their archives, and especially my colleague, Dr Rudina Toto, for her insights and review of the chapter. I would also like to thank one of my students, Reada Lemnusha, for her contributions to fieldwork and data collection for this publication.

References

Aliaj, B. (1998) 'Pilot actions for community based planning of irregular settlements in Tirana – Albania', international conference, 'City and Culture, Urban Sustainability and Cultural Processes', Stockholm.

Aliaj, B. (2003) *Albania, a Short History of Housing and Urban Development Models During 1945–1990*, Tirana: ENHR.

Aliaj, B. (2008) *Misteri i Gjashtë: Cili është kurthi që mban peng zhvillimin dhe integrimin e ekonomisë shqiptare me botën moderne?* (1st edn), Tirana: POLIS Press.

Aliaj, B., Dhamo, S. and Shutina, D. (2009) *Midis Vakumit dhe Energjise*, Tirana: POLIS Press.

Aliaj, B., Dhamo, S., Niented, P. and Stachowiak-Bogwa, K. (1997) *Proceedings of the Workshop on Urban and Regional Planning*, Tirana: Institute for Housing and Urban Development Studies.

Allkja, L. and Marjanovic, M. (2017) *Europeanization of Spatial Planning Systems – Comparative Study between Albania and Serbia*, Rome: Università Roma Tre.

Çobo, E. and Toto, R. (2010) 'Planifikimi i territorit Nga ligji në reformë', in R. Toto and D. Shutina (eds) *Politikndjekës apo Politikbërës: Alternativa mbi zhvillimin urban manaxhimin e territorit dhe të mjedisit*, Tirana: POLIS Press.

Co-PLAN, Institute for Habitat Development (2018) 'Co-PLAN: an urban chronicle', in L. Rossi and B. Aliaj (eds) *When a River Flows: Strategies for Environment, Touristic and Infrastructural Development of Albanian Rivers*, Tirana: POLIS Press, pp 12–20.

Danemark, B. (1993) 'Post-war urban and regional development in Albania', *HABITAT INTL*, 17(2): 73–90.

Janku, E., Aliaj, B., Allkja, L. and Dhamo, S. (2014) *Manifesto 2030: A Vision for Albania*, Tirana: POLIS Press.

Kelm, K., Harasani, P. and Stanfield, D. (2000) 'Land privatization in Albania', in A. Hartkoorn (ed) *City Made by People*, Tirana: Co-PLAN, Institute for Habitat Development, pp 43–59.

Ministry of Urban Development (2014) *Policy Document on Territorial Planning*, Tirana: MUD.

Misja, A. (1998) 'Organizing Tirana's land and housing market', in S.Dhamo, P. Niented (eds), *City Made by People*, Vol.1. Tirana: Co-PLAN, pp 51–67.

Pojani, D. (2011) *From Slum to Suburb: The Success Story of Bathore, Albania, ECA Housing Forum: Europe & Central Asia, Budapest, 4-6 April 2011*.

Shutina, D. and Slootweg, S. (1998) 'Bathore, pilot for an urban self-development program', in S.Dhamo, P. Niented (eds) *City Made by People, Vol. 1*. Tirana: Co-PLAN, pp 119–35.

Slootweg, S. (1998) 'Statements on urban reality in Tirana, Albania', in S.Dhamo, P. Niented (eds), *City Made by People,Vol. 1* Tirana: Co-PLAN, pp 137–52.

Toto, R. (2012a) 'Analize e situates se planifikimit te territorit ne Shqiperi', in D. Shutina and R. Toto (eds) *Politikendjekes apo Politikeberes*, Tirane: Afrojdit, pp 1–40.

Toto, R. (2012b) 'Raport i Situatës së Planifikimit të Territorit në Shqipëri', in R. Toto and D. Shutina (eds) *Politikndjekës apo Politikbërës 2: Analiza dhe Rekomandime për qeverisjen territoriale në Shqipëri*, Tirane: POLIS Press.

Universiteti Bujqesor i Tiranes (2018) 'Universiteti Bujqesor i Tiranes', September 2018 from https://ubt.edu.al/sq/misioni-vizioni-historiku/

13

Conclusion: The normalisation of moral ownership

Willem Salet, Camila D'Ottaviano, Stan Majoor and Daniël Bossuyt

Introduction

Self-building is a hybrid concept; it has several faces in different city-regions around the globe. In this book, we deliberately took a wide definition of self-build in order to involve a wide range of housing arrangements by low- and middle-income inhabitants in international city-regions. Self-building does not necessarily mean that inhabitants own the land and the home; in many cases, they do not. Therefore, the definition of self-building must also include non-ownership relations. Self-builders do not always construct their homes themselves; there may be mutual help and also often professional agencies are involved. Finally, they do not necessarily arrange their housing situation individually as a singular activity, but often cooperate with a plurality of persons and organisations, in particular, in dense city-regions where multiple housing complexes are common practice. Taking this wide scope in research on self-building enables us to pay attention to all these relevant differences. On the other hand, our analytical lens is very precise in one respect. This concerns the responsibility and active involvement of the inhabitants: their role in *commissioning* is pivotal in the analyses and case studies of this book. The inhabitants do not have a monopoly over building processes; there are always different agencies involved, among which are a number with considerable financial and political resources. However, the central research question of this book is whether and, in particular, how in this powerful arena the low- and middle-income inhabitants manage to take on a 'commissioning' role in the uses of the land and the buildings where they live. This central research question directs the research to the ways in which these inhabitants materialise the *moral ownership* of their homes and livelihoods in expansive city-regions.

The question of moral ownership is a very relevant issue at the micro-level of the home and neighbourhood but, as Harvey (1989) and Lefebvre (1996) clearly indicated, it is simultaneously an issue at the higher level of the cultural, political and economic regime conditions of the city and state. Being in charge of arranging the housing situation at the micro-level presupposes access to land, resources and social and political support. This makes civic efforts to influence the social and political regime conditions at the city-region and nation-state levels highly relevant for our research. Land, resources and social and political support are permanently contested, and the question of whether and how citizens are enabled to materialise moral ownership over their micro-level building processes therefore also depends for an important part on their active participation in the public definition of regime conditions. The struggle over *public regime conditions* is manifest in the endemic propensity of capitalism to materialise new pathways of economic growth, displacing lower financial returns of investment, on the one hand, and in the social and cultural power of inhabitants and social movements to organise their own demands via social organisation, public opinion and political and legal power, on the other. Local and national politics are in between this carrousel, being dependent on material welfare and income generation, on one side, and on the drives of the political electorate, on the other. They may be drawn to the one side or to the other, and the differences are large for those at the bottom.

The self-build performances in the selected city-regions of this book reflect the different material conditions of social and economic prosperity of national systems, as well as the uneven pressures of spatial demography and social inequality. However, they also reflect the different pay-offs of the aforementioned economic and social/cultural kinetics. City-regional pay-offs tend to be asymmetric (in many cases, highlighting the preponderance of selective economic drives rather than social/cultural drives) but the outcomes are never determinate. There are also successful social performances, even within systems characterised by the worst economic conditions. The performances differ spatially from city-region to city-region, and they differ temporally, as the historic analyses demonstrate, over periods of time. It is from comparing the different ways of organising the trade-offs between the social/cultural and the economic drives and forces that we hope to find the potential to learn from the different local cases. This analysis focuses on the dynamic interaction between housing practices and regime conditions. In this concluding chapter, we will first recapitulate the general headlines of the shifting décor of governance in the three visited continents and the relevant practices in the individual case studies in order to analyse and compare in more detail the different ways in which self-builders navigate their cases and influence the social and political regime conditions vis-a-vis the match of capitalism. In the final part, we will reflect on these findings and draw conclusions from the research.

The changing décor of governance

The level of social and economic prosperity of city-regions depends a great deal on the position of national and regional economies in global networks. The city-regions discussed in this book take completely different positions in these economic networks. Three groups of economic city-regions may roughly be distinguished. First, there is a group of city-regions with a prominent position in the advanced networks of the world economy, in particular, the city-regions in North-Western Europe. The housing situation for low- and middle-income groups is – albeit not without problems – generally established at a higher level of prosperity than in countries with lower social and economic standards. Next, there is a group of 'emerging and growth-leading economies' like Brazil and Turkey, characterised by a relatively modest standard in the international economy in absolute terms but with a tremendous pace of economic growth over the last decades. These transitional economic systems tend to jump to a higher level of economy but their explosive economic growth has not yet materialised in social growth. Both Brazil and Turkey experienced fierce material growth but also social drawbacks in times of economic peaks. The third group relates to states that are not yet strongly positioned in international economic networks and suffer drawbacks in both a social and an economic sense. This is the case with the African city-region referred to in this book. Ecuador is somewhere in between the second and third groups, with a significant recent economic growth but with a weak position in the international economic network.

A second crucial indication of the urban context is the rapid growth of the urban population occurring worldwide but explosively in Latin America and Africa. There, urban population growth is caused by high birth rates, which are presently slowing down with gradual effects over time. Further and more particularly the urban population grew because of rural–urban migration, culminating in new heights in Africa and Latin America in recent decades. As detailed more precisely in Chapter 2 for Latin America and Brazil and in Chapter 4 for city-regions in Africa, the proportion of urbanisation is climbing in Africa from 36 per cent in 2016 to an expected 50 per cent in 2030, and has already reached over 75 per cent in Latin America. This may indicate that further urbanisation over the next decades – at least for this reason – must slow down (particularly in Latin America) because of the huge shares of already-existing urbanisation. However, the existing situation reflects the growth dynamics of the recent past. For many city-regions, it simply appeared impossible to accommodate the explosive needs of housing. Even in (rare) intervals of supporting social policies, housing programmes in cities – such as São Paulo – reach only a small part of needy groups. Self-build initiatives in this context are not based on idealism; they are a matter of survival. As the case of São Paulo shows, while these self-build initiatives start extremely basic, they may grow and turn into institutionalised housing settlements over time.

The trend of extensive urbanisation is also manifest in the economic advanced countries, though to a lower degree of intensity. Here, it is not matter of high birth rates; rather, it relates to the new attractiveness of urban systems in the changing global information economy, which has repositioned the interconnected urban nodes as the new centres of international economic networks. This makes migration (also of international knowledge workers) a crucial source of the explanation of population growth in Western cities. The combination of higher economic pressure on the commercial uses of urban land, the attractiveness of the migrant population and the liberalisation of politics has resulted in the increasing social and spatial displacement of low-income segments of the urban population (via gentrification and increased segregation) and a general tendency of the residualisation of social housing systems in European city-regions (see Chapter 3).

Gradual institutionalisation of self-building in Latin America

The explosive urbanisation of Latin American cities led to a sharp increase of concentrations of urban population living in precarious areas, varying from 9 per cent in Chile to 50 per cent in Bolivia, 36 per cent in Peru, 29 per cent in Brazil and 18 per cent in Colombia (UN-Habitat, 2012). Self-build initiatives in these areas have a long tradition on this continent (see Chapter 2). Cooperative self-building has been integrated (gradually) into national and local policies since the 1960s and 1970s. Uruguay was among the first countries to have a self-build housing policy in the 1960s; its organisation of cooperative housing – instigated by a strongly embedded social movement – is still the international role model of cooperative housing. A decade later, the Brazilian government arranged (modest) financial facilities

Conclusion

for banking aimed at social housing. However, the central initiatives gave way to decentralisation to municipalities in the mid-1980s. While local government is not very powerful in promoting social housing in terms of financial support, it is decisive in issues of land distribution and it may also arrange technical assistance and basic infrastructures (water, sanitation, electricity). A leading role in the social normalisation of self-build initiatives was taken by cooperative housing movements, which were part of the wider civic movement responsible for the birth of organised civil society in Brazil during the 1970s.

Over the years, political tides fluctuate at both the urban and national levels, with some political regimes being supportive and others extremely hostile to self-build and cooperative initiatives. The pressure by inhabitants to improve the quality of their homes and facilities, social movements, and involved technical non-profit organisations are the drivers of continuity in the gradual institutionalisation of cooperative initiatives. In terms of quantity, the self-management of housing is still relatively modest, especially when compared with the large share of the prevailing mass production model. In most Latin American countries, national and local governments (aiming at economic growth) tend to facilitate big construction companies in order to produce large housing projects in urban peripheries, capturing added value by transforming cheap agrarian land in urban uses; subsidies to low-income groups are needed to exploit these mass complexes. Self-management and cooperative initiatives are still marginal to these prevailing practices but the history of the last 50 years shows their continuity and increasing endurance.

In 2009, the government of Brazil launched the My House, My Life Programme (PMCMV), with a plan to build 1 million new houses. It was a counter-cyclical programme in the midst of the global financial crisis. The programme targeted low-income residents, subsidising up to 95 per cent of the value of the unit. Most of the programme pursued the large-scale production of housing by big construction companies, in particular, in urban peripheries where they may capitalise on the low price of agrarian land. However, instigated by organised social movements, a special sub-programme was created for cooperative initiatives: the My House, My Life Programme – Entities (PMCMV-E). The programme provided subsidies to buy land and or empty buildings and to pay for technical help. This programme was implemented via associations or collective housing institutions with proven local experience.

Two cooperative projects in the centre of São Paulo (see Chapter 5) were studied. Dandara São Paulo is a commercial complex owned by the federal government, which – after continuous social struggle and negotiation – was retrofitted to create 120 housing units for low-income households. The housing movement and their technical partner organised the project. The residents actively participated in commissioning and learned to take responsibility by doing things themselves. Getting access to housing was made dependent on participating in committees and social action. One of the risks was the sharply increasing commercial value of the dwellings (more than doubling after the first year of completion), which enlarged pressure from the market and urged the housing movement to be extremely strict on entrance and exit rules. The Maria Domitila project is a new housing complex on occupied land, including 245 housing units for the very poor (paying 3 per cent of the costs, with the rest having to be raised). It was also constructed through a partnership between the housing movement and a technical organisation. The future residents actively participate both in the internal committees and in social and political action. It took 17 years (after first occupation and repossession) to realise after having mobilised public opinion and politics, and having overcome all legal and other obstacles. Also, the (horizontal) internal participation required intensive social learning to make the residents the moral owner of the housing complex and to prevent social degradation after its realisation. These PMCMV-E cases are exemplary from the point of view of participation by the poor:

- the direct connection between inhabitants and social building movements;
- the continuous social and political articulation of inhabitants via the social movements;
- the involvement of technical organisations and their co-leadership by the social movements;
- the (partial) integration of cooperative building in governmental programmes;
- the learning participation of residents (in design but also social learning); and
- the continuous pressure from commercial markets (access to land, entrance/exit and so on).

These conditions appear successful. However, the production logic has severe limits over land disputes and the location in the city. Besides this, these cooperative experiences are hardly representative in quantitative terms. Nevertheless, for the poor, they are the major way of getting access to morally owned and qualitatively good housing. The exemplary projects might have a wider influence on the prevailing supply-led models of mass housing production.

Another case of the Brazilian PMCMV-E was investigated in Rio de Janeiro: the Solano Trindade housing occupation in Duque de Caxias, on the periphery of the Rio de Janeiro metropolitan region (see Chapter 6). It is a cooperative self-management project that started in 2014 with the occupation of abandoned property by the national movement for housing rights. The cooperative movement is committed to a wide number of local occupations, struggling to get the land acquisitions recognised. It is well recognised in public opinion and socially supported, for instance, by the Catholic Church and the National Workers Party, and also cooperates with the Landless Rural Workers Movement. Besides self-building, the Solano Trindade project includes alternative technologies for urban services and agro-ecological production. To this end, a special partnership was established with the university. The movement subdivided the complex into three categories of tasks: a private category of self-building based on individual property; a public category on behalf of infrastructures (state/municipality); and the so-called 'residential association spaces' – spaces for collective use, such as planting crops through agro-ecological techniques, composting organic residue, a basin for ecological sanitation, a collective kitchen and agro-ecological restaurant, a library, lavatories, a laundry room, and an auditorium for political and technical training activities. The project is still under construction. We conclude on the following:

- the self-management project started with the close cooperation of residents and housing rights movement;
- it is well received in public opinion and linked to a supportive network of social organisations;
- it mobilised funds from governmental programmes (PMCMV);
- in this particular case, it widening its goals by experimenting with new technologies for urban services and agro-ecological products; and
- it cooperated with the university, including over technical advice, training and learning.

The final investigated case in Latin America is located in Ecuador (see Chapter 7). Ecuador has a strong tradition of cooperative civic and housing movements. In the 1970s and 1980s, cooperative movements had already acquired public funds for the production of social housing. In the liberal 1990s, however, this tradition was suppressed. Due to failing alternatives, low-income inhabitants decided to create their own alternatives, often in the form of cooperative self-building. As a reaction to poor housing conditions, a number of civic movements established the common development programme La Solidaridad (The Solidarity). One of the results of the programme was the Alianze Solidaria Housing Cooperative. This cooperative association acquired unused land on the periphery of Quito to develop a unique city quarter (not just housing, but also by ecologically transforming a large trash heap and ravine, a landmark that presently attracts external visitors). From the beginning, a process of participation was organised to develop the plans jointly; the aim was a complete neighbourhood, including amenities rather than just housing. The land was divided into large plots in order to stimulate cooperation and to avoid individual housing. Next, contracts were made with the municipality for water, sanitation and electricity. The organisation was headed by the cooperative association in cooperation with a particular technical agency. The process of deliberation with the inhabitants and the joint commitment resulted in a durable self-built city quarter. In summary:

- the case demonstrates the known characteristics of the Latin American cooperative cases outlined earlier (tight cooperation between residents and movements, the involvement of technical expertise, horizontal organisation and learning, the mobilising of public opinion, and political articulation);
- it had a focus on joint initiatives (showing solidarity between residents); and
- it included the self-arranging of public amenities (sanitation, water, ecological landscape and so on) in contract with the municipality.

Shifting governance in Europe

The shifting décor of housing governance in Europe over the last 50 years have been characterised by the rise and the liberalisation of national welfares states. The national housing policies reflect the differences of national welfare states but a common denominator in the build-up of national policy systems was the centrally arranged professionalisation of technical and social facilities. Capitalism is at the base of all Western states but it has been mitigated during the 20th-century process of modernising public policy systems: these systems arranged a higher quantity, a better quality and a fair accessibility of social amenities. Universalist housing policies, including both low- and middle-income groups, were settled, mainly in North-Western Europe but these 'affluent' housing systems have been increasingly residualised since the beginning of liberalisation in the 1980s. The process of liberalisation and residualisation also reflected the differences of national states: it took place abruptly in the UK (from affluent housing to narrowly targeting the poor and selling the better council homes) and Germany (radically withdrawing state subsidies and municipalising the housing system in the early 1990s) and more gradually ('slow-motion gradualisation') in other countries, such as in Scandinavia, France, Austria and the Netherlands. Southern Europe has always relied on the family model of the private home sector; social housing is not strongly developed in southern states. Eastern Europe radically shifted its socialist legacy in a capitalist market model after the fall of the Iron Curtain. Overall, there is no evidence of the strong institutionalisation of self-built and cooperative housing in Europe. The processes of modernisation professionalised the provision of social housing at a high level but marginalised the responsibility of the inhabitants in North-Western Europe. Also, the liberalisation from the beginning of the 1990s paved the way for the dominance of the market rather than involving inhabitants. Market conditions prevail in Eastern and Southern Europe too.

The retreat of national governments from housing policies is the most important shift in the post-war conditions of housing governance in European states. The social sector is still considerable in a number of countries but largely diminished after governmental retreat. On the other hand, the potential role of local and regional governments has become more strategic. The most challenging questions are whether the inhabitants will subsume their own responsibilities and re-articulate their constituent role in housing policies, and whether they will be able to mobilise the social and political conditions in city-regional systems. The conditions of governance have shifted but not yet crystallised into a new equilibrium. In a number of countries, new self-build initiatives are undertaken (for instance, instigated by citizens' initiatives in the UK, cooperative alternatives in Germany and social organisation in Austria) but the empowering strategies are not numerous and they are facing the residualisation of national policies and the increasing rejection of commercial uses of urban land. We investigated the following three contrasting cases in more detail: Almere in Amsterdam, Kamëz in Tirana and Istanbul.

The Dutch case of social housing in city-regions exemplifies the social embedding of capitalism in North-Western Europe. For almost a full century until recently, major cities were governed by coalitions of the political Left. As a result, the municipal ownership of land, housing production by housing corporations and numerous governmental interventions in housing markets were the prevailing conditions of housing in Amsterdam (which still has 40 per cent social housing in 2019 even after 20 years of liberalisation). Housing the poor started a hundred years ago in social associations but shifted – intensely since the 1960s – into a paternalist supply-led partnership between the government and social and commercial producers of mass housing, providing universal qualities but degrading the residents – with their (hidden) diversity of preferences – to passive end users. Over the last two decades, the government has retreated from social housing, promoting the private home sector and liberalised, residualised and decentralised social housing. New self-build and cooperative initiatives are emerging at a low scale. The Homeruskwartier in the new town of Almere (in the Amsterdam region) is the first sincere attempt to break with the tradition of universal modernism. It entails the self-building of an entire neighbourhood of 6,279 residents. The city of Almere took a unique political position to promote self-building by buying and procuring the land (as usual) but not selling it to the institutional developers (unique in the Netherlands); instead, the land was subdivided into parcels and sold to residents to develop it themselves. The needs of the residents were shown from the first day and continued even into the financial crisis of 2008. In Chapter 8, the motives of residents were investigated in depth. The chapter analyzed a wide range of rationales and strategies employed by self-builders. Rationales were related to either achieving particular living arrangements through customisation (expressing autonomous preferences and lifestyles) or achieving homeownership through an exceptional value-for-money deal. Residents appear to be motivated by a mix of use values and commercial values. To conclude on this Dutch case:

- capitalism is socially embedded;
- there was post-war paternalism in early-century associations in the central regime of the government and institutionalised producers;
- there has been functionally good and accessible but universal mass housing production and the degradation of the resident to a passive end user;
- there has been a retreat of government over recent decades – liberalisation and decentralisation;
- there has been a hesitant transition to autonomous local regimes of municipalities and producers;
- there has been a slow renaissance of the constituent role of residents; and

- the unique case of Almere demonstrates increasing self-build needs and the mix of the motives of residents (both customising individual preferences and creating commercial value for money).

Self-build initiatives were undertaken throughout post-communist Central Europe after the fall of the Iron Curtain but are far from being dominant. The market model is prevailing. The state retreated in Central European countries, though local government attempted to create new regimes in collaboration with the private sector. Albania differed from this general picture due to a lack of public budgets, private building industries and the huge administrative chaos of the public sector after the fall of the central regime. Here, individual families took their own decisions, illegally occupying abandoned and no longer administrated public properties, and developing their accommodation. As many residents migrated to the capital of Tirana (due to higher chances of employment), this kind of self-build invasion overwhelmed the peripheral areas of the metropolitan region (amounting to 50 per cent of the city-regional housing market). The case study of Kamëz suburb is an example of this development (see Chapter 12). The newcomers formed their own regime, albeit informal. The individual family was the cornerstone of the fragmented communities (some generating money elsewhere in Europe, some building, others arranging the new family complexes). The quality of these built complexes was not worse than the built environment in the central city of Tirana. However, the self-made community of singular families did not manage to organise quality public amenities at a professional level (public places, infrastructure and so on) and also suffered social problems, for instance, with regard to social distribution (such as fair entrance rules). A non-governmental organisation (CoPLAN) filled the public vacuum and successfully began to mediate, first, between the residents themselves, building up a position of social trust, and then also with external actors, in particular, the municipality and market actors (banks, developers), in order to arrange social order and the public provision of social and material facilities. In the early 2000s, constructive cooperation resulted in the legalisation of the informal suburb. Since then, the public sector has taken responsibility for the construction of public facilities. The improvement of the suburb has even spread to the whole city. In short:

- it was a self-build initiative by single families;
- it lacked social movements and social organisation;
- it lacked conditions from the government and municipality;

- it involved the coordinating role of a non-profit organisation to fill the public gap; and
- it involved the gradual normalisation of orderly relationships between autonomous families, non-profit organisations, local government and market actors.

Istanbul provides a unique case of self-build experiences. Since the 1950s, two forms of self-build are predominant modes of housing production in Istanbul: '*gecekondu*' and '*yap-sat*' (or 'build-and-sell'). *Gecekondu* entails the occupation of publically owned vacant land and building an unauthorised house on it (see Chapter 9). In the early 1960s, a third of the population already had used this informal mode of housing (35 per cent in 1963). The illegal occupation of land was tolerated by the government because it had no housing policy to accommodate the explosive flows of rural–urban migrants. The state provided only basic infrastructures to *gecekondu* areas. *Yap-sat* is a peculiar form of commissioning between plot owners and small contractors in the planned sections of the city. Owners and contractors shared the incomes generated by developing buildings. This mode was used by middle-income groups.

In the liberal period of 1980–2000, the housing market was targeted by economic investment. The economy was booming and land had become a scarce good in the expansive city, attracting foreign investment and large development projects. New amnesty legislation legitimised all unplanned and uncontrolled developments. Low-income *gecekondu* housing commercialised and became the subject of speculation. For the residents, this opened a way out of poverty. The government founded TOKI (Public Housing Development Administration) for mass production and cooperatives. However, while intended for low-income inhabitants, it moved immediately to the middle and particularly upper-middle classes. Urban land became the major means of accumulation. Since 2000, governmental commercialism became more aggressive. The government built increasingly interventionist and authoritarian economic growth strategies on the urban land market and the construction sector. New laws enabled central intervention and also discretionary authority to the government. Self-built neighbourhoods were considered as obstacles to more lucrative growth. The state and its administrative arms (TOKI, REIT) grew into real estate giants, displacing *gecekondu* residents and dominating the *yap-sat* negotiations. The urban practices and interventions of the state aroused considerable dissent and led to the emergence of new urban movements. They founded neighbourhood associations in order to organise collective opposition against these projects (through meetings, press statements and lawsuits). As the urban space became increasingly commodified, the opposition enlarged to include professional chambers, academics, NGOs and 'neighbourhood beautification associations' of middle-income groups who stood against these projects. In short:

- 1950–80 involved extensive self-building, lax land policies and a silent alliance between the state and the newcomers;
- since the 1980s there has been increasing commodification – the state enabled commercial deals with urban land and became more entrepreneurial itself (TOKI);
- there has been an authoritarian state since 2000, favouring economic transformation and displacing the urban poor; and
- there has been a renaissance of urban movements, socially well embedded and struggling for public opinion, legal rights and political representation.

African politics in between opening doors to international capitalism and inclusion of the poor

The economic and political conditions to low- and middle-income housing in Africa navigate between the international initiatives to open African markets for international capitalism and bottom-up strategies to include the poor (see Chapter 4). The economic productivity of many countries is among the lowest on earth. The combination of low productivity and rapid urbanisation has resulted in rising urban slum populations to unprecedented heights. In the poorest ten African countries, the urban slum population is higher than 80 per cent of total urban population. There is a strong international ambition to renew Africa's cities using World Bank strategies or, for instance, the model of Singapore (UN-Africa Renewal, 2016), and to promote the growth of economic and urban productivity. Urban planners from the Global North joined local policymakers to develop African cities according to Western models but the outcomes were ambiguous. It proved difficult to include the poor. Paradoxically, the promoted economic and social development of cities resulted in the shrinking of the livelihoods and spaces of the poor. The rising prices of land are exclusive and require a higher return on investment. There is a plethora of bottom-up initiatives of self-management and cooperation, in particular, on the outskirts of cities – out of necessity – not just in the field of housing, but also including home-grown productivity (producing your own food). However, they are being increasingly displaced by developing cities. As everywhere, finding ways to combine the economic and social/cultural drives and to mitigate capitalism through responsible civic initiatives is challenging, but it is nowhere as incisive as in the context of Africa.

The final case study concerned Ouagadougou, the capital of Burkina Faso. Self-construction is traditionally the main mode of housing production in this African country, but it is not optimally facilitated by the government. Its history is divided into several intervals. Until 1960, French colonisers mainly cared for the imported European cities, which included all state functions and urban facilities, but they neglected the need for public infrastructures in the peripheral areas characterised by basic forms of self-construction. Two decades after independence, a revolutionary regime shaped a well-organised order for self-built housing between 1983 and 1995. A new law on agrarian and land organisation (establishing state sovereignty over land) enabled self-production by low-income people through distributing land to families and providing amenities to communities (see Chapter 4). Framed by the slogan 'a household, a plot', the authorities adopted a policy of massive subdivisions with the production of plots, socio-economic housing, community amenities and sanitation (Folkers and Perzyna, 2017). Every family was given access to a plot for self-building and the production of food, with affordable, strictly controlled rents, and financial funds supported the needed facilities for the communities. It was the birth of a well-ordered, extensive self-built city for 500,000 people.

However, this intriguing model of centrally organised self-organisation disappeared when a liberal regime was established in 1996. The state kept some entrepreneurial activities but largely decentralised housing policies to the local governments and liberalised the building process to private developers. The state gradually disengaged from the promotion of social conditions in the housing market. As a result of the liberalisation (in the context of rapid urbanisation, the increasing scarcity of land and growing needs for housing), the urban spaces became subject to speculation, transforming existing uses and displacing less lucrative uses. Besides poor residents lacking access to the liberalised housing markets, and lacking social facilities, the housing market is in need of further professionalisation to enable reliable conditions of material prices, legal administration, building permits and so on. The era of liberalisation enabled a wild, almost uncontrolled, property boom after 2008, including large projects and foreign investment, but it simultaneously neglected public policies in support of the self-building majority of the population that should enable decent facilities. To conclude:

- The African city struggles with the dilemma of opening its economy and thus its urban spaces to the forces of international capital (including injections from the United Nations or World Bank) and building up the commodities of property – including some civic groups but displacing the many who are not involved – and building up the self-reinforcing potential of the urbanising population that appears to be excluded from liberal development.
- The case of Ouagadougou demonstrated both sides of urban development, clarifying the need to interconnect the tendencies of self-regulation and regulation but also the problems of finding a balance between these forces.
- The case of self-management flourished under the strict conditions of the radical central regime in the 1980s, with regulated access for all and supported public facilities. It demonstrated a unique case of combining regulation and self-regulation.
- Left to the forces of liberalisation since the 1990s (in times of economic globalisation and rapid urbanisation), these areas appear to be the most vulnerable to land speculation, economic transformation and the displacement of the poor.

Comparison and reflection

The analysis of different international cases demonstrates, first of all, that a successful performance of self-build housing is not yet mainstream for low- and middle-income groups in international city-regions. In terms of quantity, the amount of realised self-build homes appears to be modest in most of the cases. Even in Latin America, where the international fame of self-built *'favelas'* is almost stereotypical of the idea of social housing, *favelas* do not amount to more than 10 per cent of the housing stock, for instance, in such a needy city-region as São Paulo. The segment of mass housing production for lower classes is much larger in Brazil and it takes a much larger share of the national budget. The mass production of housing does target low- and middle-income groups but it is established for economic rather than social goals and does not respond to the real demand of the poor in many cases. In Europe, the amount of self-built housing has become even more marginal through the 20th century, though we studied some extensive cases in this book (an exemplary case in Albania and the struggle for survival of historically large cases in Istanbul). In a number of African cities, the rate of self-build practices is much higher but here we run into the qualitative problem of how to acquire a decent level of quality. Here, the extensive self-build cases often demonstrate the powerlessness of needy groups and policy systems rather than a successful practice of housing. Overall, it proves to be very difficult for low- and middle-income groups to take a constituent role in the production of housing in a context where markets and governments set their own priorities.

Self-build arrangements are apparently not abundant in international comparison; however, in many cases, they are the best option for the poor and – when successfully attempted – they may be exemplary of the active participation of the inhabitants and their appropriation of the daily living environment. For this reason, the impact may be much larger than just fulfilling their own housing needs, for instance, on non-descript mass housing production. The pursuit of this social endeavour is very laborious. We studied quite a number of inspiring self-build cases, some with deep historic roots and others still under construction, but all of them commissioned by inhabitants and social housing movements that attempt and often struggle to mobilise the attention and the energy of other actors on the housing market (with usually more resources to their disposal) to their case. This is the key to all the cases studies: self-built housing is not just the self-arrangement of a particular housing situation by specific groups; at the same time, the conditions that do or do not enable this particular housing arrangement are influenced and decided on through the committed social and political interaction of these groups with all other actors and agencies. Self-built housing is a multi-scalar and multi-actor process in which low- and middle-income inhabitants claim their role and opportunity to arrange their living situation. May we expect this multi-scalar civic mission to be fulfilled by exactly those groups that have to climb the social ladder from the bottom? Would they have the social and institutional capability to have all this ambition?

These are the dilemmas and questions that we posed in the Chapter 1 of the book, in which we also determined the framework of the study as being expressed by the contestation between the commercial and the social powers in processes of housing arrangements and urban development. The framework focused in particular on the contestation between the commercial drives of (inter)national or local market actors and the social and cultural drives of inhabitants and their organisations. All case studies confirmed this deep contestation; the outcomes differ in different cases but the tension between capitalising on the commercial values of urban land and urban resources versus the social and cultural uses of the same land and resources was visible in all cases. Many cities have become reluctant to enable bottom-up initiatives in increasingly selective and commercially highly valued urban spaces. Often, the attempts at self-building were displaced to peripheral places of the city-region or were underwent long-term struggle. In most cases, the long-term uncertainty as to whether actual processes of self-built housing were allowed to continue proved to already be a crucial part of the problem. However, the selected cases also showed a high social and cultural resilience, which found a way to persist, in some cases, with remarkable success. In the selected cases, both sides of the urban contestation apparently managed to mobilise their sources of power.

However, the cases demonstrated that the tension between capitalising on the commercial values versus the social and cultural use values of urban resources is more sophisticated than just a struggle between market and social forces. The capital of banks and developers is often used for urban investments that displace the commercially less valued uses of urban spaces, but under certain conditions, it may also be invested in social and cultural practices, such as self-build arrangements. Self-build arrangements have to mobilise the commercial injection of capital. Some governmental programmes in Brazil and other Latin American countries contained incentives (instigated by social housing movements) to enable this kind of commercial investment. Not all capital is in search of the highest return in the shortest of time; part of it (pension funds, insurances, social banks and so on) cares more for the continuity and certainty of economic value over time. Governments usually play a role in enabling social investment by private capital. From a social background, there is always pressure from inhabitants and their movements to activate this potential. On the other side, low- and middle-income inhabitants care not only about social and cultural use values, but also about the commercial value of housing, certainly in cases when they are the owners. Deep research into the motives of self-builders in the case of Almere revealed a mix of social motives, containing both the preference of inhabitants to customise the building to their authentic preferences and their material longing to make 'good value for money'. The self-build inhabitants of '*gecekondu*' and '*yap-sat*' in Istanbul were happy to live in their self-constructed areas but also appeared to be extremely vulnerable to commercial offers to sell their land when big capital arrived to develop commercial projects. The commercial value of dwellings in São Paulo's Dandara self-build complex increased so dramatically after its successful realisation that measures were needed to prevent the commercialisation of its uses. Huge areas of Ouagadougou's successful self-built housing of the 1980s appeared extremely vulnerable for commercial sale in the liberal 1990s. In one case, it is the small owners themselves; in the next case, it is the non-profit organisations and in yet another case, it is the municipalities –in all cases, though, the existence of economic value bears the potential for wider commercial exploitation by those who are in charge.

Apparently, self-build initiatives are socially and culturally driven initiatives, but in capitalist societies, they are not screened off from the endemic tendency of capitalist societies to capitalise on commercial values. This tendency is nested (with a different range of resources) in the attitudes of all participants of society, as well as in the arena of self-built housing. Obviously, social interaction is driven not solely by materialism, but also by social and cultural drives deeply normalised in societies and usually expressed more vividly in self-build arenas. However, it is important to investigate socially indicated initiatives, such as self-build housing, in an analytical way. Socially inclusive, self-build areas may shift over the course of time into closed and socially exclusive resorts of gentrification! This changeable reality calls into question whether a social initiative of self-build housing is organised as an initiative by and on behalf of a group of self-builders or whether it also includes the interests of future residents. In the latter case, the dwellings may be owned by an association or social organisation that keeps control over the entrance and exit rules of inhabitants. In the first case, the self-build development is held open for economic development depending on the decision of the owners; in the latter case, it may institutionalise as a social organisation. This may seem evident but the implications are often overlooked because at time of founding the self-build initiatives, its creation may take so much effort to be realised and the social motives may be so evident that caring for potentially different states in the future is not the first concern of the involved actors.

Keeping an open eye on the evolution of self-build initiatives also implies a search for the potentially changing roles of the different actors involved in the complex arena of self-building. In the Latin American cases, the self-build initiatives are commissioned by a very tight and horizontal relationship between the residents, the social housing movements and the committed technical experts. Given the circumstances of need and the tough social struggle to convince public opinion, public sector bodies and economic agencies, it is hard to imagine in this embryonic stage that housing movements and their associated technical experts would serve different interests than the residents themselves. Most of the involved experts share idealistic convictions. However, the Dutch examples show that a similar kind of tight residential associations in the early 20th century turned into professional organisations distant from the residents, and even established coalitions with governmental and market agencies from which residents sometimes feel excluded today. In the post-war epoch, housing non-profits grew dramatically but far removed from residents, who were gradually degraded into the role of a passive end user: the outsider on the waiting list dependent on what might be offered. Paradoxically, new self-build initiatives are taken here in order to escape this modernist evolution but they often neglect to organise these new initiatives as future-proof social associations. Social movements may grow into professional organisations and deal with the large-scale and complex financial and technical issues of large housing complexes, at far distance from residents. Their policies and external coalitions (with governmental and market agencies) may gradually lose their original social destination. Governmental organisations of social housing and governmental social programmes may also change into development vehicles taking profit from commercial value rather than serving the social interest of inhabitants, such as happened with TOKI and REIT in the cases of Istanbul, and in the case of Ouagadougou. It is crucial to pay due attention to the social conditions to enable durable self-build practices, in particular, the constituent role of inhabitants, from the very first stages onward. Questioning these conditions of social organisation early on (such as in Latin America, the case of Albania or the new cases in North-Western Europe) may sound a bit abstract because in their actual situation they are standing together closely with residents, but the older cases show that evolution over time may make these relationships more complicated.

One of the most challenging questions in this book concerns the capability of low- and middle-income citizens to arrange their own housing situation. As housing in dense city-regions requires building multiple housing complexes rather than singular buildings, this concerns specialised knowledge of, in particular, financial, architectural and construction-technical, and last but not least social capabilities. Furthermore, dealing with the conditions of self-build housing requires the social/political capability to deal with external organisations. We tested this question in the Latin American cases, in particular, where many poor rural–city migrants are involved. These people are apparently not trained in these capabilities, are often not educated, do not make an income (which made them move to the city) and many are illiterate. The active presence of a social movement is crucial in these situations; it has to organise the needed capabilities itself by hiring or cooperating with technical, financial and social experts. However, they must very impressively lead but not overtake the decision-making process of the residents. Processes of self-building are perceived as learning processes where technical experts explain the choices, tasks are divided and shared, and decisions are taken jointly in time-consuming procedures and meetings with residents because of the necessity of the participants 'learning by doing'. In particular, social expertise is important as residents have to learn what it means to be responsible for their homes and to organise and share tasks. They also learn to make their case in public. For the sake of social learning, the relationships between residents and technically informed leaders of social movements are organised in horizontal ways. In this way, civic capabilities are successfully trained. This learning process does not make technical experts of the residents (though some do actually grow into this role); rather, residents learn to be responsible for their cases, to express their preferences and to discuss and share ideas with others. The social movements also learn themselves because of the gradual expansion of their activities. Starting as spokesmen and representatives of residents, they gradually learn to implement processes by attracting and cooperating with financial and urban experts. In some cases, the subject of self-organisation extends to other activities; they are not limited to building processes, but involve the organisation of facilities and home-grown productivity (for instance, in the cases of Quito and Rio de Janeiro but also in Africa's Ouagadougou). Innovative techniques of ecological sanitation or soil productivity are learned via contacts with external experts.

Conclusion

The economic growth of cities shapes material wealth, jobs and social opportunities, and it enables public administrations to generate income, but it tends to simultaneously enlarge the social gap between groups and to repress the social and spatial perspectives of lower-income groups and less profitable activities. The increasing pressure and growing prices of urban land and resources enlarge the thresholds on the housing market for starters and low- and middle-income groups, urging them to move to economically less attractive spaces. These selections characterise urban development both in the Global North and the Global South. The resilience of the dependent groups depends on their power to organise their interests and to make a public claim for better conditions by influencing public opinion and politics, and to use their economic power by articulating their particular demand to the organisation of productivity. Citizens are not just victims of selective economic systems; they take a constituent role in urban society and define their rights to participate and to make places of quality. This is key for self-build housing. The wide array of self-build arrangements depends, first of all, on the social articulation of residents and their social movements. In this book, a central emphasis has been laid on the responsible and commissioning role of inhabitants, both in the articulation of their own livelihoods at the micro-level and – in relation to this – in their collective manifestation and claim to provide the required conditions at the level of cities and states. The role of social housing movements is crucial in the embodying of this public claim.

Next, the analysis of self-build cases in different urban contexts underlined the significant role of non-profit organisations in effectuating the civic articulation in professional housing. The requirement of expert organisations is needed in almost all initiatives of self-building. The organised power of non-profit agencies: enables the translation of the diversity of individual demands in collective action; enables expertise on finance, architecture and urbanism; enables professional construction and services of exploitation; organises external relationships with government and market organisations; efficiently organises the transaction costs of cooperation between different persons and households; enables the maintenance of the social function of the housing for future residents; and, finally, organises management and exploitation, including the costs (often rent). The role of non-profits is crucial in most self-build experiences; yet, the challenge of institutionalising this professional agency in the arena of self-regulation initiatives is not just a matter of equipping these organisations with more social and material resources. The real normative (and thus institutional) challenge is to keep these organisations in a position of being responsive and effective to actual and future low- and middle-income groups. This requires a legal recognition of the residents and the interest of future residents in the formal arrangement of non-profit organisations. The best chances to recognise the commissioning role of residents appears to be in associational forms of organisation.

Arranging this role in formal statutes is important but even more important is the growing and continuing challenge of residents in order to make this responsibility work in practice. Non-profit organisations need a critical following and permanent check by residents. Non-profit organisations fulfil an important social function, but as hybrid organisations navigating between the defined positions of state and market, they are vulnerable to getting entangled in interdependent relationships with one or the other, or even both. Almost all historic cases demonstrated the high relevance but also the vulnerability of non-profit organisations. The long history of non-profit social housing in Europe demonstrated: how social non-profits may become entangled with the state in an epoch of social politics but may be marginalised in the next political epoch; how the affiliation of non-profits with commercial markets may grow at times, leading to economic perspectives; and how the constituting relationships with their residents may become flawed, alienating them from dynamically changing needs in practice. Non-profit organisations, like other organisations, do not automatically perform as might be expected from their origins or formal statutes. Institutions do not work in practice if their normative meaning is not permanently articulated and innovated in ongoing practices and critical debate. It is the challenge of citizens and residents to keep the non-profit organisations in the right position. Residents do not have the professional knowledge and capabilities to fulfil the task of non-profit organisations; they are not the technical experts, but they know about the problems and the needs that have to be served. Keeping professional organisations in line with legitimacy is a difficult challenge, especially for low-income groups that often do not have the knowledge and experience, but they may grow into this role. This is the key to social normalisation of self-build processes: the institutionalisation of moral ownership. Ironically, this process appears to be more dynamic and vivid in the embryonic context of Latin American processes of self-build housing than in the professionalised systems of the Global North.

Finally, the intervention of politics is needed to set the conditions to correct the negative sides of commercial development. However, politics does not solely care about social housing arrangements, and the positions of governments fluctuate. At worst, they turn against the social interests of bottom-up initiatives. The worldwide tendency of liberalisation over the last two decades has resulted in a retreat of national governments in social policies. In some of the case studies, the government did not retreat, but shifted itself into the role of economic transformer (a sort of state-capitalism or authoritative interventionism) rather than providing a shield for needed groups. There are also many attempts to 'liberalise' the intermediating non-profit organisations but a well-organised social sector and a well-organised social non-profit sector may be resilient and should function as a buffer against the volatility of political and economic fluctuation. Their social resilience also depends on social articulation. Moreover, politics does not stand on its own; in the end, it depends on civic articulation. Considering the repositioning of national states, there may be a large potential for new regimes at the city-regional level, where local and regional administrations cooperate with market organisations and non-profits to fulfil social needs. The inhabitants and social movements will have to make certain that it is their needs that are organised and will have to march through the institutions.

References

Folkers, A. and Perzyna, I. (2017) *The Beeker Method: Planning and Working on the Redevelopment of the African City*, Leiden: ASC Leiden.

Harvey, D. (1989) *The Urban Experience*, Oxford: Blackwell.

Lefebvre, H. (1996) *Writings on Cities*, Oxford: Blackwell.

UN-Africa Renewal (United Nations Africa Renewal) (2016) 'Africa's cities of the future', *Africa Renewal*, 30(1): 4–5, www.un.org/africarenewal/magazine/april-2016/africa's-cities-future

UN-Habitat (United Nations Human Settlements Programme) (2012) *State of the World's Cities 2010/2011: Bridging the Urban Divide*, London: Earthscan.

Index

A

Accra, Ghana 62, 63, 64
Acosta, A 123
Addis Ababa 63, 64
Affordable Housing Foundation 80
Africa 2, 247
  cities 58–64, 71
  housing policies 257–9
  self-building 57–61
  social deficits in 191
Agricultural University of Tirana 230
Agro-ecological Exchange 114
agro-ecological front 113–16, 251
agro-export economy 122, 212
Agro-Forest System (SAF) 114
Albania 50, 236, 255
  history of housing 231–3
  informal development 233–8
  urban development 229–31
Alianza Solidaria Housing Cooperative (COOVIAS) 121, 127, 129–35, 251
Almere 144, 148, 149, 151–3, 253
alternative technologies 101, 110, 251
Amnesty Law 173–4, 178
Amsterdam 144, 148
  history of urban development 218–23
  and Sao Paulo 210–11
Andino & Asociados (architects) 131
apartment blocks 172, 231
architects 131, 149, 157, 232
Association of Multiple Cooperatives of Quito (ACMQ) 129
Austria 45, 46

B

banking 28, 82, 94, 127, 236
Bank of the Ecuadorian Institute of Social Security (BIESS) 127
Bank of the Habitat 194
basin, evaporation-transpiration (BET) 106, 115
Bathore 230, 236, 239
Belgium 50, 51–2, 146
BET *see* basin, evaporation-transpiration
Bobo-Dioulasso 66, 193, 195, 197, 202

Bolivia 24, 248
Brazil 23, 24, 26, 31
  cities 27, 79, 96
  history of self-building in 27–33
  housing policies 30, 38, 39, 80–3, 104
  new constitution 103
  population 25, 79, 216, 217
Brazil and Latin America 38
Buenos Aires 24
building materials 196, 198
building regulations 159–61, 198
building strategies 157–9
building workforce 27
bureaucracy 199–203
Burkinabe Movement of Human Rights and Peoples (MBDHP) 205
Burkina Faso 59
  history of urban development 192–4
  housing costs 197–9
  infrastructure 191
  public housing 194–200

C

Caixa (federal bank) 37, 82, 94, 104, 109
capitalism 6, 9, 246
case studies 14, 70, 79, 101, 149–51
catalogue building 149, 159
Catholic Church 31, 34, 105, 251
Central African Republic 57
Central Bank of Ecuador 128
Chile 24, 39, 121, 248
Christian Democratic policies 219
cities 58, 61–4
  Albania 229–31
  distribution of wealth in 7
  migration to 23, 59, 167, 229
  spatial design 223–4
citizen-empowering programmes (England) 49
citizen rights 225
City Management Centre (CEGECI) 197
City Statute 83–4, 88
civic movements 256

civil society, and housing
  planning 205–6
'class consciousness' 102
collaborative housing 145
collective action 35–6, 101, 230, 232, 239–40
College of Architecture and Fine Arts 31
colonial legacy 122, 192
Columbia 248
commissioning role 4, 48–52, 245, 250, 264–5
Communitarian Village 31, 32
compensation 235
Conakry, Niger 62, 63
condominiums 88, 172, 214
Construction Financing, of Social Interest Housing (FICAM) 215
construction process 110–13, 211, 232
Construction Works Follow-Up (CAO) 86
contested urban governance 13, 24, 43–4, 246, 260
  Africa 57–61
Cooperation of Movements of Housing Associations, Mutual Aid and Self-Management 81
cooperative movement 127
cooperatives 129–35, 171, 174, 232, 235, 251
Co-PLAN 239
costs 146, 153–5
council houses 46
Covas, Mário 35

D

Dandara building 90–3, 96, 249
Dar es salaam 63
da Silva, President Luis 37
De Bruijne, G.A 61
Denmark 45, 47, 146
de Soto, Hernando 9–10
'Disaster Law' 178, 179
Droste, C 51
Dutch housing 162, 220, 254

E

earthquakes 178
Eastern Europe 50, 229
  social housing 47

ecological park 133–4
Ecuador 123, 131, 247, 251
  cooperatives 127–9
  rural migration 121
Ecuadorian Housing Bank (BEV) 123, 131
Emlak Konut REIT 179–80
England 48–9
  citizen-empowering programmes 49
  council/social housing 45, 46
environmental conservation 113, 134
environmental quality 134, 135, 173, 183
Erundina, Luiza 32, 33, 34
Ethiopia 57, 64
Europe 2, 43–5, 50
  housing policies 252–7
  urban regimes in 209–10
  welfare economies 48
European Union housing regulations 222

F

families 24, 32, 38, 103, 113, 237
  eligibility for housing 86
  participation of 94
Family Collective Effort 29
family networks 47, 58, 215
favelas 23, 28, 39, 214, 216, 259
Federal Constitution 82
Federal Housing and Urbanism Service (SERFAU) 80
Federal Savings Bank *see* Caixa (federal bank)
Federal University of Rio de Janeiro (UFRJ) 101, 105, 106
Federation of Housing Cooperatives (EECOVI) 128
finance for housing 38, 149, 160, 161, 197
  Albania 236
  Brazil 103
  Ecuador 124, 126–8
  Istanbul 171, 174
financial considerations 155–6
financial crash 37, 84
Financial Housing System 34, 80
Financing for Urbanised Lots (PROFILURB) 80
Fire Department licence 93

food producers 65–70
food production 58, 113, 231, 258
foreign investment 61, 71, 256
France 44, 45, 46
Freire, Paulo 132
French West Africa, land registration system 193
Fund for Social Development (FDS) 37
Fund for the Service to the Population in Sub-Normal Housing (FUNAPS) 32, 34
Fund for the Service to the Population in Sub-Normal Housing Communal (FUNACOM) 32, 33–5, 34, 82

G

garbage collection 212, 214
gated communities 218
gecekondu 169–71, 177, 181
General Law of Financial System Institutions 124
Germany 44, 46, 50, 127
Ghana 57, 62
globalisation 8, 13, 214
Gohn, M 29
Gomide, R 29
Government Platform of Social Development 127
Government Severance Indemnity Fund for Workers (FGTS) 82
grass-roots initiatives 48, 50, 125, 205
Growth Acceleration Programme (PAC) 83, 217
Guayaquil 121, 122, 128
Guislain, Pierre 60–1

H

Habitat Fund 197
Harvey, David 9, 10, 246
Homeruskwartier, Almere 148
 case study 149–51
 demographics 151–2
 self-building scheme 144
Housing, Transport and Mobility, Sanitation and Urban Programmes 217
Housing and Urban Development Company (CDHU) 32, 33
Housing and Urban Development Ministry (MIDUVI) 126

housing associations 6, 220–1
Housing Campaign, Turkey 179
housing cooperatives 127–9
housing costs, Burkina Faso 197–9
Housing Finance System (SFH) 215
Housing Incentive Scheme (SIV) 126
Housing Movements, First Meeting of 81
Housing of Social interest (HIS) 84
housing rights movements 104
Housing Team 31
Hungary, social housing 45

I

industrialisation 66, 168, 212, 229
Industry Labour Force (IAPI) 80
inequality, in Africa 62
informal settlements 27, 60, 60–4, 230, 256
infrastructure 23, 29, 172, 195, 211, 217
 basic 249
 Burkina Faso 191
 sewage 113, 214
 in Tirana 241
Infrastructure & Industrialization of the African Development Bank (AFDB) 60
Institute of Agriculture 231
Institute of Retirement and Pension 80
Institutions of the Financial System (1994) 129
Integra (technical advisory team) 93
Inter-American Development Bank (IBD) 126
irrigation 68–9
Istanbul 256
 aggressive neoliberalism 176–82
 emergent neoliberalism 172–6
 housing regimes 167–71
 property exchange values 182–5

J

Juliana Revolution 127
Justice and Development Party (AKP) 177

K

Kamëz 230, 232
Kampala 63

Knorr-Siedow, T 51
knowledge workers 7, 222
kossodo 66

L

labour force 59, 169, 215, 232
Lagos 63, 64
Lai, D 59
land banks 88
land disputes 87
Landless Rural Workers Movement (MST) 105
land prices 81, 121, 155, 167, 175, 202
land titles 10, 193, 237
Las Cuadras Park 127
'La Solidaridad' 130
Latin America 2, 33, 39, 247
 cities 23–6, 102
League of Tenants 123
Lefebvre, H 44, 184, 246
 Writings on Cities 12
legal city 211, 215
Linear Park 134
living space 160
López, Sandra 133, 135
Lula, President 36, 82, 217

M

mapping arrangements of housing, in Europe 45–7
Maria Domitila building 89, 93–5, 250
Marmara 178
Maricato, E 96
Marx, Karl 10
mass housing 39, 85, 180, 249, 254, 259
Mass Housing Administration (TOKI) 174, 178, 179–81, 184
Melo, Fabián 132, 137
methodology 12–14, 148
Mexico 24, 39
migration to the city 23, 59, 121, 167, 229, 235
Ministry of Environment and Urbanism 178
Ministry of Habitat 194
Ministry of Housing and Urban Planning 197
Ministry of the Cities 24, 82, 85, 86, 104, 217

Ministry of Urban Planning and Construction 202
moral ownership 245–57
Municipal Corporation of Environmental Health 134
Municipal Housing Office 33
My House, My Life Programme-Entities (PMCMVE) 79, 83, 85–9, 103, 109–10, 249
My House, My Life Programme-FAR (PMCMV- FAR) 94
My House, My Life Programme (PMCMV) 37–8, 83, 84–5, 214

N

National Collective Efforts Programme of the Special Office of Communal Action (SEAC) 34
National Forum for Urban Reform (FNRU) 103
National Housing Bank (BNH) 28, 80, 213
National Housing Board (INV) 123
National Housing Fund of Social Interest (FNHIS) 84
National Housing Plan (PLANHAB) 80, 84, 94
National Housing System of Social Interest (SNHIS) 84
National Movement for Housing Rights in Brazil (MNLM) 101, 105–8
National Movement for Urban Reform 81
National Popular Housing Union (UNMP) 36
National Urban Land Development Company (SONTAUR) 197
neoliberalism 9, 168, 173
Netherlands 6, 45, 46, 144, 218–23
 social housing 44, 49
 turnkey housing 162
New Labour, tenant management 48
Niger 57, 62
non-governmental organisations (NGOs) 49, 135, 184, 230, 239, 255
non-state actors 238–40
North American subprime crisis 37
North-Western Europe 2, 14, 247
 social housing 43–5, 52–3

Index

O

occupations of buildings 5, 27, 89, 96, 105, 255
Odriozola, Jones 124, 126
Öncü, A 167
Organizing Entity - EO 86, 87
Ouagadougou 58, 61, 191–6, 197, 202, 258
  food producers 65–70
Owen, Robert 127
ownership 196, 245–57
  in Belgium 51–2
  definition of 5
  in Europe 44

P

PAC- Urbanisation of the Slums 83
parcel subdivision 204
Peru 24, 248
Pieterse, Edgar 60
popular movements 29, 32, 33, 36
Portugal 47
Pouw, N.R.M 61
poverty 57, 59, 61, 62
precarious housing 23, 24, 34, 122, 195
prestigious residences 218
privatisation 102, 172
productivity levels 62, 65
Programme for the Eradication of Sub-habitation (PROMORAR) 215
Programme of Sub-Housing Eradication (Promorar) 28
Promotion of Local Building Materials (LOCOMAT) 197
public amenities 126, 127, 219, 242
public spaces 105, 134, 232
Purcell, M 12, 44

Q

Quito 121, 122, 123, 124, 128, 135
Quitumbe Bus Terminal 127
Quitumbe plan 125–7

R

real estate developers 126, 197, 201–2
Real Estate Investment Trusts (REITs) 179
Recanto de Alegria (Joy Place) 31
regulation 15–16, 178, 234, 258

renting 5, 27, 52
Representatives (CRE) 86
Residental Lease Programme (PAR) 82
Residential Leasing Fund 38
residents 48–52, 143–7
revolution in Ecuador 127
Right to Buy 46
right to the city 3, 12, 83, 105, 122, 184
Rio de Janeiro 24, 27, 101
Rodrigues, Evaniza 37
Rotterdam 50, 220

S

São Bento Environmental Protection Area (APA) 113
São Bernando do Campo 31, 81
São Paulo 24, 26, 29–31, 79, 81
  and Amsterdam 210–11
  history of urban development 211–17
  self-management experience 89–94
São Paulo City Hall 82
São Paulo Collective Efforts Programme 32, 35–6
São Paulo Housing Movements (UMM/SP) 81
Scandinavian countries 45, 46
self-building 3–9, 143–7, 149–51
  customisation 153–5
  history in Brazil 27
  motivations of builders 151–2
  by the poor in Africa 64–8
  rationales and strategies 145–8
Self-Building Programme/Ovenbird Project 29
Self-management in São Paulo 29–33
Senegal 57
Single Window Land (GUF) 199–200
Skidelsky, R 10
slums 57, 60, 63, 79, 195
Smith, Adam 10
Social Development Fund 85, 86
'social dispossesion' 10
social function of property 83–4
social housing 211
  Burkina Faso 199–201
  Dutch 254
  in England 44–6
  in Europe 43–51, 253

Socialist Party 229, 232
social movements 103
Social Rental Programme 96
social unrest 241
Social Welfare Office (SEBES) 29
soil survey 198
Solano Trinidade 101, 102, 110–13, 251
  and growing food 114
  occupation 104–7
Solidaridad Quitumbe 130, 136
Solidarity Association for the Right to Housing (ASP/DROL) 205
Solidary Loan Programme 36–7, 103
Southern Europe, social housing 47
spatial development 71
speculation 196, 256
Squatter Housing Law 170, 174
squatting 31, 60, 64, 169–70
subprime crisis 37
Superintendence of Popular housing (HABI) 34
Sweden 44, 45, 47

T

Taksim Gezi Park 184
Tanaka, M 29
Tax on Commerce of Goods and Services 35
technical advice 28, 31, 34, 93, 104–8, 131
Tekeli 176
Thatcher, Margaret 46
Tirana 229, 231, 236
Turkey 50, 172
  Amnesty Law 173–4
  cities in 167
  'Disaster Law' 178
  housing regimes 167–71
  squatting 170, 174
Turner, John 28
turnkey housing 162

U

Unification of the Tenements and Housing struggles Movement (ULCM) 89, 94
United Nations 1, 9
  Human Settlements Programme (UN-Habitat) 23, 60, 71
  State of the World Cities 2016 58
urban development
  in Africa 59–61
  Albania 229–31
  in Quito 122–7
  in Turkey 180
Urbanised Allotments Financing Programme (PROFILURB) 215
Urbanised Allotments Financing Programme (Profilurb) 28
urban populations 63, 64, 247
urban regime theory 210
urban transformation 175, 179
Uruguay 81, 121, 248
  housing cooperatives 31, 36, 39
Uruguayan Federation of Cooperative Housing for Mutual aid (FUCVAM)
  housing co-operatives 81
USA 10, 37, 128, 146

V

Van der Vegt, J 152
Vargas, Getulio 80
Venezuela 24, 39

W

water 23, 58, 62, 66, 214
welfare economies 43, 48, 219–20
women 59, 115
Workers' Party 31, 103, 251
World Bank 28, 239
Writings on Cities 12

Y

yap-sat 168, 174, 177, 181
young adults 58, 195

www.ingramcontent.com/pod-product-compliance
Lightning Source LLC
Chambersburg PA
CBHW071151070526
44584CB00019B/2746